D1417766

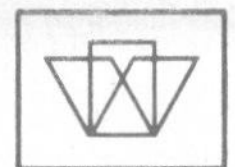

The Bookmark Reading Program

Prereading Language Development

Primary Readers

Skills Readers

- **Goals in Reading**
- **Reading to Learn**
- **Reading Power**

Literature Readers

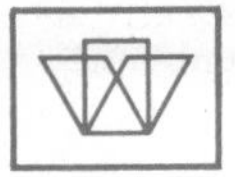

The Bookmark Reading Program

Reading to Learn

Second Edition

MARGARET EARLY

ROBERT CANFIELD

ROBERT KARLIN

THOMAS A. SCHOTTMAN

Harcourt Brace Jovanovich, Inc.

New York Chicago San Francisco Atlanta Dallas

PRINTED IN THE UNITED STATES OF AMERICA

ISBN 0-15-332255-1

ACKNOWLEDGMENTS: *For permission to reprint copyrighted material, grateful acknowledgment is made to the following sources:*

ABELARD-SCHUMAN LIMITED: An excerpt (titled: "Whirling Wheels") adapted from *Motorcycles: Whirling Wire Wheels* by Edward Radlauer, copyright 1969. All rights reserved.

BEACON PRESS: Excerpts on p. 353 and p. 354 adapted from *Hands* by Dorothy T. Spoerl, copyright © 1961 by the Beacon Press.

F. E. COMPTON CO., DIVISION OF ENCYCLOPAEDIA BRITANNICA, INC., CHICAGO, ILLINOIS: Chart on p. 311 "Food Value in 1 Quart of Milk for Teen-Agers" from *Compton's Pictured Encyclopedia.*

COWARD-MCCANN & GEOGHEGAN, INC.: "Communication Is More than Words" adapted from *Breaking the Language Barrier* by Fred West, copyright © 1961 by Coward-McCann, Inc. "Bananas Grow in Iceland" (retitled: "Hot Springs in Iceland") adapted from *Volcanoes and Glaciers* by Sturges F. Cary, copyright © 1959 by Coward-McCann, Inc.

THOMAS Y. CROWELL COMPANY, INC., PUBLISHERS: "If They Want a War–" from *Land of the Free* by Enid La Monte Meadowcroft, copyright © 1961 by Enid La Monte Meadowcroft.

CROWN PUBLISHERS, INC.: "Frederic Remington, Painter of the Last Frontier" from *Cavalcade of America,* edited by Carl Carmer, © 1956 by Lothrop, Lee & Shepard Co., Inc.

DODD, MEAD & COMPANY, INC.: An excerpt on p. 147 from *Wonders of the Woods and Desert at Night* by Jacquelyn Berrill.

DOUBLEDAY & COMPANY, INC.: "The Tools Came First" (retitled: "Man's First Inventions") adapted from *The Real Book About Inventions* by Samuel Epstein and Beryl Williams, copyright 1951 by Franklin Watts, Inc. "Paul Cuffe" (retitled: "The Secret of the Sea") and "Benjamin Banneker" (retitled: "He Reached for the Stars") adapted from *Pioneers and Patriots* by Lavinia Dobler and Edgar A. Toppin, copyright © 1965 by Doubleday & Company, Inc. "The Voyage of the *Beagle*" by Millicent E. Selsam adapted from *Nature and Science,* May 15, 1964, copyright © 1964 by The American Museum of Natural History.

E. P. DUTTON & CO., INC.: An excerpt (titled: "A Boy and a Raccoon") from *Little Rascal* by Sterling North, copyright © 1965 by Sterling North.

FAIRE EDWARDS: An excerpt on p. 154 from "Barns" by Faire Edwards from *Vermont Life,* Summer 1966.

FOLLETT PUBLISHING COMPANY, DIVISION OF FOLLETT CORPORATION: An excerpt (titled: "From Bowstring to Violin") adapted from *How Man Made Music* by Fannie R. Buchanan and Charles L. Luckenbill, copyright © 1959 by Follett Publishing Company, division of Fellett Corporation. Previous copyright 1951. An excerpt on pp. 356–57 from *George Washington, Leader of the People* by Clara Ingram Judson, copyright © 1951 by Clara Ingram Judson. An excerpt on p. 345 and an illustration on p. 345 from *Exploring Regions of the Western Hemisphere* by Herbert H. Gross, Dwight W. Follett, Robert E. Gabler, William L. Burton, and Ben F. Ahlschwede, copyright © 1971, 1966 by Follett Publishing Company, division of Follett Corporation.

FOUR WINDS PRESS, A DIVISION OF SCHOLASTIC MAGAZINES, INC.: An excerpt (titled: "Man on the Moon") adapted from *The Moon Explorers* by Tony Simon, copyright © 1970 by Tony Simon.

GARRARD PUBLISHING COMPANY: An excerpt on p. 209 adapted from *Junior Science Book of Sound* by Dorothy Anderson, copyright 1962 by Dorothy S. Anderson.

GENERAL LEARNING CORPORATION: Excerpts and illustrations on pp. 97–98 from *Modern Mathematics Through Discovery (Grade 5),* pp. 391–94, © 1970 General Learning Corporation. Excerpts on p. 295 and pp. 381–83 from *The American Continents,* © 1968 General Learning Corporation. An excerpt on p. 341 from *Science 5,* p. 305, © 1968 General Learning Corporation. An excerpt on pp. 242–43 from *Man and Society,* p. 156, © 1972 General Learning Corporation.

GINN AND COMPANY: An excerpt on p. 135 from *Your Country and Mine* by Tiegs, Adams, Brown, © copyright 1965 by Ginn and Company.

THE STEPHEN GREENE PRESS, BRATTLEBORO, VERMONT: An adaptation of "Busman's Holiday" (retitled: "The Pony Auction") from *The Loon in My Bathtub,* by Ronald Rood, copyright © 1964 by Ronald N. Rood. An excerpt on p. 149 adapted from *The Loon in My Bathtub,* by Ronald Rood, copyright © 1964 by Ronald N. Rood.

GROSSET & DUNLAP, INC.: An excerpt on pp. 202–03 adapted from *How and Why Wonder Book of Basic Inventions* by Irving Robbin, copyright © 1965 by Wonder Books, a division of Grosset & Dunlap, Inc.

HARCOURT BRACE JOVANOVICH, INC.: Excerpts on p. 302, p. 305 and p. 306 from *And Everything Nice, The Story of Sugar, Spice, and Flavoring,* copyright © 1966 by Elizabeth K. Cooper. Excerpts on pp. 150–51 and pp. 152–53 from *The Story of India* by Jean Bothwell. Entry on p. 50 for *apt* from *The Harcourt Brace School Dictionary.* Long pronunciation key on p. 390, short pronunciation key on pp. 393, 395, 397, 399, 401, 403, 405, and 407, all Glossary entries on pp. 391–407, and illustrations on pp. 392(a), 393(a and b), 395(a and b), 396(b), 399(b), 404(a), 405(b), and 407(a) from *The Harcourt Brace School Dictionary,* copyright, © 1972, 1968, by Harcourt Brace Jovanovich, Inc. An excerpt from Table of Contents on pp. 336–37 and excerpt on pp. 136–37 from *Roberts English Series: Fifth Book* by Paul Roberts. Exercises on pp. 191–92 and excerpt on pp. 247–48 from *Harbrace Mathematics, Purple* by Payne, *et al.,* copyright © 1972 by Harcourt Brace Jovanovich, Inc. Introduction on p. 100, Pronunciation Key on p. 100, selected Glossary entries on p. 101 from "Key Concept Terms: A Beginning Vocabulary for Science"; section of Table of Contents on pp. 338–39, excerpts on p. 137 from *Concepts in Science: Purple,* Third Edition, by Paul Brandwein, *et al.* An excerpt on p. 253 from *The Negro in American Life* by Mabel Morsback. Excerpts on pp. 112 and 113 from *A Letter to Anywhere* by Al Hine and John Alcorn. An adaptation of "Men in the Sea" by Peter R. Limburg, © 1970 by Harcourt Brace Jovanovich, Inc.

HARPER & ROW, PUBLISHERS, INCORPORATED: Excerpts on p. 136 and pp. 138–39 from *Basic Social Studies, 5* by Burnette, *et al.* Excerpts on pp. 40–41 and pp. 244–45 from *Today's Basic Science 5,* 1967 Edition, by Navarra and Zafforoni.

D. C. HEATH AND COMPANY: An excerpt on pp. 186–88 from *Science in Our World 5* (*Heath Science Series,* Third Edition), by Herman and Nina Schneider.

HOLT, RINEHART AND WINSTON, INC.: An excerpt on pp. 189–90 from *Knowing Our Neighbors in the United States* by Carls, *et al.,* copyright © 1966. Excerpts on p. 136, p. 137 and pp. 294–95 from *Science: A Modern Approach 5* by Fischler, *et al.,* copyright © 1966. Illustration on p. 294 adapted from *Science: A Modern Approach 5* by Fischler, *et al.,* copyright © 1966.

JOHNSON PUBLISHING COMPANY: An adaptation of "Hollywood Stunt Girl" by Walter Price Burrell from *Ebony* Magazine, December 1971, copyright 1971 by Johnson Publishing Company, Inc.

LAIDLAW BROTHERS: An excerpt on p. 296 from *Health* (Second Edition) 5 by Byrd, *et al.* An excerpt and illustration on pp. 37–39 from *The Social Studies and Our Country: Concepts in Social Studies* by King, Rudman, and Eppenly. An excerpt on p. 340 from *Our Country* by Krug and McCall. An excerpt on pp. 386–87 adapted from *Great Names in Our Country's Story* by Eibling, *et al.*

LION BOOKS: "Helen Keller – Conqueror of Darkness" adapted from *Great American Heroines* by Arnold Dolin.

MACMILLAN PUBLISHING CO., INC.: Excerpt on pp. 240–41 and illustration on p. 241 from *Science for Tomorrow's World,* 5 by Dr. J. Darrell Barnard, Celia B. Stendler, and Dr. J. Myron Atkins, copyright © by The Macmillan Company 1966. Illustration on p. 297 adapted from *The Story of American Freedom* by Edna McGuire, copyright © by The Macmillan Company 1971.

JULIAN MESSNER, A DIVISION OF SIMON & SCHUSTER, INC.: An excerpt (titled: "The Beginnings of Printing") adapted from *Black on White and Read All Over: The Story of Printing,* by Albert Barker, copyright © 1971 by Albert Barker. An adaptation of "The Parachute Pioneers" (retitled: "Skydiving – Sport in Space") from *The Space Age Sport: Skydiving* by Ray Darby, copyright © 1964 by Ray Darby.

WILLIAM MORROW AND COMPANY, INC.: An adaptation of "Village in the Wilderness" (retitled: "John Smith, Wilderness Leader") from *America Is Born: A History for Peter* by Gerald W. Johnson, copyright © 1959 by Gerald W. Johnson.

NOBLE AND NOBLE, PUBLISHERS, INC.: An excerpt on p. 293 from *When Greatness Called; Stories of Courage in America* by Lavinia Dobley, copyright © 1970.

PARENTS' MAGAZINE PRESS: An adaptation of "Rails Across the West" from *The Golden Spike* by Harold Littledale, copyright © 1963 by Parents' Magazine Press.

RAND MCNALLY & COMPANY: An excerpt on p. 146 from *Animals on the Move* by Ann and Myron Sutton, copyright 1965 by Ann and Myron Sutton.

RANDOM HOUSE, INC.: Chapters 1 and 2 (titled: "Man's First Dog") condensed from *All About Dogs,* by Carl Burger, copyright © 1962 by Carl Burger. "Sacajawea" condensed from *Heroines of the Early West,* by Nancy Wilson Ross, copyright 1944, © 1960 by Nancy Wilson Ross. "Four Boys and the French Cave of Lascaux" from *All About Prehistoric Cave Men,* by Sam and Beryl Epstein, copyright © 1959 by Sam and Beryl Epstein. "Floyd Little" adapted from *Star Running Backs of the NFL,* by Bill Libby, copyright © 1971 by Random House, Inc. An excerpt on p. 14 from *All About Volcanoes and Earthquakes* by Frederick H. Pough, copyright 1953 by Frederick H. Pough. An excerpt on pp. 384–85 from "John Smith Sets an Example" from *This Is Our Land,* by Patterson, Patterson, Hunnicutt, Grambs, and Smith, copyright © 1963, 1967 by The L. W. Singer Company, Inc.

HENRY REGNERY COMPANY PUBLISHERS: "Light My Fire" (retitled: "Feliciano!") adapted from *Challenged by Handicap* by Richard B. Lyttle.

SCOTT, FORESMAN AND COMPANY: An excerpt on p. 51 from *Thorndike-Barnhart Junior Dictionary,* Sixth Edition, copyright © 1964 by Scott, Foresman and Company. An excerpt on p. 340 from *In the Americas* by Hanna, *et al.*, copyright © 1965 by Scott, Foresman and Company. Extracts on pp. 343–44 and illustrations on pp. 342–45 from *Health for All, Book 5* by Bauer, *et al.*, copyright © 1966 by Scott, Foresman and Company. An excerpt on p. 291 from *Science Is Discovering* by Beauchamp, *et al.*, copyright © 1968 by Scott, Foresman and Company.

CHARLES SCRIBNER'S SONS, THE BOBBS-MERRILL COMPANY, INC., AND G. P. PUTNAM'S SONS: "Learning About Penguins" (retitled: "Penguin Paradise") adapted from *Explorers and Penguins,* pp. 1–34, by Edna M. Andreas, copyright © 1959 by Edna M. Andreas. Parts of "Learning About Penguins" were adapted by permission of The Bobbs-Merrill Company, Inc., from *Whaling in the Frozen South* by Alan J. Villiers, copyright 1925, 1931 by The Bobbs-Merrill Company, Inc., 1953, 1959 by Alan J. Villiers; or adapted by permission of G. P. Putnam's Sons from *Little America* by Richard E. Byrd, copyright 1930 by Richard E. Byrd, renewed 1958 by Richard E. Byrd.

EVELYN SINGER LITERARY AGENCY AND HARVEY HOUSE: "Ancient Engineers" (retitled: "America's Earliest Engineers") from *The Story of Archeology in the Americas* by Mary Elting and Franklin Folsom, © 1960 by Mary Elting and Franklin Folsom. Adapted illustration on p. 218 and illustrations on pp. 219–22 from *The Story of Archeology in the Americas* by Mary Elting and Franklin Folsom, © 1960 by Mary Elting and Franklin Folsom.

STRAVON EDUCATIONAL PRESS: An excerpt on p. 259 adapted from *The Man Who Painted the Sun: The Story of Vincent Van Gogh* by Kerwin Bowles.

VANGUARD PRESS, INC.: Chapters 1 and 6 (titled: "A River in the Ocean") adapted from *The Gulf Stream* by Ruth Brindze, copyright 1945 by The Vanguard Press, Inc.

The artists in this book and the pages on which their work appears are as follows:

MONROE EISENBERG: pp. 156, 158, 160–61, 210, 212, 215–16, 272, 274, 277. MARVIN FRIEDMAN: pp. 122, 124, 127, 176, 178, 181, 183–84. MANNY HALLER: pp. 4–5, 7–13, 46–53, 106–09, 111–13, 115, 144–55, 196–203, 205–09, 252–61, 302–09, 350–52, 355–59. MICHAEL HAMPSHIRE: pp. 60, 63, 87, 89–90, 96. TED LEWIN: 57–58, 76, 78, 81, 83, 321, 323. CARL OWENS: 65, 67–68, 71, 73, 131, 229–30, 232, 235, 237–38.

All Maps: Harbrace. Illustration on p. 345 adapted by ORIN KINCAIDE. All adapted illustrations: Harbrace. The illustrations on pages 394a, 394b, 396, 397, 400b, 401, 402a, 404, and 406 are reproduced from *The Harcourt School Dictionary,* copyright © 1972, 1968 by Harcourt Brace Jovanovich, Inc.

Photographs are from the sources listed below:

KEY: MP Magnum Photos, Inc.; PR Photo Researchers, Inc.; WCA Woodfin Camp and Associates.

Page ii, David Falconer, BLACK STAR; 2, NASA; 16, 18, 20 (2), Parachutes Inc., Orange, Mass.; 22–36, NASA; 38, The Mariner's Museum, Newport News, Virginia; 44, WASHINGTON UNIVERSITY GALLERY OF ART, St. Louis, Missouri; 55, New York Public Library; 75, Washington State Park, Portland, Oregon; 95, Union Pacific Railroad Museum Collection; 104, Bruce Davidson, MP; 117, UNIVERSITY OF CHICAGO PRESS; 119, 121, New York Public Library; 128, 133, Courtesy American Foundation for the Blind; 142, Marc and Evelyn Bernheim, WCA; 163, Russ Kinne, PR; 165, Robert Rheinhold; 166, Phillipa Scott, PR; 169, National Park Service Photo by Cecil W. Stoughton; 172, J. D. Pennewell, Pennewell Pictures; 189, Albert Bierstadt, *The Last of the Buffalo,* in the collection of the Corcoran Gallery of Art; 194, René Burri, MP; 223, 226, Mats Wibe Lund, Jr.; 225, SHOSTAL AND ASSOCIATES; 250, Katrina Thomas, PR; 263, 264, French Government Tourist Office; 267, Languepin, RAPHO GUILLUMETTE PICTURES; 268, *Permission S.P.A.D.E.M.,* 1972 by French Reproduction Rights, Inc. Photo by Giraudon; 271, Archives Photographiques – Paris; 279, 281, Thomas Gilcrease Institute, Tulsa, Oklahoma; 283, Collection, Remington Art Memorial Museum, Ogdensburg, New York; 284, United Press International; 287, 289, Feliciano Enterprises; 292, Dan Budnik, WCA; 300, Barry Hennings, PR; 314, 317, R. T. Peterson, PR; 325, 326, Official U.S. Navy Photographs; 329, United Press International; 330, 333, Official U.S. Navy Photographs; 348, Erich Hartmann, MP; 360–66, PHOTO ASSOCIATES; 369, A. DEVANEY, INC.; 371, Hiroji Kubota, MP; 373, Sepp Seitz, MP; 375, A. DEVANEY, INC.; 376, G. Peress, MP; 377, 379, 380, Sidney Baldwin for EBONY MAGAZINE.

Contents

Unit 1 Venturing into Space

Unit 2 Building America

Unit 3 Communicating with Others

Unit 4 Man Meets Beast

Unit 5 Putting Ideas to Work

Unit 6 Communicating Through Art

Unit 7 **Learning About the Earth**

Unit 8 **Action!**

To the Reader

This is a book about learning. In it you will read how men and women have learned many things, such as:

–how they learned to tame wild animals,
–how they learned about the earth they live on,
–how they learned to live in space and in the ocean.

As you read about how others have learned, you will also be studying how to learn yourself. You will learn how to read better and how to study. You will learn how to remember ideas and facts that are important. You will learn how to think clearly about what you read.

This book is divided into eight units. Each unit begins with Skills Lessons, which will show you ways to read and study. You can use these skills when you read the articles that follow.

Many of the articles are like books you read for history, science, mathematics, and other school subjects. In fact, your big purpose for using *this* book is to learn how to read and study better in all the other books you use in school.

Each unit in this book has a section called "Textbook Study." In some ways, reading a textbook is like reading anything else. But in other ways, reading a textbook is a little different. You study a textbook to learn how to do something, or to understand new ideas and remember important information. In the sections called "Textbook Study," you will learn ways to get the most out of your textbooks.

Unit 1

Venturing into Space

A spaceship and docking vehicle with Earth in the background.

SKILLS LESSON

CLUES TO PRONUNCIATION

You find new words everywhere—in your textbooks, in the reading you do for fun, in watching television, and in listening to people talk. Some words you pick up without realizing you're learning them. Others you learn on purpose.

When you learn new words through reading, you do these things:

—You think of sound-letter relationships and look for syllables and other word parts. You try to pronounce the word.
—You look for clues to meaning *within* the word.
—You look for clues to meaning in the *context*.
—You use a dictionary.

Of course, you don't do all these things with every word. Often a combination of clues helps you understand a word—a context clue and a familiar prefix, for example.

The lessons in this unit will help you to review the first three ways of adding to your reading vocabulary. The fourth way—the dictionary—will be discussed in the next unit.

Using Sound-Letter Relationships

You know what sounds letters stand for. So you can often decode a word that you've never seen in print before. When you do so, you often recognize a word you know "by ear." Perhaps this word—**squint**—is one you have not seen before. You can pronounce it because you know what sounds its letters represent. Once you have said the word, you know what it means.

Syllables Help in Pronouncing Words

A one-syllable word like **squint** is easy to read. But how do you tackle a long, unfamiliar word? Dividing a word into syllables can help you to say it. Look at this example:

There is danger of **spontaneous combustion.**

If you don't know how to pronounce those last two words, you should divide them into syllables:

spon ta ne ous com bus tion

You remember that a syllable is a word part that has one vowel *sound.* The last syllable in **spontaneous (-ous)** and the last

Different things can give you clues.

syllable in **combustion (-tion)** each have two vowel *letters* but only one vowel *sound.*

After you have said the syllables in each word separately, put the sounds together and say the whole word. Your first try may not be exactly right, but probably it is close enough for you to recognize the two words. Have you ever heard these words spoken? Do you know their meaning? Spontaneous combustion is a fire that starts by itself. Spontaneous combustion may happen with oily rags, for example.

TRY THIS

How many syllables are there in each of the following words? Write the number of syllables on your paper. Then write the meaning of the word. Use a dictionary if you need to.

1. accidental
2. vertical
3. gymnastics
4. emergencies
5. parachute
6. together

SKILLS LESSON

CLUES TO MEANING WITHIN THE WORD

Once you can pronounce a word, you must find out what it means. Sometimes word parts give you clues to meaning.

Morphemes Help with Meaning

A **morpheme** is a unit of meaning in a word. The word *spacesuit* has two units of meaning: *space* and *suit*. There are two morphemes in *spacesuit*.

The word *talk* has only one morpheme, but *talked* has two: the meaning of *talk* and the meaning of the past tense, shown by the suffix *-ed*.

In *cheerful* there are also two morphemes: the root word *cheer* means "state of gladness," and the suffix *-ful* means "full of." A morpheme may be a syllable by itself (like the *space* in *spacesuit*), or it may be only part of a syllable (like the *-ed* in *talked*).

Recognizing morphemes is helpful to a reader, for a morpheme may give you a clue to the meaning of a word. For example how does the morpheme *metal* give a clue to the meaning of *metallic* in this sentence?

The object has a **metallic** glow in the firelight.

In some compound words, it is easy to see how the separate morphemes contribute to the meaning of the whole word. *Campfire* is such a word. The meanings of those two morphemes – *camp* and *fire* – combine to make a word that means "a fire at an outdoor camp."

In other compound words, the meaning of the morphemes may not be so clearly reflected. In these compound words, you have to use your imagination to see where the whole word gets its meaning:

babysit **graybeard** **shoehorn** **skydiving**

Roots, Prefixes, and Suffixes

How many morphemes are there in *unhelpful?* If you said three, you are right. You recognized the root word *help,* the familiar prefix *un-,* and the suffix *-ful.* Since *un-* means "not," you know that the word means "not full of help." Do these three morphemes help you to interpret meaning in these words?

uncover **helpless** **frightful**

Prefixes are morphemes added to the beginning of a word, and suffixes are morphemes added to the end. The words to which they are added are root words.

A prefix always makes at least one separate syllable (*mis place, inter state*). A suffix may be one or more separate syllables *(wait ed, work able),* or it may not be a separate syllable *(walked).*

Prefixes and suffixes always have meaning, so they add meaning to the root word. A familiar prefix, suffix, or root word gives you a clue to meaning. For example, do you know the word in boldface type in the sentence on the next page?

The ski pants are made of **stretchable** fabric.

Stretchable is easy to decode when you see its two morphemes: *stretch* and *-able*. Do you know what the word means?

TRY THIS

Find the root in each word in boldface type and write it on your paper. Be prepared to pronounce each word and to tell what you think it means.

1. A door mat should have a **nonskid** backing.
2. He attended school so **irregularly** that he did not make passing grades.
3. We could hear a faint **insectlike** buzz from the motor.
4. A wild animal may smell a hunter who is **upwind** of him.
5. The teacher viewed Harold's science exhibit—a garter snake—with some **disfavor.**
6. Many all-purpose coats for men and boys have **detachable** linings and hoods.
7. For miles around, everyone felt the **thunderous** power of the Saturn V rocket.
8. The herd ran **unchecked** toward the river.

SKILLS LESSON

THERE MAY BE A CONTEXT CLUE

You may be unfamiliar with the meaning of some morphemes in a word. Or a morpheme may have a different meaning from the one you know. You know what *re-* and *treat* mean, but you also know **retreat** does *not* mean "*to take care of again.*" When you cannot figure out meaning from word parts, you must look for clues to meaning in the context.

Context, you remember, means the words or sentences that surround a particular word. Writers often tell you what a new word means by defining it in context. Here is an example:

Physical **coordination** – the smooth working together of parts of the body – is necessary for an athlete.

The context often helps to explain an unfamiliar word even if a definition is not given. Consider this sentence:

He cut a path through the jungle with his **machete.**

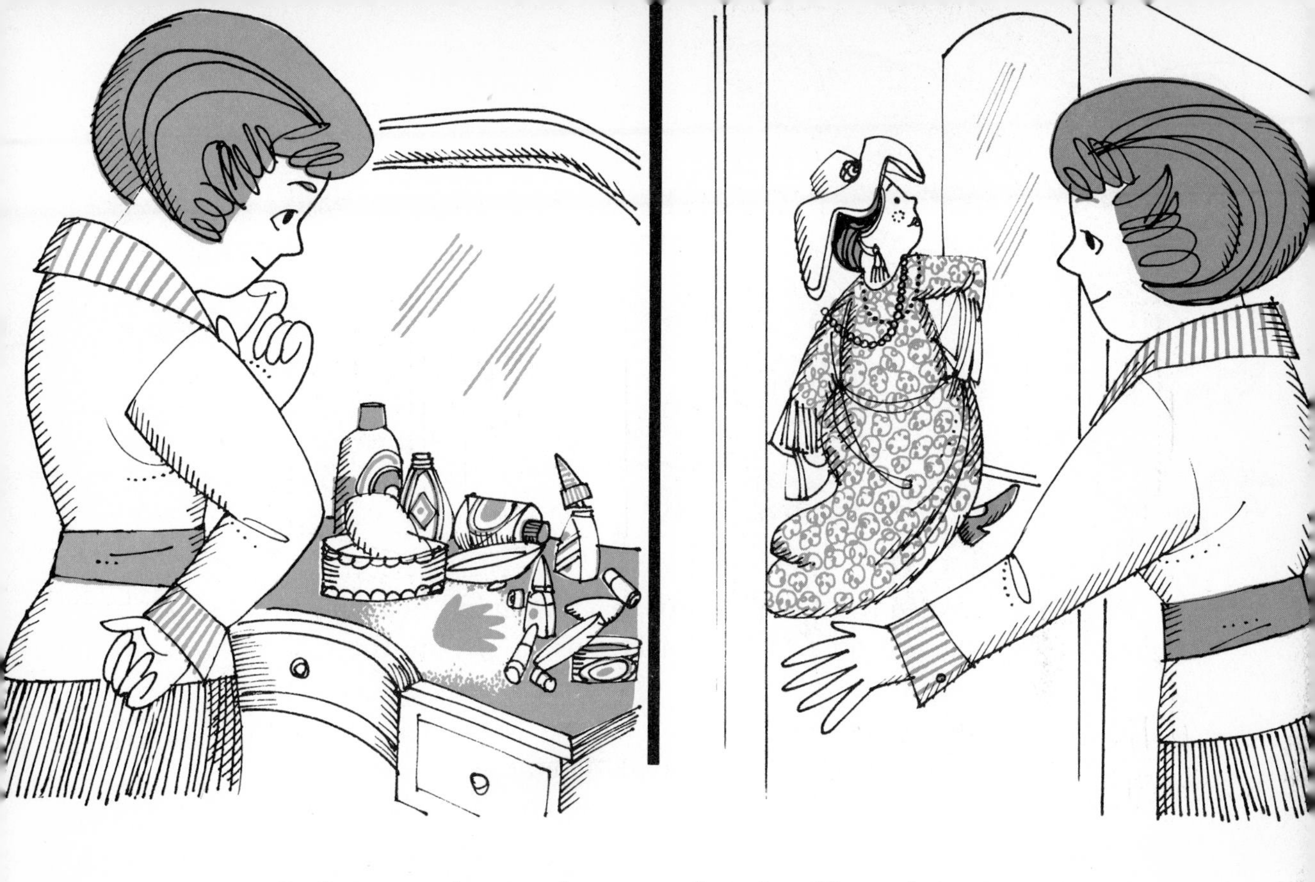

Perhaps you know what a *machete* is. If you do not, you can tell from the context that a *machete* must be a sharp tool of some kind that a person can use to cut away thick shrubs and vines. You may not know how to pronounce *machete,* but you know something about its meaning because of its context.

TRY THIS

On a piece of paper write each word that is in boldface type in the sentences below. Decide from the context what each word means and write its meaning beside it. Be ready to tell how the context helped you.

1. The pilot had to **abandon** his burning plane and jump to safety.
2. The wind lifted the front flap of the tent, one of the poles swayed sideways, and then the whole tent **collapsed.**
3. Scientists train the **technicians** who will operate the instruments and machines needed for a space flight.

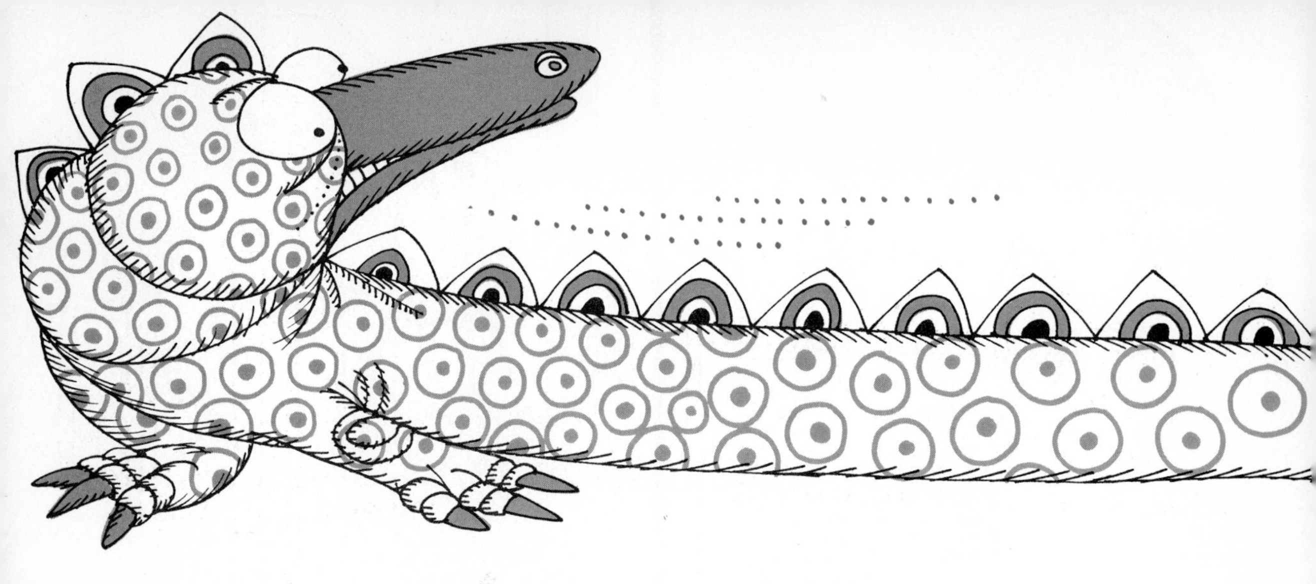

4. She was studying so **intently** that she didn't hear me.
5. The operator broke in and asked us to give up the line for an **urgent** call.
6. The **navigator** studied the maps, took star sightings, checked the instruments, and plotted the ship's course.
7. The jumper's fall was **checked** when his parachute opened.

Similar Meanings and Opposite Meanings

The clue to an unfamiliar word may be a word with a similar meaning. Thinking about what you are reading helps you to see such likenesses. Read these sentences.

The trail **terminated** in a thick tangle of thorns and bushes. Since the afternoon was coming to an end, too, the boys decided to turn back.

You can tell that *terminated* must mean "came to an end." The word *too* after "coming to an end" tells you that.

Unfamiliar words may be explained by contrast, too. The next paragraph explains *vivid* by using words that are not like it in meaning.

The colors on the TV screen in the space capsule were blurred and cloudy. But through the window the astronaut saw **vivid** colors.

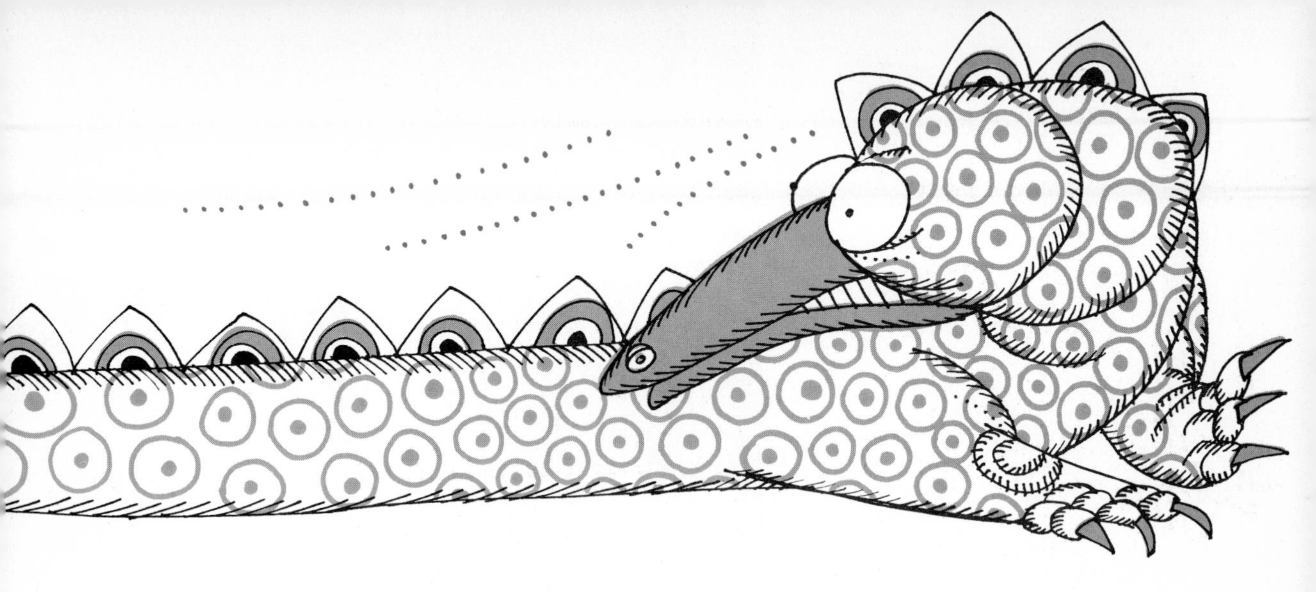

If you do not know what *vivid* means, what clues will help you? First, you know that *vivid* can describe colors. Second, the word *but* is a signal for a contrasting idea. It tells you *vivid* must mean *not* blurred and cloudy—that is, *vivid* means bright and sharp. The context helps you by using words with opposite meanings.

TRY THIS

Write the numerals 1 to 6 on a piece of paper. After each, write what you think is the meaning of the word in boldface type in the sentences below.

1. The broken tubing wasted valuable fuel, but the pilot was able to **conserve** some power in free flight.
2. Some plastic leaves look so real that you can hardly believe they are **artificial.**
3. A cat may look big to a mouse, and a mouse probably looks **monstrous** to a bug.
4. Elevators used to be operated by persons, but today most of them are **automatic.**
5. Many of the buildings on the fairgrounds were built to last, since they are intended for **permanent** use.
6. He usually gave a prepared speech, but today he made some **impromptu** remarks.

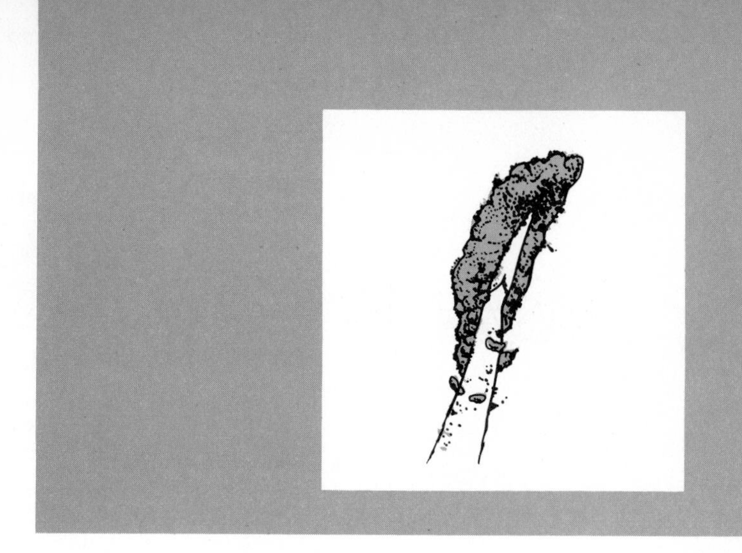

The Larger Context

Clues to meaning are often right in the sentence that contains the word. But sometimes you need to look further. Does this sentence help you know what pumice (pum′is) is?

Pumice is one.

You cannot tell what pumice is from this sentence. But now look at the sentence that comes before it:

All sorts of stones of a much less precious sort come out of volcanos. **Pumice** is one.

Now you see the word in a larger context. You know it is a volcanic stone that is not precious. Additional context tells you more about pumice.

It looks like a brittle sponge and is the lightest stone in the world, so light, that if you put it in the water, it will float. That's because it's filled with bubbles of gas. The lava got thrown out with such violence that the gas in it never had a chance to escape. It made a froth of hot stone. Before it could get out, the lava became solid.

Now you know quite a lot about *pumice.* The entire paragraph explained it. Remember to look for *all* the information you can find about an unfamiliar word.

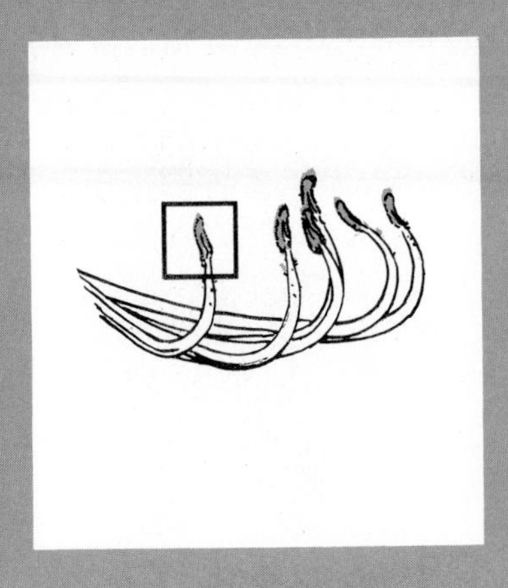

TRY THIS

Read the following paragraphs. Look for clues to the meaning of the term **relay satellite.** Then write an explanation of a relay satellite.

A man-made satellite is an object that has been launched by rocket and is revolving around the earth. Satellites are equipped to do various things. A satellite may be equipped to receive and broadcast television signals. A television station in England, for example, broadcasts a program and rebroadcasts it to a city in the United States.

This satellite is something like a runner in a relay race. It receives and passes on live television programs over great distances. This is why it is called a relay satellite.

WHAT DID YOU LEARN?

1. How does knowing sound-letter relationships help in reading?
2. How can dividing a long word into syllables help you to understand it? Give two examples. Does it always help?
3. What is a morpheme? Tell how many morphemes are in each of these words: **inkstand, accidents, preview.**
4. Where can you look for context clues to the meaning of a new word? What kinds of clues may you find?

A man falls through the sky. Down, down he goes. What is happening?

Spread-eagled, the skydiver descends through space in free fall.

Skydiving—Sport in Space

by RAY DARBY

To pronounce any words that are new to you, use your knowledge of sound-letter relationships and look for familiar word parts. Note the many figures of speech.

The small plane looks like a mosquito up there at 12,000 feet. You can barely hear its insectlike buzz as it makes a lazy circle against the bright blue of the sky. It is a beautiful day. The wind is blowing gently about five miles per hour, judging by the half-filled wind sock on its pole above the hangar. There are a few soft, white clouds drifting by, their shadows creeping across the low, brush-covered hills that surround the private airfield where you are standing.

It is a perfect day for parachute jumping.

You strain your eyes to keep the plane in sight. It is almost time. At any moment now, a tiny black speck will separate itself from the plane, a speck no larger than the period at the end of this sentence. Because you have been watching this sort of thing before, you know what will happen. The speck will appear to hover as the plane flies away from it, as though it had been marked on the blue page of the sky with the point of a sharp pencil. Then, suddenly, it will appear to grow larger. It will begin to take shape.

You squint your eyes, trying to focus them on that tiny dot up there. The plane has flown out of your line of vision. You can't see it any more, or use it to help locate the speck, so you don't even blink for fear you may lose it.

Perhaps ten seconds have passed. The time always seems to be longer than it actually is. But now the speck is easier to see. It has grown larger. In another few seconds, like a tadpole turning into a frog, it sprouts arms and legs. Now, for the first time, you are able to see it as the figure of a man, spread-eagled in the sky. A mile and a half above you, a man is plummeting down out of nowhere, completely detached from the earth. He has no wings, nothing to hold him up. He is simply tumbling through space with his arms and legs outstretched. You are still struck with the strange sight of a man up there in the nothingness of the sky. Men walk on the ground, climb hills, jump across ditches, but always with that established relationship to the ground. Men just don't fly all by themselves, higher than eagles. It takes a while to get used to the idea each time you see it. You recall nightmares you've had, in which you found yourself falling helplessly, shaking with terror. But this is not a nightmare. You are wide awake on a bright, crisp fall day and the man up there in the heavens is still falling . . . falling.

You shake your head. Suddenly you see a flutter of nylon above the man, as though he were waving a handkerchief at you. The flutter blossoms into a huge, brightly colored umbrella, and a fraction of a second later, you hear a sharp, crackling sound. It reminds you of someone snapping a bed sheet like a whip.

Now the jumper's fall is checked. He hangs beneath his open parachute, swinging gently back and forth. He is not too far above you, maybe a thousand feet or so. You

can make him out quite clearly. He is wearing coveralls and heavy boots and what looks like a pilot's helmet, and he is tugging at the lines that extend up to the parachute. The chute revolves slowly, turning him to face the wind . . . what there is of it. He is looking down at the ground, and as you watch, you hear him shout at you.

"Clear the target!"

For an instant you are unable to move. The strangest thing of all is to hear a voice bellowing down at you from the height of a twenty-story building. Then you realize you are standing right beside the crossed strips of white cloth that mark the spot where the jumper wants to land, and you back quickly away.

He seems to be coming down very fast. He is still working those control lines, keeping his face to the breeze. He hits the ground about ten feet away from the target, falls, rolls over and bounds up again, running a few steps as the collapsing parachute tugs at him. Then the chute becomes a heap of red, white, and blue cloth on the ground, and the jumper is calmly unbuckling the straps that held him to it. You walk over to him, and he turns to you with a broad grin on his face.

"How was it up there?" you ask. What else do you say to a man who has just fallen from a height of nearly three miles? "Have a good trip?"

You are talking to a skydiver, one of the many thousands in this country and abroad who spend their weekends and holidays—and often their evenings—jumping out of airplanes.

THE PARACHUTE

The thing that has made all this possible is the parachute. The word "parachute" originated in France, and is derived from two French words, *para*, meaning that which shields or protects, and *chute*, meaning a fall. By combining these two source words, we come up with a very appropriate name which means "to protect from a fall." The modern parachute has removed almost all the risk of jumping. It has taken the jumper out of the classification of reckless daredevil and made him a respected and accepted sportsman, an athlete of sorts, in a game that doesn't require great strength or speed. Except for the first couple of jumps, it doesn't even require a lot of courage.

THE TECHNIQUES OF FREE FALL

Our skydiver's jump started with a free fall—leaving the plane and falling through space before opening the parachute. When the

◄ **The parachute begins to open, and the diver's free fall is checked.**

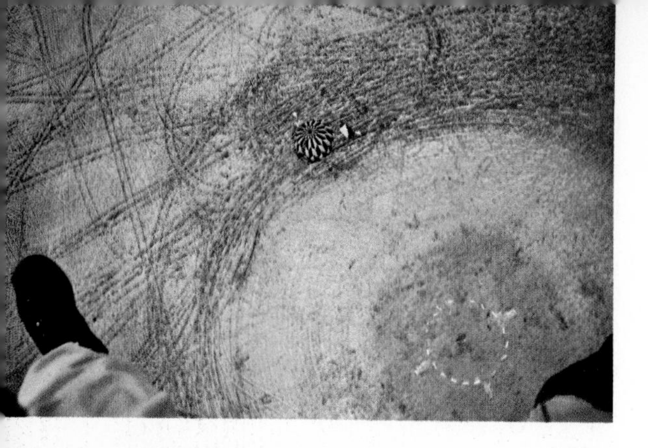

From far above, one skydiver sees another moving toward the target.

The skydiver has worked his control lines well. He has landed on the target.

French perfected the techniques of free fall, they opened up a whole new field to the sport parachutist. They also disproved a number of mistaken beliefs. For example, it was widely believed that a person would black out, or lose consciousness, if he fell any great distance. It was also believed that a jumper would continue to fall faster and faster the farther he dropped, that at such speeds he would not be able to breathe, and that a man would simply tumble over and over as he fell.

But these early jumpers proved that we are more like the birds than we ever knew. With the experience gained from the French as well as by jumpers the world over, the free-falling jumper is in complete control of both mind and body. And the method used is so simple that almost anyone can do it. All it takes is bodily coordination and a cool head.

There are four basic body positions in free fall. With all of them it is important that the movements of the chutist be fast and smooth. If a jumper should go out of control when he pulls his ripcord, he can wind up in serious trouble. The parachute may not function, or it may be damaged. The opening may be delayed too long. There have been cases where a careless jumper hunched his shoulders or pulled the ripcord too slowly, and was flipped completely over. The danger in this, of course, lies in the possibility that his feet may become tangled in the suspension lines.

FALLING WITH THE OPEN CHUTE

When the jumper opens his chute, his falling speed drops to sixteen feet per second in a matter of three seconds, at most. But the opening shock is not as violent as you might think. The parachute and the lines are made of stretchable material, and they absorb much of the jolt. The rest is distributed over various parts of the body by the harness. It might be compared to the feeling you get in a descending elevator when it comes to a fast halt.

The first thing the parachutist does after opening his chute is to look up at it to make sure everything is in good order. Then he looks down at the target and checks the direction and speed of his drift. He steers himself to land as close as possible to the target by pulling on left or right steering lines, which causes the chute to turn in the direction he wants. In this way he can compensate for unexpected gusts of wind and change the direction in which he is heading, if necessary. Most chutes have certain sections removed from the rear. This causes the parachutist to move along at about three to thirteen miles per hour as the trapped air is forced out through the opening.

The jumper tries to stay upwind of the target when descending. If he allows himself to drift downwind, he must work his way back against the breeze, which is rather like sailing a boat head-on into a stiff gale. He always faces into the wind when landing, as this reduces his forward speed and prevents tumbles. If he lands with the wind at his back, his landing speed will be the normal three to thirteen miles per hour, plus the speed of the wind itself, and this could get him into trouble.

It may be that some of these details, which every parachutist must learn, can be simplified as new designs and new methods of skydiving are introduced.

■ "One small step for a man, one giant leap for mankind."

Man on the Moon

by TONY SIMON

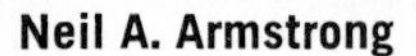

Neil A. Armstrong

Edwin E. (Buzz) Aldrin, Jr.

Michael Collins

Use the context clues to help you understand new words.

It was the start of a new age for man. No one would forget 1969, just as no one has forgotten 1492.

OFF TO THE MOON

On the morning of July 16, three men got up about 4:15 A.M. They had a healthy breakfast of orange juice, steak, scrambled eggs, toast, coffee. Soon they were in white spacesuits and on the way to Pad 39A. An elevator lifted them to the top of the Saturn V. They were Neil A. Armstrong, the commander of the first moon-landing flight; Edwin E. (Buzz) Aldrin, Jr., the LM (Lunar Module) pilot; and Michael Collins, the command-ship pilot. The men had much in common. Each had been born in 1930. Each was an experienced jet pilot. And each had been on space missions before.

Armstrong, calm and quick-thinking, had been the commander of Gemini 8. He had performed the first space-docking in history. Later, when Gemini 8 tumbled out of control, he brought it down safely in a wild emergency splashdown in the Pacific Ocean.

Aldrin, a brilliant space scientist,

had served as co-pilot of Gemini 12. He had made a five-and-a-half-hour spacewalk, evaluating new equipment and space tools.

Collins, an all-around astronaut, had been the co-pilot of Gemini 10. He had walked in space twice and had performed a difficult double-docking task.

Armstrong would be the first man to walk on the moon, and Aldrin would be the second. Collins, orbiting overhead in the command ship, would not touch down on the moon. But he was pleased to be part of the crew. "I'm going 99.99 percent of the way," he explained.

Armstrong boarded the Apollo 11 ship and sat on the left side. Then came Collins on the right, with Aldrin in the center. The command ship was code-named *Columbia*. LM, code-named *Eagle*, was stored, with legs folded, between the service module and the front of the third-stage rocket.

At Pad 39A, a million faces were turned to the rocket. Millions upon millions more watched on TV that was beamed around the world. What they could not see were Armstrong, Aldrin, and Collins inside Apollo 11. They were running through testing patterns and checking out systems and switch settings on the control panel. All was in perfect order.

Apollo 11 lifting off. ►

"LIFT-OFF . . . WE HAVE A LIFT-OFF. . . ."

The countdown minutes dwindled into the final seconds.

"Twenty seconds and counting," called flight control. ". . . twelve . . . eleven . . . ten . . . nine . . . ignition sequence starts . . . six . . . five . . . four . . . three . . . two . . . one . . . zero . . . all engines running." As the countdown ended, powerful jets of steam spurted from the pad below the rocket. Blinding orange flame leaped out, slamming into the ground. Intense, glaring light dazzled onlookers. Black clouds of smoke billowed up and spread far. Then the flame turned white and formed into a thick column that seemed to push the rocket up through its own fiery cloud into the clouds above.

The battle against Earth's gravity was on. Slowly, silently, the rocket rose straight up like a giant elevator. Then came a deafening, shattering roar of explosions. The ground shook, and for miles around everyone felt the thunderous power of Saturn V as its 7,500,000 pounds of thrust lifted 6,500,000 pounds of weight.

"Lift-off... we have a lift-off thirty-two minutes past the hour," came the call from flight control.

Apollo was on target for the moon. At lift-off, the moon was exactly 218,096 miles away.

In two-and-a-half minutes, Saturn V was out of sight, swallowed up by a blue sky. The second-stage rocket fired. Ten minutes later, the third-stage rocket fired and put Apollo 11 into Earth orbit, at a speed of 17,500 miles an hour, 118 miles above the surface.

The men were now weightless. While circling Earth, they again checked out systems and switches and replotted their moon course. Then, two-and-a-half hours after lift-off, the third-stage rocket fired again, for nearly six minutes. This raised Apollo 11's speed to 24,250 miles an hour and drove it out of Earth orbit.

"WE HAVE A HAPPY HOME."

The important and tricky maneuver of docking with LM was at hand. The command ship, *Columbia,* had to pull the LM, *Eagle,* out of the front end of the third-stage booster. As pilot of the command ship, Collins was in charge.

First, Collins separated *Columbia* (and its service module) from *Eagle* and the booster rocket. *Eagle* was now visible at the front end of the spent rocket. Collins flew *Columbia* off to one side and turned the ship so that it faced *Eagle.* Then he flew back to it.

Gently and easily, Collins linked

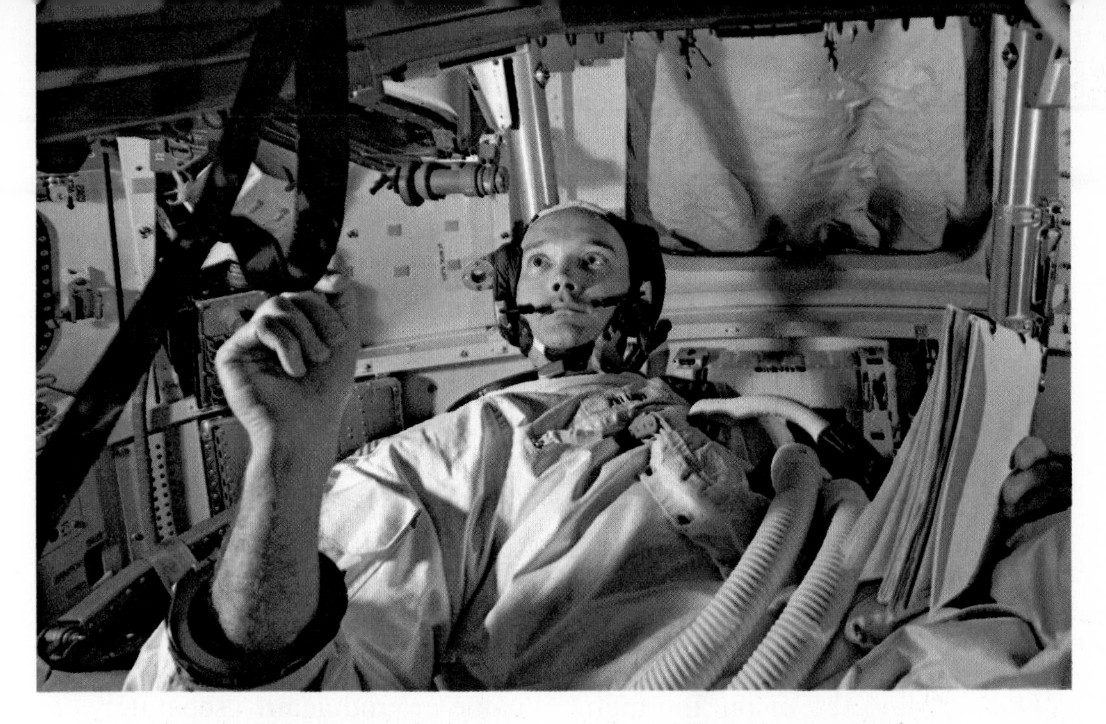

Michael Collins checking out systems in the command module, Columbia.

Columbia nose-to-nose with *Eagle.* The used-up rocket booster was released and sent into orbit around the sun. *Columbia* and *Eagle,* flying together, turned again and headed toward the moon. The next time they separated would be during moon orbit.

After the docking, the crew settled down to the routine duties of the eight-day mission. They checked equipment, studied their flight plan, made navigational readings. Like fussy housewives, they tidied their moon ship. And they prepared TV shows for Earthlings.

"We have a happy home," Collins said during a telecast. "There's plenty of room for the three of us, and I think we're all learning to find our favorite little corner to sit in."

The food was good, too. Collins radioed back, "My compliments to the chef. The salmon salad is outstanding." Other food, mostly in plastic bags, included bacon squares, shrimp cocktail, spaghetti and meat sauce, chicken and rice, chicken stew, pork and potatoes, brownies, butterscotch pudding, coffee. The men squirted water into the bags with a water pistol to "mush up" their food. But they also had fresh apples and oranges.

By July 18, the third day, Apollo 11 was three quarters of the way to the moon. Armstrong and Aldrin showed Earthlings the inside of *Eagle,* the moon-lander, by way of TV. As the hatch leading into *Eagle* opened, Collins said, "It's just like a refrigerator, when you open the door. The light goes on." They reported that *Eagle* was in perfect working order.

"IT WAS LIKE PERFECT."

On July 19, the ship slowed down to seventeen hundred miles an hour, its slowest speed. Then Apollo 11 came under the control of the moon's gravity, and it picked up speed again. Soon it was ready to make its first swing around the moon.

Once behind the moon, the men had to fire the main rocket to slow down Apollo 11. It would have to fire just right to allow Apollo to be captured by the moon's gravity. When the ship came out from behind the moon, Armstrong radioed back to mission control in Houston, Texas: "It was like perfect."

The pull of the moon's gravity now gripped Apollo 11 in orbit. Its speed dipped to around thirty-seven hundred miles an hour. Each full orbit of the moon took two hours.

As they orbited, the men sent more TV pictures back to Earth. Then they began to prepare for the big day ahead – July 20 – and the landing on the moon.

During the ship's eleventh orbit, Armstrong and Aldrin put their spacesuits on and crawled into *Eagle* through a small tunnel for a final check of equipment.

On the thirteenth orbit, with both men aboard, *Eagle* would leave *Columbia* and start down to the moon.

Just before the thirteenth orbit of the moon, mission control radioed: "Apollo 11, Houston. We're go for undocking." This was the signal to separate *Eagle* from *Columbia.*

Apollo 11 disappeared behind the moon and the world waited for word that both ships were flying alone. About forty-five minutes later they came around again – separately.

"How does it look?" mission control asked.

"The *Eagle* has wings," answered Armstrong. Then he added, "Looking good."

For fifteen minutes, the two ships flew only a few feet apart. During this time, Armstrong and Aldrin checked the *Eagle* inside, while Collins, from *Columbia's* window, looked over its outside, especially the landing gear. Then *Columbia* fired small rockets and moved into a new orbit, about two miles from *Eagle.*

"I think you've got a fine-looking flying machine there, *Eagle,* despite the fact that you're upside down," Collins radioed jokingly.

"*Somebody's* upside down," Armstrong replied.

The view of Earth seen from Apollo 11.

No one could say who *was* upside down. In space without gravity or landmarks, there is no "up" or "down."

Now both *Columbia* and *Eagle* went behind the moon again. On the far side, *Eagle* was to fire the rocket engine to start it down toward the surface.

Two minutes later, *Eagle* radioed Houston that all was well and continued its drop into the unknown.

Now, every foot of the way was a new adventure for man. Apollo 10's LM, *Snoopy,* had come to about forty-five thousand feet from the surface. But now, *Eagle* was below that point. Never before had man come so close to the moon.

Inside the ship, the number ninety-nine flashed on a computer—a code signal that Armstrong had a few seconds to make a decision: to refire the engine and drop to the surface . . . or to stay in moon orbit, link up with *Columbia,* and go home.

Armstrong pushed a "proceed" button. The engine restarted. Down flew *Eagle,* its rocket engine acting as a brake. As it slowed, it began to "fall" out of orbit—forty thousand feet . . . twenty thousand feet . . . fifteen thousand feet . . . five thousand feet. Houston radioed, "You are go for landing."

Moving forward tail first, *Eagle's* windows were still tilted upward, away from the surface. Armstrong at the controls, and Aldrin next to him, calling out the ship's forward speed and rate of drop, were flying blind. They were relying on computers and flight instruments.

A smooth target landing-area seven miles long and three miles wide had been charted out before the flight. But now, below the ship and not too far ahead of it, appeared a crater filled with rocks and boulders. It was unseen by Armstrong and Aldrin. *Eagle's* computer, had guided the ship to the crater instead of to the target area.

Now, as *Eagle* arched toward the surface, it turned its legs downward into touchdown position. For the first time, the men could see the surface from *Eagle's* window. Instead of the smooth landing area he expected, Armstrong saw the rock-filled crater below.

"What," he wondered, "was wrong?" Armstrong had to make a fast decision whether to let the computer guide *Eagle* in for a landing, or whether to work the controls manually. Armstrong decided to let the computer guide *Eagle* for a few moments—then to take over himself.

There was nothing to rely on now but years of training and tremendous skill as a pilot. The ship was supposed to be dropping *down* faster than it was moving forward. Instead, it was suddenly moving *forward* fast, and barely dropping. *Eagle* was dropping only one foot a second, but was skimming right above the surface at forty-seven feet a second. And as it swept over the center, there was little fuel left.

Aldrin called in the position: ". . . Three hundred feet, down 3½, forty-seven forward . . . down one a minute. One-and-one-half down. Seventy. Got the shadow out there. Fifty, down at 2½. Nineteen . . . 3½ down. Two hundred twenty feet. Thirteen forward . . . coming down nicely . . . seventy-five feet . . . things looking good. Down half. Six forward."

Mission control reported back: *"Sixty seconds."*

Computer warnings were flashing. *Eagle's* fuel supply kept dropping. Mission control radioed: "Go for landing."

Eagle answered: "Lights on. Down 2½. Forward, forward. Good. Forty feet, down 2½. Picking up some dust. Thrity feet, 2½ down. Faint shadow. Four forward. Four forward. Drifting to the right a little . . . down a half."

"Thirty seconds," called mission control.

The view of the Moon seen from Apollo 11.

Skillfully working the hand controls, Armstrong had steered *Eagle* past the crater. The ship blew out a swirling cloud of dust as it inched down to the surface.

Long metal probes on *Eagle's* legs touched the surface. As they did, a blue light flashed in the cockpit. "Contact light," called in *Eagle*. "O.K. engine stop. Engine arm off. 413 is in."

"We copy you down, *Eagle*," said mission control.

"Tranquillity Base here," answered Armstrong again. "The *Eagle* has landed."

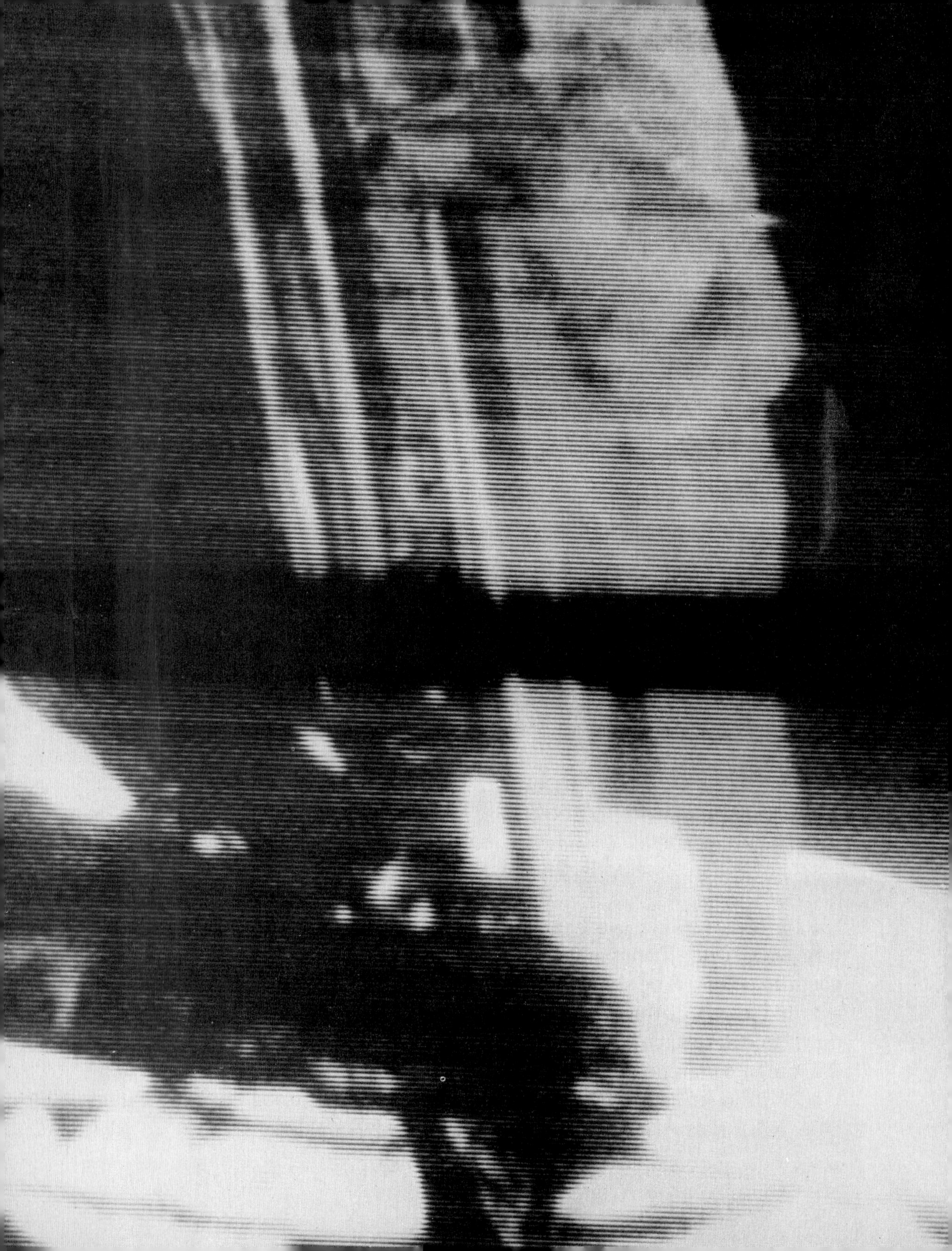

The ship was down. It had landed safely on a flat plain in the Sea of Tranquillity, about twelve hundred feet from the rocky crater. And it had come to within thirty to forty seconds of running out of fuel.

"Roger, Tranquillity," mission control said. "We copy you on the ground. You've got a bunch of guys about to turn blue. We're breathing again. Thanks a lot."

It was 4:17 P.M., Eastern Daylight Time. The moon which never had known man or his time, now had both.

Armstrong had shown that man is needed in space flight. A computer can't do everything. Certainly, it can't work out answers to *unforeseen* emergencies.

"Be advised there are lots of smiling faces in this room," said mission control, after *Eagle* landed.

"There are two of them up here," said the *Eagle* crew.

"And don't forget one in the command module," said Collins, who *had* been almost forgotten as he circled in *Columbia,* seventy miles above the moon.

ONE SMALL STEP

Now Aldrin and Armstrong had time to rest. Several hours later, they struggled into their spacesuits, boots, helmets, gloves. They also put on their "portable life-support systems," back packs that carried oxygen for breathing, a water-cooling system, and communications. Then they depressurized the LM cabin. When the pressure was down to zero, Armstrong opened the hatch, turned around, and backed out onto the porch, a small platform above the ship's nine-step ladder.

"O.K., Houston, I'm on the porch," he reported. On the second step Armstrong pulled a rope to release a section on the side of *Eagle.* A TV camera automatically began to take pictures. And for the first time, Earthlings, clustered around their TV sets, could see, as well as hear, the man on the moon.

"We can see you coming down the ladder now," said Houston.

Armstrong answered, "I'm at the foot of the ladder. The LM footpads are only depressed in the surface about one or two inches, although the surface appears to be very, very fine-grained as you get close to it. It's almost like a powder. It's very fine. I'm going to step off the LM now."

Seconds later his booted left foot pressed down on the moon's surface.

"That's one small step for a man, one giant leap for mankind," said Armstrong.

◄ **Armstrong taking the first step on the moon.**

Space Stations

Once people had learned to travel in space, they began to think about ways of staying in space—to observe and explore. Space stations would provide a place for space vehicles and travelers to come to and "park" for a while.

These pages show some designs that have been imagined for spaceships and stations.

Traffic between Earth and space could be by a shuttle system—vehicles going back and forth between the two. In the design pictured below, the shuttle has a double-decker seating arrangement with the pilot and co-pilot on top and the cargo specialists below. The shuttle would leave Earth and head for

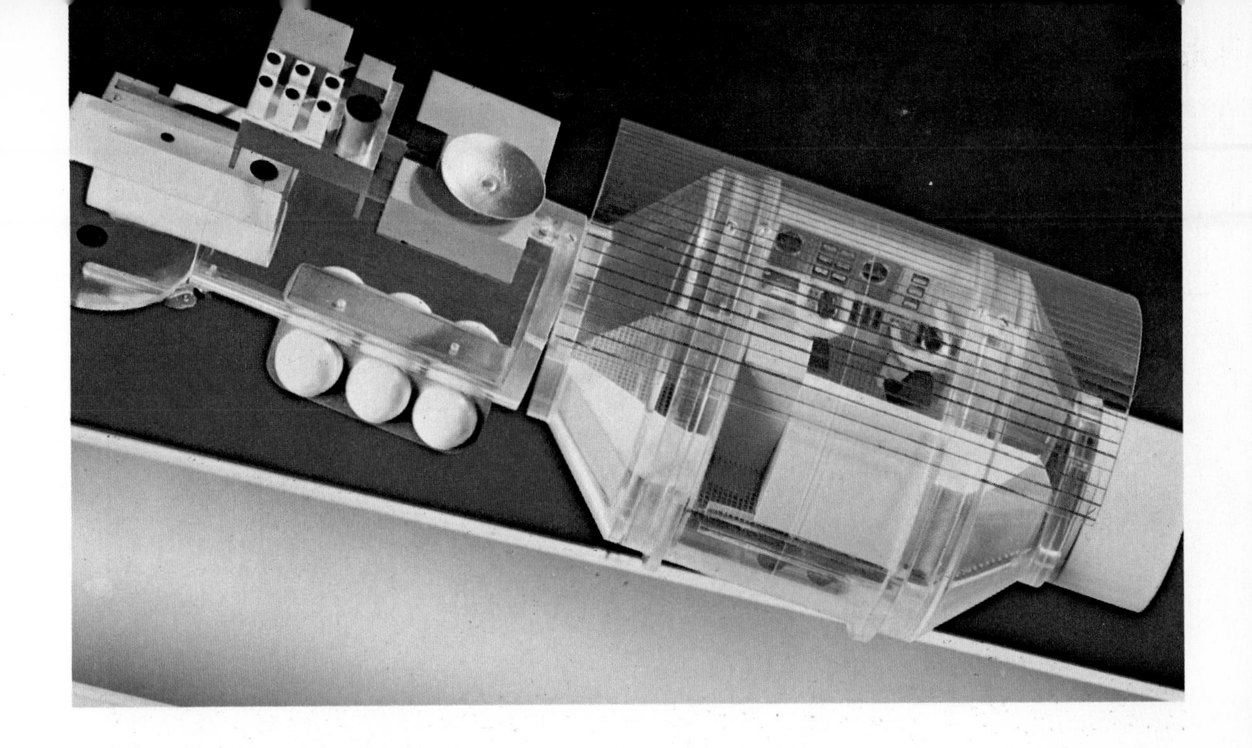

the space station, perhaps making stops along the way. It might act as a "flying mechanic," inspecting unmanned satellites to make sure they were in working order. It would deliver its cargo to its destination, pick up new cargo, and then return to Earth.

Of course, shuttles will carry people, as well as cargo. They will carry supplies for spaceships, for space stations, and for passengers. But most important, they will carry space stations themselves. Some little space stations may be carried into space by one shuttle. Above is a model of a laboratory that would remain attached to a shuttle while orbiting the Earth. It could carry up to four people and remain in orbit for as long as seven days. The lab, which measures 14 feet by 26 feet, would be equipped to conduct many experiments. There is room for telescopes and antennae at one end. Bunks, kitchen, and bathroom are included, too. Other equipment would control atmosphere and temperature, provide power, and record information.

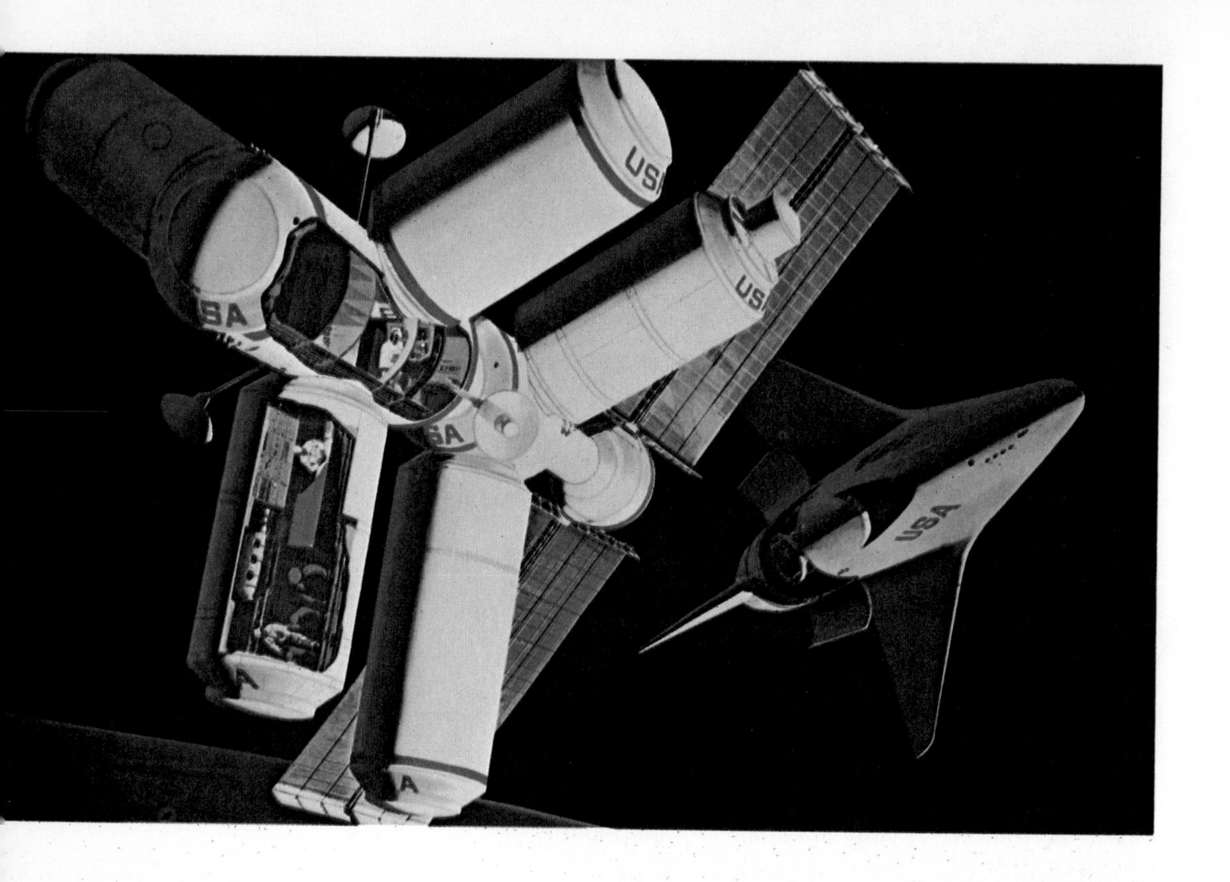

What about larger space stations? Instead of carrying a whole station, shuttles may carry *parts* of stations. These parts would be put together in space. In this way an entire station could be built in space out of "blocks" made to fit together. In the space station above, there is a central core. Laboratory modules are attached to, or docked with, this central core. If a new or different section is needed, it can be added to the central core in the way a new room is added to a house. It could also be detached and returned to Earth by shuttle.

Shuttles will also be able to carry satellites. The shuttle below can carry up to 65,000 pounds. It is designed to place a communications satellite into orbit. It might also send satellites to Mars, Jupiter, Mercury, or other planets. Such satellites would float free in space. They would be unmanned. Space stations could guide them by remote control, bringing them back to the stations to deliver their information and to be repaired as necessary.

Most of the work in space stations will probably be scientific. Laboratories will be equipped to conduct experiments in astronomy, space physics, life sciences, and navigation. Using precise and sensitive instruments, experimenters will be able to gather information that is very accurate. They will investigate the stars, the planets, and other things in space, such as radiation. Some scientists will be looking at Earth.

Here is what a large space station might be like. This model would be launched in three parts by rockets and then put together in space. The living quarters at the left and the laboratory space in the center are made out of parts of an old rocket.

Although this manned station would be fixed in space, it would rotate. The station turning in space would make its own gravity so that people could walk around inside the station the way they do on Earth. Floating at the lower left is a telescope. A ferry-shuttle is approaching the telescope to check it and pick up information before going on to the space station. In the middle, a small satellite that has been brought in by remote control is approaching the hangar, where it will be repaired. You can see how a miniature Earth-world has been transported to space, to become a bustling space station.

Adding to Your Reading Vocabulary

In this section you will learn how to use your word-study skills in reading textbooks. Textbooks usually explain the meanings of new words, but you must look for the explanations. Sometimes a new word is underlined, or printed in a special type called italics, *like this*, or in boldface type, **like this.**

In these lessons, read the sidenotes as you come to them. They will help you increase your skill in word study.

New Words in Social Studies

In this section, use both the context and the picture to learn the meanings of new words.

A Famous School

The subheading tells you the topic of this section.

[1] Have you ever ridden in a motorboat or in a sailboat? [2] If so, then you know how the person guiding the boat along its way used certain landmarks to help him guide the boat. [3] In large ships, such a person is known as a **navigator** (nav′əgā′tor).

The meaning of **navigator** was given in the sentence before. What is the meaning?

[4] A famous prince of Portugal, who became known as Prince Henry the Navigator, thought that navigators should learn to guide their ships when they could not see landmarks. [5] He decided to set up a school for navigators.

[6] Prince Henry brought some of the best mathematicians, astronomers, mapmakers, sailors, and shipbuilders to his school.

The roots of these words will tell you what these men do.

[7] By sharing information, these people were able to make better charts for navigators. [8] They were also able to design better ships for long voyages and to bring about a wider use of instruments for navigation.

[9] Two instruments that people in Prince Henry's school improved upon and brought into wider use were the **compass** (kum′pəs) and the **astrolabe** (as′trə·lāb). [10] The compass helped navigators solve their problem of knowing in what direction they were sailing. [11] It is an instrument

Be sure to pronounce this new word each time you see it. Watch for clues to its meaning.

What new information does the picture give you about an **astrolabe?**

that shows direction. [12] A compass helped a navigator set the course of his ship.

[13] The astrolabe helped navigators solve their problem of knowing where they were. [14] An astrolabe is an instrument that measures the height of the sun or the stars from the horizon. [15] This measurement enabled navigators to determine their north-south position at sea. [16] The picture shows an astrolabe. [17] The numerals stand for degrees.

—from *The Social Studies and Our Country: Concepts in Social Studies*

The context should help you to understand the meaning of **course.** What is the meaning?

Each sentence in this paragraph gives you information about an **astrolabe.**

Building Skills

To Write

1. What sentences helped you understand the meaning of **astrolabe?**
2. In Sentence 8, does **wider** mean *less narrow, more common,* or *not so small?*
3. The word **instrument(s)** is used four times in this selection. Does it mean *tool, device for making music,* or a *measuring device?*
4. What different kinds of information did the navigator learn from the compass and from the astrolabe?
5. Find and write four compound words in the selection.

To Discuss

1. Three new words in this selection have been respelled to help you pronounce them. Try to pronounce them.
2. What information about the astrolabe did you get from the picture that you did not get from the words alone?
3. What information did you get from the words about the astrolabe that you could not get from a picture?
4. Tell how you figured out the meaning of **course.**

New Words in Science

Do you know the meaning of the following words: **refract, objective, converge, eyepiece, convex?** These words are used in discussing telescopes. As you read the paragraphs on the next pages, notice the context clues, the sidenotes, and the illustrations. They will help you to understand the new words.

The Telescope, a Basic Tool

The telescope was invented some time in 1608. It is said that a Dutch spectacle maker held one lens near his eye and looked through it at another lens held farther away. The objects he observed through the two lenses seemed close to his eye—closer than ordinarily.

There are several clues in this sentence to help you understand the meaning of **lens** and **lenses.**

Galileo heard of this remarkable discovery. He applied it to make a simple two-lens telescope. The lenses were contained in a sliding wood tube. Many telescopes of today have two lenses arranged in much the same way.

Galileo has four syllables: gal · ə · lē′ ō. The stress is on the third syllable. Galileo was an Italian scientist.

Such telescopes are called *refracting* telescopes. The lenses are shaped in a

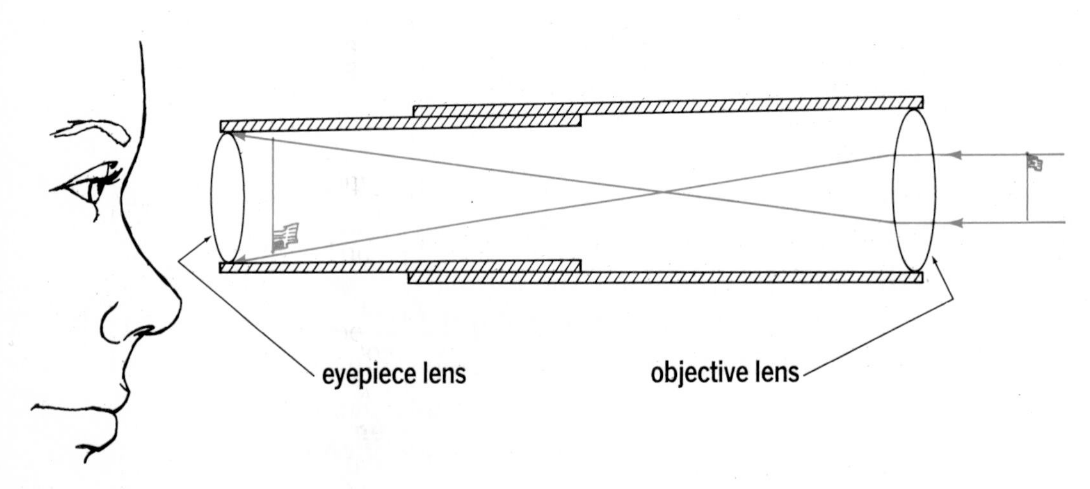

special way. Their shape causes the light rays to bend, or to *refract.* The refracted light rays make an image appear larger than normally.

The meaning that is given for **refract** helps you to understand the meaning of **refracting** and **refracted.**

How a Telescope Works

A refracting telescope is a tube containing lenses. At one end of the tube is a large lens. This big lens is called the *objective.* It is pointed toward the object you wish to see.

Look at the **objective lens** in the illustration on page 40.

The objective lens is made of glass. The sides of the glass are curved. The curved glass bends, or *refracts,* the light rays as they pass through the lens.

The bent light rays *converge,* or come to a point. The converging rays form an image inside the tube at the other end. This image is what the viewer sees when he looks through the *eyepiece.*

The meaning of **converge** follows the word.

Look at the point in the illustration on page 40 where the light rays converge. Then look at the **eyepiece lens.**

The eyepiece is the small lens at the viewing end of the telescope. This lens magnifies the image formed by the objective lens. It seems to bring the object close to the viewer's eyes.

This sentence explains the word **magnifies.**

A lens that causes light to converge is called a *convex* lens. A convex lens is thicker in the center than at the edges.

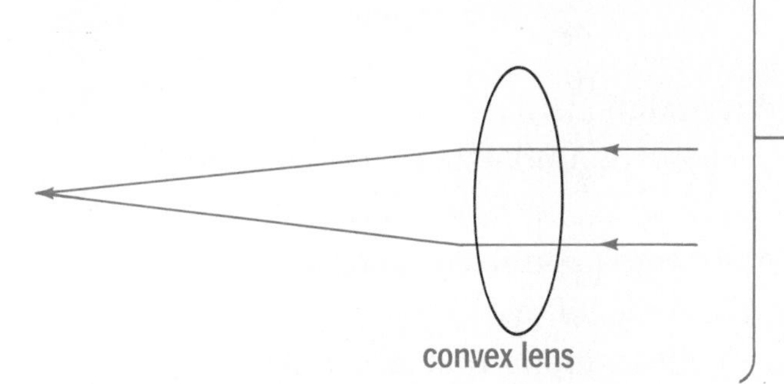

Context and the picture together make the meaning of **convex** clear.

—from *Today's Basic Science* 5

Building Skills

To Write

1. The author introduces several new words: *refract, converge, eyepiece, convex.* Which two words are explained by similar meanings given either before or after the word *or*?
2. Write the suffixes added to *refract* to make new words.
3. The context and pictures help you to understand the meaning of convex lens. Is the objective lens a convex lens? Write a sentence telling what a convex lens does.

To Discuss

1. Where do you find clues to the meaning of *eyepiece*? Is eyepiece a compound word? What part of the word helps you to remember where the eyepiece is in the telescope?
2. What familiar word do you find in the word *objective*?
3. In order to understand how a telescope works, the reader must understand the word *refracts*. How many times is it explained?

Summary

As you read, you add to your vocabulary by using your word-study skills. Sometimes you use only one skill to learn an unfamiliar word; at other times you use a combination of skills. Skills that give help are:

– Remembering sound-letter relationships.
– Using all the context clues to understand the meaning of new words.
– Looking for familiar root words, prefixes, and suffixes to help with pronunciation and meaning.
– Studying any pictures or illustrations that accompany the text.

Books About Venturing into Space

What Makes a Plane Fly? by Scott Corbett.

The story of aircraft from gliders to jets is told in this book. There are many excellent diagrams.

First Book of Mars by David C. Knight.

This introduction to the Red Planet tells of the flight of Mariner IV. It contains many of the famous pictures that were taken of Mars during that flight.

Man in Space to the Moon by Franklyn M. Branley.

This is another description of man's first journey to the moon. What was life like in that space capsule as it sped toward the moon? This great adventure of Armstrong, Aldrin, and Collins is recounted with clear illustrations.

American Women of the Space Age by Mary F. Hoyt.

Since the beginning of space exploration, women have worked in the United States space program as mathematicians, engineers, doctors, nurses, artists, and designers. They are presented here in words and pictures.

Skyhooks: The Story of Helicopters by Charles Coombs.

Take off straight up, stand still in mid-air, fly backward or forward or in any direction—this describes the helicopter. This is an easy-to-read book with striking photographs.

All Kinds of Airplanes by Maurice Allward.

The first airplane to fly was built by the Wright brothers in 1903. This book begins with a picture of that airplane. Beautiful pictures of airplanes that man has built for many purposes fill the rest of the book.

Environments Out There by Isaac Asimov.

A famous scientist discusses the possibility that other planets may support human life. He begins with our own solar system and works out into distant galaxies.

Unit 2

Building America

"Daniel Boone Escorting a Band of Pioneers into the Western Country" by George Caleb Bingham.

Finding the right entry will help you to unlock the meaning of a word.

SKILLS LESSON

THE DICTIONARY: FINDING THE ENTRY WORD

Have you ever looked for a word in the dictionary and not been able to find it? Maybe it wasn't in your dictionary, because only the very largest, complete dictionaries have nearly all words in them. Perhaps it was there but was not listed among the **entry words.** Entry words are the words printed in boldface type at the left-hand side of each column in the dictionary.

Many times the word you need is related to an entry word but has a different form – that is, its spelling is changed by the addition of a prefix or suffix. When that is true, you must be able to recognize the root word and look for it as an entry word. Suppose you do not understand the word in boldface type in this sentence:

This weather makes the cabin seem **mustier** than ever.

You won't find *mustier* among the entry words in a dictionary. What do you do now? Notice that *mustier* is a describing word. What would the root word be? You can guess that it is *musty*. The suffix *-er* has been added to the root. (Most words ending in *y* change the *y* to *i* before adding a suffix.) **Musty** is the entry word. When you find that word, you see that **mustier** is part of the entry. (Would a musty cabin smell damp?)

TRY THIS

Write the entry word you would look for to find each numbered word.

1. resembled
2. mysteriously
3. fancied
4. nourishing
5. sentries
6. apparently

SKILLS LESSON

USING THE PRONUNCIATION KEY

Since a dictionary can't speak, it must use printed symbols—letters, apostrophes, dots, and special marks—to show what sounds are represented by the letters. Entry words are respelled with these symbols according to the way they are spoken. If you know what each symbol stands for, you can put sounds together to say the word. Sometimes this is easy to do; sometimes it isn't. The more you use the symbols to pronounce new words, the better you become at doing it.

You can learn what sound each symbol represents by using the *pronunciation key* in the dictionary. Look at page 390 of this book. You will find there the pronunciation key for the Glossary. It tells you, for example, that an *e* marked like this, **ē,** is sounded like the first *e* in even. The symbol **ə,** which looks like an upside-down *e,* is called **schwa.** Look at the key to see what sound schwa stands for. With this knowledge, can you pronounce these respelled words? They are all names of animals.

el′ə·fənt **lep′ərd** **kam′əl** **zē′brə**

Pronunciation keys are not all the same, but some common symbols appear in most of them. Probably you have learned many symbols without even trying. Once you get used to the symbols in your dictionary, you will be able to say many of

the respelled words without referring to the key. Of course, the pronunciation key is always there, at the bottom of the page and in the front of the dictionary, when you do need it for reference.

When you are working out the pronunciation of words that have two or more syllables, you have to know which syllable to accent or stress. Most dictionaries use a mark like this ′ to show which syllable receives the strongest stress. Even a familiar word sounds strange if you accent the wrong syllable. Suppose you said *si LAB uhl* and *glo SAR ee*?

In some long words, like **revolution,** two syllables are accented, one more than the other. This mark ′ represents the stronger stress; this mark ′, the weaker one. Which syllable gets the stronger accent in rev′ə·lo͞o′shən?

TRY THIS

Use the pronunciation key in the Glossary. Say each respelled word below to yourself. Then write the words the symbols represent.

1. kāk	4. rē′zon	7. kən·tin′yoo
2. mī	5. rek′ləs	8. sel·ə·brā′shən
3. thro͞o	6. nûr′ish	9. al′fə·bet′i·kəl

SKILLS LESSON

FINDING THE DEFINITION THAT FITS THE SENTENCE

If a dictionary gives only one definition for a word, you can be sure that it is the right definition for your sentence. But sometimes you have to choose among several definitions. When you find the one that seems right for the sentence, try substituting the definition in place of the word in the sentence. If the sentence makes sense, you have probably chosen the right definition.

Let us find the meaning for *apt* and fit it into this sentence:

At that moment Henry made an **apt** remark, and everyone fell silent.

Suppose you find this dictionary entry for *apt*. Which of the three meanings is the right one for this sentence?

apt [apt] *adj.* **1** Having a natural tendency; likely: Fish are *apt* to be biting then. **2** Quick to learn: an *apt pupil.* **3** To the point; fitting: an *apt* suggestion. **–apt′ly** *adv.* **–apt′ness** *n.*

–from *The Harcourt Brace School Dictionary*

A chair or a definition—

Henry would not make a remark "having a natural tendency," so that you know Definition 1 is not the right one. Definition 2 will not fit either, since a remark cannot be "quick to learn." Can a remark be "to the point or fitting"? Yes. Try substituting the meaning in Definition 3 for *apt* in the sentence:

At that moment Henry made a **fitting** remark, and everyone fell silent.

This sentence makes sense, so you know that the third meaning is the right one for *apt* in your sentence.

It is sometimes necessary to change the definition slightly so that it will fit smoothly into the sentence. Read the following sentence, and choose the right definition for *factors*.

The time of the broadcast and the length of the program seem to be **factors** in the popularity of a television show.

> **fac tor** (fak′tər), **1.** any one of the causes of a result; one element in a situation: *Ability, industry, and health are factors of his success in school.* **2.** any of the numbers or expressions which, when multiplied together, form a product: *2 and 5 are factors of 10.* **3.** separate into factors. **4.** person who does business for another; agent. *n., v.*

—from *Thorndike Barnhart Junior Dictionary, Sixth Edition*

You can see that the first definition is the right one for this sentence. The second definition has to do with numbers; that does not seem right here. The third definition is given as a verb, and you can tell that **factors** in your sentence is a noun. The fourth definition, although it starts with a noun, is not right because you know that the **factors** in your sentence are not persons.

If you replace *factors* with all the words of the first definition, you will have a sentence that does not make sense. Since *factors* is plural, you will have to change the definition to make it plural, too. As you reread the sentence, you can see that "the time of the broadcast" and "the length of the program" are causes. "The popularity of a television show" is the result. If you substitute the definition for the word *factors*, the sentence will read like this:

The time of the broadcast and the length of the program seem to be **causes of** the popularity of a television show.

That sentence makes sense, so you know that your understanding of *factors* is correct.

TRY THIS

The definition of each word in boldface type is in parentheses. Rewrite each sentence substituting the definition for the word in boldface type.

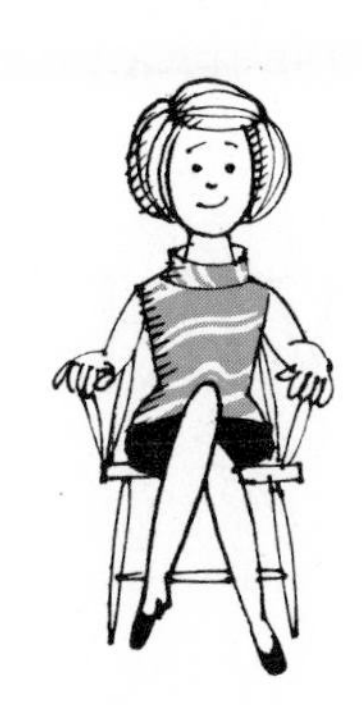

it's important to find one that fits.

1. He must have **inherited** his talent from his grandfather.
   (**inherit:** get or possess from one's ancestors)

2. Mr. Williams was asked to **survey** the land for the new high school and athletic field.
   (**survey:** measure and determine the boundaries or other features of)

3. It takes an experienced sailor to know what to do when a boat **capsizes.**
   (**capsize:** upset; turn over)

4. The loss of their maps and compass was of **vital** concern to the explorers.
   (**vital:** very important; essential)

WHAT DID YOU LEARN?

---

1. How do you find a word like **beauties** or **distributing** in a dictionary?
2. How does a dictionary tell you how to pronounce a word?
3. How can you tell that you have chosen the correct definition for a word?
4. What is meant by "making the definition fit the sentence"?

■ The men who had to work with John Smith were quick to say that he was hard to get along with. And yet, more than any other man, he kept the struggling colony of Jamestown alive. How did this happen?

John Smith, Wilderness Leader

by GERALD W. JOHNSON

Sometimes a word only looks strange. As soon as you hear it pronounced, you recognize it. Here are two words you will meet in this selection: **apparently, surveying.** Can you pronounce them? If not, use the dictionary now to learn how to pronounce each one. What entry words will you look for?

The kind of men who came to Virginia in 1607 were not careful men. If they had been, they would have stayed at home. Most of them were wild, reckless fellows who loved excitement more than they feared danger. They had all heard stories of Mexico and Peru. They had heard that men who went there as poor soldiers, men who hadn't had two pennies to clink together when they left, had come back to Spain after a few years loaded with gold and pearls and jewels. They had bought fine houses and thereafter lived like rich men. If it could happen to Spaniards in Mexico and Peru, why couldn't it happen to Englishmen in Virginia?

Of course, the answer was that most of the gold in North America was on the other side of the continent, thousands of miles from Virginia. But nobody knew that. Most of the men who came to Jamestown with that first group expected to find rich mines without much trouble. They wasted a great deal of time looking for them when they should have been at work clearing the forest and planting seed, so they would have something to eat when winter came. But no, they must be looking for gold. There was great excitement when they found a kind of clay filled with bright yellow specks that looked like gold. It was not. It was only what they called in England "fool's gold," because it fooled so many people into believing it was the real thing.

But there were a few among them who were not so foolish. These men understood that the important thing was not the discovery of gold but possession of the land itself. The London Company had sent sealed orders which were not to be opened until the landing, concerning the management of the colony. When the orders were opened, it appeared that things were to be run by a council of seven men, of whom Captain Christopher Newport was one. But among the other six was a man who was already under arrest because of a row he had had with some of the ship's officers on the voyage. For a month they would not allow him to sit in the council, so he took a small boat and began to explore the country. This was the famous Captain John Smith, who in the end did more than any other man to bring about English possession of America.

This is the only known likeness of Captain John Smith. It was published in his book *A Description of New England.*

The men who had to work with him would never have believed that this would be true. He really was a very tough character—loudmouthed, boastful, hard to get along with. Some of them felt sure he was the biggest liar in the New World. The story of his life, as he told it, is pretty hard to believe, and for a long time historians refused to accept it. Part of it is certainly true. About the rest we simply don't know.

It is true that Smith was born into a fairly good family, that he attended a good grammar school but not a university, and that he inherited a little money from his father. It is true that he refused to go into his father's business, but instead went abroad and became a soldier. Apparently he didn't care much on which side of a war he fought; he served first in one army, then in another.

Smith was very strong and very active. His mind was as active as his body. When he went exploring, he did not merely look and come away. He took surveying instruments, made measurements, and drew maps that were remarkably accurate, considering what poor instruments he had. He made note of rivers, islands, and bays; he carefully examined plants and animals; he wrote down the nature of the soil in different places. In 1608 he took a barge, a large rowboat with twelve oarsmen, and went north from Jamestown up the Chesapeake Bay, looking into the creeks and rivers and finding good places for future settlements. All this information he sent back to England.

But what impressed people most at the time was the way he handled things at Jamestown. Smith didn't like a good deal that was going on there—for instance, all that rushing around looking for gold, when the colonists should have been making sure of something to eat. He said so, loudly and frequently. This angered the other members of the council, and they talked back. One quarrel followed another. But after Captain Newport had left for England, things began to get worse and worse. Many of the settlers began to see that John Smith was right and to take his part. Once, though, they came very near to hanging him, and would have done so had not Newport come back at that moment, bringing new settlers and more supplies. He listened to both sides of the argument and at the end, instead of hanging Smith, made him governor!

Two stories about Smith have always been remembered. The settlers included all kinds of people. Among them were some who called themselves gentlemen and fancied that they were too good to work in the fields like common laborers. They felt this way even though it was plain that unless everybody worked to raise food, they were all going to starve. When it was reported to Governor Smith that the gentlemen were refusing to hoe corn, he issued a rule that Americans ever since have regarded as rough but fair. He said, "He that will not work, neither shall he eat." They knew that he would enforce it, too, so the gentlemen thereafter went out with the rest.

The other is one of his own yarns, which may or may not be true. The Indians were divided into small tribes, each with its chief. Over them all was a chief of chiefs,

named Powhatan. Once when food in Jamestown was very scarce, John Smith went to Powhatan's camp to try to buy or beg corn to tide the settlers over. But for some reason Powhatan was in a bad mood at the time. Instead of giving the white men anything, he ordered his warriors to seize them and tie them up while he decided what to do with them. His mood must have been very bad, for after some time he decided to kill them, or at least the leader, John Smith. The warriors threw Smith to the ground and put his head on a stump. Then one of them picked up a big club, intending to smash his skull. But at that

moment Powhatan's little twelve-year-old daughter ran out and threw herself on Smith, so that the men couldn't strike without hitting the princess. She begged her father to spare Smith's life. The child, Pocahontas, was Powhatan's favorite, so after a little hesitation, he ordered the Indians to let the white man live. Soon afterward he released him.

Here, again, we have only Smith's word for it, and some people think he made up the story many years later. But we do know that such things sometimes happened among the Indians. If a woman took a fancy to a prisoner, she might ask the chief for him, and the chief might agree. So it could have happened just as Smith said it did.

But the best work that Captain John Smith did for America was not done in Virginia. Before he went back to England he made a voyage to the northern part of the land. Later he drew maps of the coast so carefully and accurately that ship captains could use them as guides. All the land was then called Virginia, but to this northern part of it he gave a special name—New England. Soon everybody was in the habit of dividing America into two parts, Virginia and New England.

What the new country needed above all else was more people, and John Smith did more to bring people to it than any other one man. He could do it because he was, among other things, a writer. Even before he left Jamestown he had written one small book praising the country, telling what it was like and explaining that it was a fine place to live. Captain Newport took it back to England, and the company had it printed to advertise the new land. In those days they gave long titles to books, and the spelling was very different from ours. The title of Smith's first book was *A True Relation of Such Occurrences and Accidents of Noate as Hath Hapned in Virginia since the First Planting of That Collony.*

Later Smith wrote a great many other books and pamphlets, all meant to persuade people to settle in America. There is no doubt that he skipped over a good many of the bad features and made life in America seem easier than it really was. But in general he told the truth. From him thousands of people learned more about America than they had learned from anyone else. It seems certain that a great many of those who went there to live were persuaded to go by John Smith.

There was a growing quarrel between the American colonies and their mother country. Every act of the English king made the colonists angrier.

"If They Want a War—"

by ENID LA MONTE MEADOWCROFT

Context may help you to recognize this word: **disguised.** If it doesn't, turn to the dictionary. Think of the root word for **disguised,** and then look for that root as the entry word.

Tramp, tramp, tramp, tramp. In a pouring rain, four regiments of red-coated soldiers marched down the gangplanks of English ships and onto the wharfs of Boston. Tramp, tramp, tramp, along the wharfs and through the puddles in the cobblestoned streets.

Men, women, and children lined those streets, watching the soldiers in silence. Faces peered soberly through rain-streaked windows as the redcoats passed by. Everyone in Boston knew why the soldiers had come, and nearly everyone was angry or afraid.

It was May 1774, more than ten years after the end of the French and Indian War. During those years there had been much trouble between the colonists and their mother country.

The trouble had started because the King of England wanted money for his government. So he had commanded the colonists to pay taxes on some of the things sent to them from England. But the colonists were not used to being ordered about.

"We are English," they had reminded the King. "We have the right of all English people to help decide how we shall be governed and taxed. And we will not pay taxes unless we have a chance to vote for them first."

"Oh, yes you will," insisted King George III, who was a stubborn young man and not very wise. "You'll pay any taxes we tell you to pay and obey any laws that we make."

So a quarrel began and grew steadily worse. The colonists refused angrily to buy anything from England which was taxed. The English merchants lost a great deal of money. And at last the King and his friends in the English government lifted the taxes on everything except tea.

"Don't send us tea with a tax on it," the American colonists warned the English merchants. "We won't buy it."

But ships loaded with tea were soon on their way across the ocean. When they reached America, the colonists were ready for them. In New York and Philadelphia, angry crowds would not let the tea be brought ashore. In Charleston, the people unloaded the tea and locked it up in damp cellars. In Boston, on a dark December night, colonists disguised as Indians boarded the three tea ships anchored in the harbor. Then they threw all the precious tea overboard.

News of this Boston tea party had made King George III furious. Now soldiers had come from England to punish the people of Boston. They had been commanded to close the port. Not a ship belonging to the American colonists was to leave the harbor or to enter it until all the tea which had been destroyed had been paid for.

This was a cruel punishment. Boston was a large shipping center and almost surrounded by water. With the harbor closed, thousands of men would be out of work. Farmers could not bring meat and vegetables into the Boston markets by boat. Fishermen could not put out to sea. Soon food would become so scarce that the people of Boston would be hungry, and many of them might starve.

But even as the red-coated soldiers were marching down the rain-soaked streets, express riders were galloping out of town. North, south, and west they rode, to spread the news of the trouble in Boston and to ask for help.

And help came quickly. Farmers in Connecticut and Rhode Island sent herds of cows and flocks of sheep to Boston. Virginia and the Carolinas sent wagons loaded with grain. Other colonies sent money and messages.

"Don't give in. Don't pay for that tea. We'll stand by you."

Until this time the thirteen colonies had been almost like thirteen separate little countries. Each one had managed most of its own affairs, and had not been much concerned with the affairs of other colonies. Now they decided that they must work together to put a stop to the long quarrel with England. In every colony except Georgia, men were chosen by the people to meet in Philadelphia to talk things over.

The men who made up this Continental Congress met many times. Finally they decided to send a letter to King George III. In it they asked him to change the laws they thought were unfair and to take his soldiers out of Boston.

The King's only answer was to send more soldiers. Thousands more.

By this time many colonists felt sure that they would soon have to fight for their rights, and, in New England, they began to get ready. Week after week, companies of men and older boys drilled on every village green. Some of them were prepared to fight at a minute's notice and so were called Minute Men.

In Massachusetts the leaders of the colony quietly collected guns, ammunition, and other supplies. They hid them in the village of Concord, eighteen miles from Boston.

Boston itself was swarming with redcoats. Paul Revere and other colonists kept a secret watch on the English soldiers at all times. On the 18th of April, 1775, they learned that the British had found out about the hidden supplies. They learned also that British troops had been ordered to march to Concord before daylight next morning and to seize every gun and every barrel of powder.

Somehow the villagers must be warned and the Minute Men called out. Quickly Paul Revere and his friends made their plans.

Late that night, with the help of their friends, Paul Revere and William Dawes managed to steal past the British sentries and get out of town. Then, each taking a separate way, they galloped toward Concord, down roads bright with moonlight.

"To arms!" they shouted, as they rode through quiet villages. They

banged on doors and windows. "The British are coming! To arms!"

Sleepy farmers, storekeepers, teachers, and preachers tumbled out of their beds, pulled on their clothes, and grabbed their guns. By the time the British troops drew near Lexington, on their way to Concord, seventy Minute Men waited bravely on the village green to meet them.

"Stand your ground!" ordered the captain of the Minute Men as the British troops advanced. "Don't fire unless you are fired upon. But if they want a war, let it begin here."

On came the long, long column of red-coated soldiers, marching smartly now to the music of fifes and drums. Their bayonets gleamed and the gold on the scarlet coats of the officers glittered in the light of the rising sun.

Obeying a sharp command, they formed a battle line. The Minute Men fingered their muskets and eyed them grimly. Then, suddenly, somewhere, a shot was fired. No one has ever known from which side it came. Instantly both sides began shooting. Eight of the Minute Men fell dead, the others scattered, and the British marched on toward Concord.

By this time, Minute Men had hurried to Concord from every direction and were waiting to face the British. After some brisk fighting, they drove the redcoats out of the village and chased them back along the road to Boston. Now, all along that road, hundreds of angry colonists came running from their homes to join in the fight. They shot at the soldiers from behind houses, barns, rocks, stone fences, trees, and woodpiles.

All during that long sunny afternoon, the British retreated. It was after dark when at last they reached Boston. Nearly three hundred of the British had been killed or wounded. Forty-nine American colonists would never see the sun rise again. And a war between the colonies and their mother country had begun.

In Massachusetts in the 1760's, young Paul Cuffe was finding out everything possible about ships. He had one dream, to learn—

The Secret of the Sea

by LAVINIA DOBLER *and* EDGAR A. TOPPIN

As you read, if you come to a word you do not know, write it on a paper with its page number. When you have finished reading, use the dictionary to find the meaning of the words you have listed.

A boy stood on a windy shore in southern Massachusetts. He was spellbound by the restless ocean.

Paul Cuffe waited impatiently for the ridge he knew would appear on the surface of the dark gray water. He was so absorbed in watching the sea that he had forgotten his sister was with him. The wave moved slowly toward the shore, towering above the boy and girl. Then it crashed like thunder and the water rushed toward them.

His sister screamed. "I'm afraid!" she said, and covered her ears with her hands as she ran for the nearest hill.

The restless sea that made his sister afraid seemed to give Paul strength and courage. When the waves rose high in the air with a roar, Paul was sure the ocean was trying to tell him something he should know. Other times, when the sea was as calm as glass, he looked far away to the horizon. What was beyond?

Paul Cuffe was born on a cold winter day, January 17, 1759, on Cuttyhunk Island, about seven miles from the Massachusetts coast. At the time of Paul's birth, the French and Indian War was being fought in America.

His parents were Cuffe Slocum and Ruth Moses Slocum, an Indian girl. They both were members of the Society of Friends, better known as Quakers. They were married in their home town of Dartmouth and moved to Cuttyhunk Island. Paul was the seventh child and youngest son of the ten children born to Cuffe and Ruth Slocum.

When Paul was a small boy, Cuttyhunk Island was a lonely place. There were more wild animals than people. The only house on Cuttyhunk belonged to Paul's family. Fishermen in small boats sailed along the coast.

The family had to work long hours on the farm to make a meager living. Sometimes when he had finished his chores for the day, Paul slung his fishing rod over his shoulder and headed for Buzzards Bay. The tall, athletic boy was a good fisherman, so he generally returned with enough fish for supper.

Since there was no meeting house, or other church, on Cuttyhunk Island, the family had religious services on Sunday evening in the big kitchen in front of the stone fireplace. Paul listened to his father as he sat close to the hearth, watching the logs crackle. He liked the Twenty-third Psalm, the Shepherd Psalm, which the family recited together.

"Even though the Lord will take care of you," Paul's father warned, "you must work hard for the Lord." Then he paused, and added, "The Lord sees all of his people as his children. But many people do not see others as the Lord does." He closed the Bible and studied his family. "Never forget that all your lives you will have to work harder than others to earn your living, even though you are free-born Negroes." It was not said harshly, nor was his father resentful. He was telling his sons and daughters that because they were part Indian and Negro, often they would not be accepted as equals by the white man. "Remember, my children, you are bigger than anything that can ever

happen to you. But you must be strong!" This advice was to help Paul through many trying experiences in his life.

In 1766, when Paul was almost eight years old, his parents bought land in Dartmouth, and the family moved. This was the year of the repeal of the hated Stamp Act which had so angered the colonists in America, especially the people of Massachusetts. Since Paul's family raised most of the things they needed, they probably did not know too much about what Britain was doing to its American colonies.

Six years later, in March 1772, when Paul was thirteen, his father died. Paul and his brother John took on much of the responsibility of the farm. By this time several of the older children had their own homes. But there was his mother to care for, as well as his three younger sisters.

Paul had always resented the fact that his last name, Slocum, was the name of the man who had once owned his father as a slave. He persuaded his brothers and sisters to drop the name Slocum and use their father's first name, Cuffe, for their last name.

This responsibility of caring for his family and managing the farm made Paul older than his years. It also meant a great sacrifice—his dream of getting an education. At the time of his father's death, Paul had learned little more than his alphabet, but he was eager to learn more.

And more than ever he seemed determined to find out about ships. Whenever he had a free moment, he hurried to the shore to study them, their full sails filled with wind as they rode over the rough waves.

If he saw a sailor, he longed to ask him a question. Sometimes he did ask one politely. Sometimes the sailor would answer him. Other times he would hunch his shoulders and walk rudely away. When this happened, Paul sensibly realized that many sailors were from other countries and did not understand English. Often, though, he feared he was being ignored because of his dark skin.

But if a sailor took time to explain the kind of work he did on board ship, Paul was excited. The very fact that a sailor's work was risky and dangerous, especially when

there were storms, made Paul more determined than ever to work on a ship.

Paul never forgot the day he had his first lesson in navigation. He had looked forward to it eagerly. At last he was going to learn about ships! He not only counted the hours, but also the minutes, he was so impatient for the lesson.

When the teacher started explaining the use of mathematics to calculate position and direction, Paul was lost. As soon as the lesson was over, Paul walked out of the room, his head down, dragging his feet, back to the farm.

His sister was waiting at the door.

"Paul, tell me about the lesson," she asked.

Her brother looked at her, pain written on his face. "It was all black as midnight," he said.

Paul did not tell her that the instructor kept talking about certain principles of geometry and astronomy which he knew nothing about. He walked toward the field that needed to be plowed.

His sister caught up with him. "After a while you will understand it," she said.

"I hope so," he said, "because some day I am going to sea!"

After the second lesson, he ran all the way back to the farm in his eagerness to tell his sister about the class. "I see a little gleam of light," he said breathlessly. He studied whenever he could. After the third lesson he told his sister, "I see more light."

At the age of sixteen, part of his dream came true. This was in 1775, the first year of the American Revolution. He went as a seaman on a whaling ship bound for the Gulf of Mexico. On his second trip, he sailed to the West Indies.

On his third voyage the following year, in 1776, when he was seventeen years old, Paul was captured by the British. He was in prison in New York City for three months.

While behind bars, Paul made up his mind that, when he was released, he would study harder than ever. He was determined that some day he would own a ship. He couldn't afford to buy one, but he might build it. But if his dream was to come true, he had to know geometry.

When the British released him from prison, Paul Cuffe went to Westport, a village in Massachusetts not too many miles from his birthplace. He farmed and studied, never forgetting his dream. Whenever he sold any of his farm produce, he tried to save part of the money. Slowly the leather pouch that held the coins became heavier and heavier. He hid it carefully.

Sometimes he became discouraged, for he was impatient for his ship.

Three years later, in 1779, while the British and the American colonists were still at war, Paul built a boat. His brother David helped him.

Paul was certain he could make money by having his own ship. He planned to trade with the people of Connecticut who lived on the coast, some fifty miles to the southwest.

But there were many difficulties. The sea was often rough with storms; there was constant trouble with pirates. During the American Revolution, when the British and the American colonies were at war, there were no patrols protecting the coast, so pirates were able to menace all the ships on the Atlantic seaboard.

His brother David, who did not have the same interest and enthusiasm for the sea, told him, "It's too risky to take the ship and sail along this coast."

"Of course it's risky, but I'm willing to take a chance," Paul argued.

"It's too dangerous," David insisted. "I can't and won't risk my life on another trip."

"I can't manage the business and this ship without you," Paul said, trying to reason with his brother.

"I know that, but this is not good business," David declared. "At least I feel safe working on the farm."

So David went back to the farm.

Paul was still determined, however, to continue on the sea. He began an inspiring struggle against great odds.

If Paul had not had his dream, plus his intense love for the sea, he would not have made it. His drive kept him going, while others without a similar vision would have given up.

Paul still had the boat he and David had built together. So the following year, in 1780, he set out to sea alone. But his boat, loaded with valuable cargo, was lost in a bad storm that raged along the Connecticut coast.

Undaunted, Paul Cuffe built another boat. It was hard, lonely work. At times he feared he would never finish.

The day he launched his boat, Paul's heart beat fast. He wasted no time sailing it out into the bay.

That night as his boat ran smoothly in the water, he had an uneasy feeling. Were pirates nearby? His heart sank.

In the distance a big black object was moving slowly toward him. It could be a whale, but he feared it was a ship filled with thieves.

The brave young man prayed silently. If only there was more wind,

then maybe he could get away from the pirates. That was his only chance.

Unfortunately luck was not with him on this journey. Pirates seized his boat.

There are no records telling how Paul Cuffe finally reached land. He escaped from the pirates and probably swam to shore.

When Paul finally got back to his home town, he was in despair. He certainly could not expect any sympathy from David. Perhaps it would be more sensible to give up the plan to trade along the seacoast.

Whenever he glanced at the water and the rolling waves, though, they held the same fascination for him as when he was a boy. His deep interest was still in ships.

He would take the risk for the third time.

Paul assembled the materials to build another boat. He was gratified when David offered to help him again. He also had the good fortune to borrow money to buy a cargo.

Even though the route was still dangerous, Paul dared to take the risk. He started bravely for Nantucket, some sixty miles southeast of Westport.

Pirates chased him.

As he tried desperately to get away, his boat hit a rock. This time, however, the pirates did not capture him or his boat. Even though the vessel was badly damaged, he finally got back to Westport. He wasted no time, working night and day, to repair the boat.

Later he sailed to Nantucket with his cargo, but he lost money on this venture. On a second voyage to Nantucket, pirates robbed him of his cargo, beating him severely. Paul still would not give up. He set out on a third voyage to Nantucket. This time he made a profit.

When he returned, David said, "Paul, you'll be a rich man one of these days! I don't think it will be too many years, either." He looked directly at his brother. "What makes you so determined?"

"I like the sea," Paul answered. "I like to sail."

Paul Cuffe continued to make voyages along the coast.

"If I can make some more money, I intend to buy a larger ship and hire a sailor to help me," Paul told his brother.

"You'll have them," David prophesied.

Some months later Paul purchased a ship. He also found a good seaman who was willing to be his crew. By the time the Revolutionary War ended in 1783, the hazards on the ocean were not so great. The pirates were forced to

seek other waters. Paul soon started to make larger profits.

That year was important for Paul Cuffe, now twenty-four. He married Alice Pequit, an Indian girl of the same tribe that his mother belonged to. The ceremony took place in Dartmouth where his parents were married.

The Cuffes had two sons, Paul Jr. and William, and six daughters. They lived in a rented house for some time, but in 1797, Paul was unusually successful. With profits from Maryland corn, he bought property. He paid $3,500 for a large farm located on the west bank of the Westport River. A number of years later, he built a wharf and a storehouse. Westport was his home for the rest of his life.

In 1797, when he and his family settled in Westport, he found no schoolhouse or tutor in the neighborhood. Paul Cuffe was disturbed and troubled, for he wanted his children to have a good education. He could now afford to educate them, for he was a successful businessman.

He called a meeting of his neighbors, all white people, to help him work out a plan. Nothing was resolved at this first meeting or others that followed. Unfortunately, the people could not agree on a plan.

At last, in desperation, Cuffe built a schoolhouse on his farm with his own money. Then he offered it to the public. Cuffe also paid the teacher's salary as well as all expenses of operating the school. Negro and white students studied together.

Throughout his life, Paul Cuffe was generous with his money. He was especially interested in trying to help others get an education. He even taught navigation. Some of his apprentices were African Negroes, American Negroes, and at least one white student.

The Society of Friends was an essential part of Cuffe's life. He had been brought up in that faith, and he continued in it. In 1808, at the age of forty-nine, Paul Cuffe joined the Westport Society of Friends. He not only became a devoted worker, but occasionally spoke at Sunday services. In 1813, the Westport Friends had many more members and needed a larger building. It was an expensive project, but Paul Cuffe helped finance the new building. The meeting house cost over one thousand dollars. The records show that Paul Cuffe furnished nearly $600 worth of building materials. He probably donated most of it.

Paul Cuffe's first years of shipbuilding and sailing the seas were hard. He worked, and he succeeded. A less determined young man would have given up many times. But Paul Cuffe did not! Between the years 1793 and 1806, Paul's fleet grew to include: the 268-ton ship *Alpha*; two brigs, the *Traveller* (109 tons) and the *Hero* (162 tons); the 69-ton *Ranger*; and the 42-ton schooner *Mary*. He owned all these vessels outright or in partnership. Despite his many philanthropies, he left a fortune of twenty thousand dollars at his death.

In 1817 Paul Cuffe's health began to fail. He died at his home in Westport on September 9 of that year, which was the first year of James Monroe's presidency. He was buried in the Friends' cemetery at the Old Meeting House in Westport. Almost a hundred years later, in 1913, Cuffe's great grandson erected a five-foot granite monument in the front part of the Meeting House at Westport. Cut into the stone are the words:

In memory of Captain Cuffe,
Patriot, Navigator, Educator,
Philanthropist, Friend.

A fitting tribute to one of the most widely known and respected of all American Negroes.

■ When Lewis and Clark set out to explore the great lands north and west of the Mississippi River, Sacajawea went along, with her husband, carrying their baby on her back. How did this young Indian girl prove to be one of the most valuable members of the party?

Sacajawea

by NANCY WILSON ROSS

A statue of Sacajawea in Portland, Oregon.

Watch for new words. Use all your skills to get their meaning. If necessary, go to the dictionary.

Early settlers went overland by horse and wagon or on foot, or traveled a long, dangerous journey by sea in order to settle in the Far West. They might never have played their historic roles if it had not been for a young Indian woman named Sacajawea. This young Indian, a captured Shoshone "slave," deserves to be honored among "the greatest women in American history." So says a famed historian, James Truslow Adams, who nominated her to a place in the Hall of Fame among the heroes and heroines of our country.

Sacajawea, or Bird Woman, as

she is sometimes called, won this high honor because of the help she gave an exploring party. It was the first official expedition sent out from the capital of the then young United States to explore an unmapped continent. This was the Lewis and Clark Expedition which, in the years 1804 to 1806, crossed America as far as the north Pacific Coast. It then came back to report its findings to President Jefferson. It was an important exploration that helped the young United States claim the far western lands.

It now seems clear that without the guidance and aid of this little Shoshone squaw, Sacajawea, the adventurous members of the historic band might not have gone through to the Pacific Coast.

It was not much more than a hundred and fifty years ago when Meriwether Lewis and William Clark were sent by President Jefferson to explore and report on that vast stretch of mysterious land lying west and north of the Mississippi River.

When you look at a map today, it seems hard to imagine that all that great stretch of western country, now so thickly dotted with the names of towns and cities, was once as free of all landmarks as a large stretch of fresh, white tablecloth. The western United States—not yet a part of the States at all—was quite as "foreign" as any distant land overseas. Much less was known about this part of America than we know today about remote sections of Africa or Manchuria.

In the year 1804, Lewis and Clark with twenty-nine handpicked followers were camping on the Missouri River. They were trying to find an interpreter to accompany them and translate for them among the hostile Indians to the north and west.

The interpreter Lewis and Clark finally chose was a man named Charbonneau, of French and Indian parents. Charbonneau had a young Indian wife named Sacajawea.

By birth, Sacajawea belonged to the Shoshone tribe. She had been captured in a raid by enemy Indians and sold into captivity as a slave. It was said that her husband had won her as a prize in a gambling game.

Wherever he got her, it was plain Charbonneau did not want to lose her. He insisted that she must go with him on the long western adventure. Since Charbonneau would not leave her behind, and Lewis and Clark needed his services as interpreter, they finally had to give in to his demand.

It was a very lucky day for them, but they did not yet know it. Even though she was an Indian and used to the hardships of primitive travel, they feared she would be a burden in the many strenuous months ahead. The fact that she was carrying a papoose strapped to her back presented a particular difficulty, in their minds. She would have to carry this child all the way across the continent and back again. On the return journey the infant would be at the toddling stage and a much heavier load.

However, since there was no way to hire Charbonneau without taking his wife too, Sacajawea and her baby joined the little band of white men. It was not long before the kindly, redheaded William Clark had decided not to try to pronounce Sacajawea in the proper style but to call the little Indian "Janey" instead. As for the papoose who had been given the French name Baptiste, Clark chose to call him "Pompey." And as "Little Pomp" the baby was known to all the men on the long, grueling journey that was to last almost two and a half years.

They were only a short distance out on their great overland adventure when Sacajawea won the undying gratitude of Lewis and Clark by an act of singular coolheadedness.

The expedition had come by boat to the upper reaches of the Missouri River. Sacajawea was riding in the lead canoe with her baby, little black-eyed Pompey. In the same canoe were the expedition's surveying instruments, maps, medicine, and other vital supplies. A squall struck without warning, and since the canoe was at the time carrying sail, it keeled over dangerously. Charbonneau, who was guiding this crude boat, completely lost his head. Amid wild cursing, shouting, and general confusion, the boat all but capsized.

Although Sacajawea had herself and her baby to save, she was also aware of the importance of the lead canoe's equipment. With extraordinary courage, quick thinking, and quicker action, she managed to snatch from the swirling current the most precious papers and supplies, just as they were washed overboard.

That night in his journal, Clark acknowledged their tremendous debt to the Indian woman. They were already 2,200 miles from home and the sources of their necessary equipment. Had it been

lost in the river that day, the expedition would have faced disaster. They would have had to turn back and start all over again, and the delay might well have cost the United States the lands of the far Northwest. (Great Britain also had her eye on these lands. In the end it was to be nip and tuck as to whether they would become British or American.)

Sacajawea proved to be valuable to the expedition in many other ways as well. She knew, for instance, the hidden foods of the unexplored western land. She was able to find the delicious wild artichoke hearts stored by gophers in their prairie holes. She knew where wild carrot, wild fennel, and the far western "wapato" or wild potato would be growing, and she would dig for their roots to put in soups. She knew how to break and boil the shank bones of elk and other wild animals to extract the nourishing marrow.

All this was of the greatest value, since the matter of getting proper food in the wilderness was of first importance. Men living too long on diets of salt fish, dried meat, and rough bread often became too sick and weak to travel. As it was, there were many times on the long journey when Lewis and Clark and their men had only tallow candles to eat—nothing else at all. This was when winter weather caught them high in the mountains with no game to be found.

The Journals of the expedition kept by Lewis and Clark reveal Sacajawea's many remarkable qualities. They tell us, for example, of her courage. On one hunting expedition Charbonneau, Lewis, Sacajawea, and Little Pomp were caught in a sudden flood and nearly drowned. Lewis lost his compass. It was the only one the expedition had. He dived into the water over and over again hoping to recover it. And who dived with him? Not Charbonneau, but Sacajawea. The little squaw, who had learned the importance of this magic instrument whose needle always pointed mysteriously to the north, dived and swam until she became exhausted trying to find the compass. Neither she nor Lewis succeeded in their efforts. The expedition had to go on without this most valuable piece of equipment.

Sacajawea knew many other ways to be useful, too. She could mend the men's clothes with her needles of small bird bones, her thread of fiber and hide. She could even provide them with leather moccasins when their own stout shoes gave out on the rough trails.

Together with two men of the party, she made 338 moccasins for the long return journey from the Pacific Ocean to St. Louis.

But perhaps the most important of all her natural gifts was her sense of direction. Lewis and Clark had only a rough, rather inaccurate elk-hide map of the western region to guide them. Sacajawea, however, possessed an ability that seemed to the white men almost uncanny. She would look at a row of distant mountains that appeared to them only as a jagged ridge of blue on the distant sky. As if by instinct, she would seem to know just where the hidden passes lay. Streams and rivers also yielded to her the secrets of their distant sources.

There had been many weary days and weeks of unbroken travel when at last the little group came to the natural barrier known as the Great Divide. This is the place where the waters of streams and rivers no longer flow eastward, toward the homes the white men had left so far behind them, but westward instead, toward the setting sun and the farthest wilderness.

Soon Sacajawea found herself again in the landscape of her childhood. Among the first landmarks she recognized were strange red clay banks. They were so curiously shaped that the expedition named them "The Beaverhead Rocks," thinking that they resembled mountain beaver. The bright crimson clay of these banks, Sacajawea told them, was used by her people to make their war paint. War paint! This was hardly a reassuring thought for the travel-worn expedition. They were not sure yet whether the Shoshones would prove friends or enemies.

Though Sacajawea let them know they had reached Shoshone country, they saw no signs of any Indians. Yet they were uneasily aware that they were being watched by invisible eyes. Once in a while they did catch sight of distant smoke signals rising into the clear sky. What were the signals saying? They did not know. One day Clark's quick eye saw moccasin tracks in a damp place on the trail. They knew then that the Indians were nearby. But still they did not see any of them. It was an uncanny feeling to be spied on secretly.

It was Sacajawea who suggested one night that they make a fire and leave on a rock near it some blue beads, a looking glass, and a knife for cutting out moccasins. This would show their friendly intentions to any Indians who might be lurking about, watching them from behind rocks and bushes as they plodded westward.

After they laid the offerings on the rock, they all stole away and slept some distance off.

In the morning the offerings were gone. But still no Indians appeared.

At last there came a day when they heard the sound of many horses' hoofs far in the distance. In a short time a band of sixty Shoshones in full regalia of paint and feathers appeared on the horizon. Every heart stood still. Every man fastened his hand on his rifle and waited tensely. The Indians numbered two to their one.

The chieftain heading the Indian party rode with impressive dignity toward Lewis, who was walking guardedly towards the Shoshones.

Suddenly Sacajawea gave a loud, glad cry and darted forward from among the white men. To the amazement of them all, they saw the Shoshone chief himself dismount. Then they saw their little squaw, Janey, throw her blanket over him and burst out weeping. It was Sacajawea's brother Cameahwait, whom she had not seen since she was captured many years before in the raid by the Blackfeet that had made her a slave.

This chance encounter with Cameahwait was the greatest possible piece of good fortune for Lewis and Clark. Through the influence of this powerful chief they would be able to get the horses they must have in order to travel on through the mountains to the shores of the Pacific Ocean.

Cameahwait was very much impressed with the position of honor his sister enjoyed among such important envoys from the Great White Father in Washington. To his pride in his sister there was also added gratitude when she was able to give him, from the expedition's meager stores, gifts of food that he had never seen before. These were white men's luxuries: sugar, squash, corn, and beans.

Shrewd Sacajawea knew what importance gifts of food would have for the Shoshones. A wandering tribe with no knowledge of agriculture, they were never free of the pressing problem of finding enough to eat for all their people. No gift could have been more welcome to these particular Indians, with their unvarying diet of buffalo, fish, wild roots, and mountain berries.

Impressed and grateful, Cameahwait agreed to ask his people to postpone their annual buffalo-hunting expedition until they had guided Lewis and Clark and Sacajawea further on their westward journey. In return, so Sacajawea told the Shoshones, the Great White Father, President Jefferson, would help them to hunt for game farther south than usual without danger from enemy tribes. Also, someone would soon come to teach them to grow their own beans and squash and corn. What was more, the Great White Father would establish trading posts nearby, and there the Shoshones could get guns to make hunting easier for them.

Perhaps it was at Sacajawea's suggestion that Lewis and Clark staged a great entertainment for the Indians, with pipe-smoking, dancing and singing. The expedition had brought along a fiddler named Cruzatte. Cruzatte and his fiddle had often helped to cheer the men when they grew weary, dispirited, or homesick in the long exile from their families.

So Cruzatte got out his fiddle to entertain the Indians. He played old country tunes, and all the men danced the Virginia Reel and the Irish Jig.

Then York, a Negro, danced too: cakewalks, clogs, and shuffles. The Indians, who had never seen a Negro, were delighted with York.

After a while the Indians rose and also danced, beating the earth with their moccasined feet and chanting their eerie songs that sounded like rising winds.

At last the pipe of peace was brought out, lit, and passed from hand to hand. Good will and friendship were pledged. The expedition went over the Rocky Mountains and down into the unknown land where the fabled Oregon River, now called the Columbia, rolled on its way to the Pacific Ocean.

But even after leaving her own people, Sacajawea's usefulness was not yet at an end. She went right on helping. She tended the sick, found food, mended clothes, made new garments of elk skin.

At Christmas time in 1805, spent at Clatsop in what is now the state of Washington, all the homesick party tried to give gifts to one another and celebrate the day as best they could in the rainy wilderness. Sacajawea presented Captain Clark, the cheerful redhead who seems to have been her favorite, with twenty-four skins of the whitest ermine. She had carried them with her hidden under her garments all the way from Fort Mandan, many hundreds of miles back on the journey.

Over and over again Sacajawea's presence helped keep trouble from the party. Among western Indians no war party ever took women with them on raids. When the tribes saw Sacajawea, it was proof to them that the white strangers' intentions were peaceful.

She was useful too as an interpreter near the shores of the Pacific Ocean. Some of the difficulties of communication with Indians of unknown language can be imagined from an entry made in one of the expedition's Journals:

"In the first place, we spoke in English to one of our men, who translated it into French to Charbonneau; he interpreted it to his wife in the Minnetaree language, and she then put it into Shoshonee, and the young Shoshonee prisoner explained it to the Chopunnish in their own dialect."

There is no record anywhere in the journals of any complaint on Sacajawea's part, or any weakening of her energies. She was at one time sick—but so, for that matter, were all the men of the expedition in those months of deprivation. When she fell ill, she was tenderly cared for. They all valued her now. She slept in the main tent.

For her services in the two and a half years of hardship, Sacajawea asked only one thing: She begged to go with the men to view the "Big Water," the Pacific Ocean. Lewis and Chief Red Head, as she called Clark, permitted her to go along.

Sacajawea's awe at the sight of the ocean, however, was lost in her amazement at the carcass of a whale cast up on the Pacific sands. In later years she told her "fish story" to hundreds of inland Indians, and when she measured out quite accurately from hitching post to

The solid line shows the route of Sacajawea's long journey.

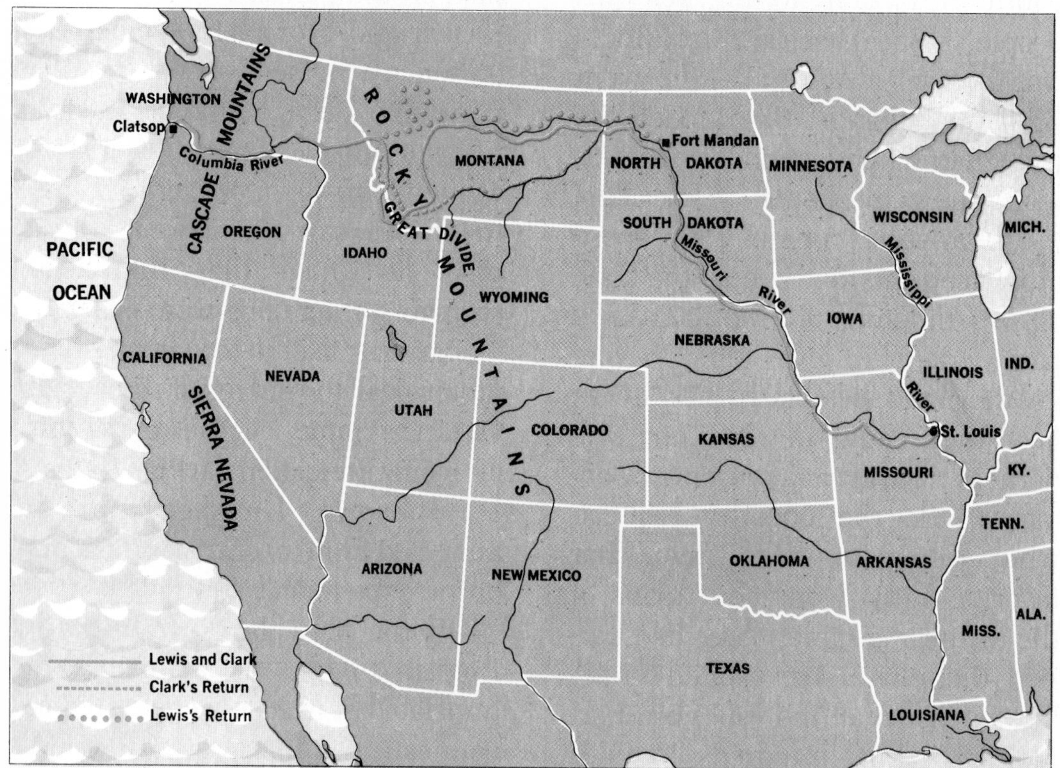

tepee the whale's great length, they would yell with joy at her "big lie." At the same time she would describe her first sight of the seals she had seen on the Oregon shore as "people who lived in the water," with no one doubting the story at all!

As for her baby, Little Pomp, Captain Clark gave him an education in St. Louis. He grew up to be an interpreter and a traveler like his mother—with one big difference. Baptiste was paid for his work! Baptiste acted as guide and interpreter for expeditions of rich European noblemen who came all the way by slow boat across the Atlantic to see, in the early days of the frontier, the American wilderness and its strange natives.

Sacajawea, who lived to be more than one hundred years of age, kept on traveling too. She crossed the western country many times as an old woman, on the free passes with which early stagecoach companies provided her. Wherever she went, she acted as an unpaid agent of good will for the white people. Known among Indians by a variety of names—Chief, Lost Woman, Great Woman—she spent the remainder of her long life spreading good feeling between the Americans and the people of her own race. In the days when the buffalo were fast disappearing, it is said she did her best to persuade the Plains Indians to change their wandering way of life, settle down to learn agriculture, and enjoy a peaceful existence.

Since her death in 1884, Sacajawea's fame has grown steadily. The monuments raised in her honor in Far Western towns salute the intelligence, courage, and kindness of this little Indian woman. She played a truly important role in saving for the young United States the great natural riches and beauties of the country where the states of Montana, Idaho, Washington, and Oregon now appear on our maps.

In all her wanderings with the men of the Lewis and Clark Expedition, she had traveled on foot not only through parts of the four states just named but also large parts of what are now Kansas, Iowa, Nebraska, South Dakota, North Dakota, and Wyoming.

Find on a map the area through which these brave men and this equally brave little Indian woman tramped—often in danger of violent death, frequently hungry, sometimes even starving, footsore, anxious, exhausted, but always determined. You will agree that Sacajawea does indeed belong in our Hall of Fame.

The growing nation needed a railroad from the Atlantic to the Pacific. Not one but two railroad companies started to build it, one from the east, the other from the west. Thus began one of the strangest and most exciting races in history.

Rails Across the West

by HAROLD LITTLEDALE

You may find several new words in this selection. If context doesn't help you with their meanings, try to pronounce them. Do they sound familiar? Look for morphemes you know. Turn to the Glossary or a dictionary if you need further help.

By the middle of the nineteenth century, more and more people were going west. Railroads had been built as far west as the Mississippi River. In 1853 Congress asked for a government survey to find the best railroad route from the Missouri River across the continent to the Pacific Coast.

In California, a year later, a brilliant young engineer decided that, if there was to be a transcontinental railroad, he was going to build it. His name was Theodore Dehone Judah.

JUDAH'S DREAM

Theodore Judah was twenty-eight years old when he arrived in California early in 1854. He was tall and he wore a thick black beard —to make him look older, some people said. He was a dreamer. There was a far-away look in his eyes when he strode down the muddy streets of Sacramento. Children ran after him shouting, "Crazy Judah! Cra-a-zy Judah!"

The California that Judah had come to was booming. Gold had been discovered in 1848, and people had been pouring into the state ever since. Tiny San Francisco and Sacramento had grown into thriving cities almost overnight. The shopkeepers were making fortunes selling dry goods, food, and hardware to the gold hunters.

But transportation was a problem in the California of the Gold Rush days. People and goods could hardly get around on the winding footpaths and rutted wagon trails of the new state. Railroads were needed, and wider, carefully graded wagon roads. This is where Judah came into the picture.

A group of Sacramento businessmen had hired Judah to do two jobs. The first was to survey for a railroad—California's first—to run twenty-one miles between Sacramento and Folsom. The second job was to map out a wagon road running east from Sacramento, up over the jagged Sierra Nevada mountain peaks and on to Nevada, where silver mines were opening up.

The first job went quickly. In a year a train was running regular trips to Folsom. But the more Judah worked at mapping out a route to Nevada, the more he became sure that the wagon road

should be a railroad—and not just to Nevada, but beyond, all the way to the Atlantic coast.

Judah asked his employers to back this plan, but they refused. He talked to leading California citizens, but people laughed at the idea and said "Crazy Judah" was a good nickname.

Judah decided to ask the government to back his plan, so he went to Washington. He found members of Congress more and more interested in the transcontinental railroad. But now they couldn't agree on a route for the road to follow. It's not hard to understand why. The railroad would carry settlers and new business to the states it ran through. Each congressman wanted the route to run as close to his state as possible so that his people would benefit.

Judah was discouraged. But his luck was about to change. Four Sacramento businessmen had caught his railroad fever. The four were Leland Stanford, a grocer, Collis Porter Huntington and Mark Hopkins, partners in a hardware and mining equipment business, and Charles Crocker, a dry-goods man. They were rich and getting richer. Later they were called "The Big Four."

The Big Four listened to Judah. They looked at his maps and surveys. Finally they agreed to give him money to build his railroad over the mountains to the silver mines in Nevada, where they could sell lots of supplies and equipment to the miners. They formed a company—The Central Pacific Railroad of California. They made Judah chief engineer.

In Washington, Judah's luck changed, too. In the spring of 1862 Congress passed a Pacific Railroad Act. The Act gave Judah's Central Pacific Railroad the right to build east from Sacramento. It set up a Union Pacific Railroad and Telegraph Company to start building west from the Missouri River near Omaha, Nebraska. President Abraham Lincoln signed the bill on the first of July, 1862. And one of the longest, most exciting, and strangest races in history began.

THE CENTRAL PACIFIC RAILROAD

Building a railroad is a slow business at best. But the conditions under which the Central Pacific Railroad began to build early in 1863 were the worst possible. There was plenty of good California redwood around for railroad ties. But everything else—every nail, every spike, every hammer, every pickaxe—had to be brought to California from the East, 18,000 miles by sailing ship around stormy Cape Horn at the southern tip of South America.

Worse still, there was a shortage of workers. Many of the younger men had gone to war. The gold-mining boom was slowing down, but the settlers had found the California farming good and were busy with their land. Only a few drifters were willing to take on the dangerous, back-breaking work Judah's railroad offered. And these worked slowly. At the end of 1863 only eighteen miles of track were laid.

The Big Four blamed Judah for the railroad's slow pace. Thousands of dollars were at stake, they said. Speed was the most important thing.

Judah was angry. He said the most important thing was to build a good railroad. The argument went back and forth. Neither Judah nor The Big Four would budge an inch. Finally, Judah quit. Once again he made the long trip back east. This trip was his last. Judah died of yellow fever just after he arrived in New York.

THE UNION PACIFIC RAILROAD

In the East the Union Pacific Railroad and Telegraph Company was having troubles of its own. A marvelous ground-breaking ceremony had been held near Omaha in 1863. But when the Civil War

ended in 1865, not a rail had been laid.

The Union Pacific needed a leader—someone able to handle the rowdy bunch of ex-soldiers, tough Irish immigrants, and freewheeling muleskinners who had signed on to build the road. Such a leader was General Grenville M. Dodge, who became the Union Pacific's chief engineer in 1866.

Dodge quickly took charge of the Union Pacific's construction. Two hundred and sixty miles of

tracks were laid down during his first year as the railroad's chief engineer. This was more than eight times as many miles as had been built in the three previous years. And this was only the warm-up. The Union Pacific was humming at last.

"CROCKER'S PETS"

Things were humming back in California, too. Charles Crocker, one of The Big Four, had taken over leadership of the Central Pacific Railroad. A roaring, big man—250 pounds of stubborn courage and pure energy—Charlie Crocker had none of Judah's engineering know-how, but he could lead men. And at last he had found good men to lead. They were Chinese laborers—small, wiry men in odd, down-turned basket hats and sagging blue-denim suits.

By 1866 Crocker had two thousand Chinese working for his Central Pacific Railroad. In the years that followed, the number grew to ten thousand. People called them "Crocker's Pets."

They were demons for work, these Chinese laborers, and it was a good thing. The work ahead was going to be harder than any railroad building ever done before.

By the spring of 1866, more than forty miles of Central Pacific track had been laid to Colfax. It had been uphill work, a climb of one thousand feet. Now there was a further climb of seven thousand feet to the summit of the Sierra Nevada.

Slowly the Central Pacific edged up into the mountains. "Crocker's Pets" worked from baskets swinging high above the raging American River, chipping a road along the sides of towering granite cliffs. Slowly they toiled their way up past mining camps with colorful names—Red Dog, You Bet, Dutch Flat, Little York.

Winter came, and heavy snows. Many of the men worked in damp semidarkness in tunnels built underneath the snow. Others took their chances outside in screaming winds where avalanches could sweep them to sudden death in the canyons below. Half the men worked simply at shoveling the tons and tons of snow that fell in the high passes. Many died of sickness and plain exhaustion.

Hammers and pickaxes rang against the solid granite mountainside. Progress could be as little as eight inches a day. But the work went on, through winter, spring, and summer.

By September of 1867 the passage across the mountains was open for train travel. Crocker said the worst was over. From now on his men could lay a mile of track a day. Nevada was in sight.

INDIANS!

While Crocker's men were fighting their way through the blizzards of the high Sierra Nevada, General Dodge's Union Pacific men were fighting the Indians of the Nebraska and Wyoming plains.

They had been warned. Shortly after the Union Pacific had laid its first tracks, Red Cloud, a great Sioux warrior chief, had sent the railroad men a message. "We do not want you here," he said. "You are scaring away the buffalo." But the railroad had pushed ahead, and the Sioux and the Cheyenne Indians had gone on the warpath.

Their attempts to stop the railroad were almost funny at first. One Indian brave tied the end of a rawhide rope around his waist

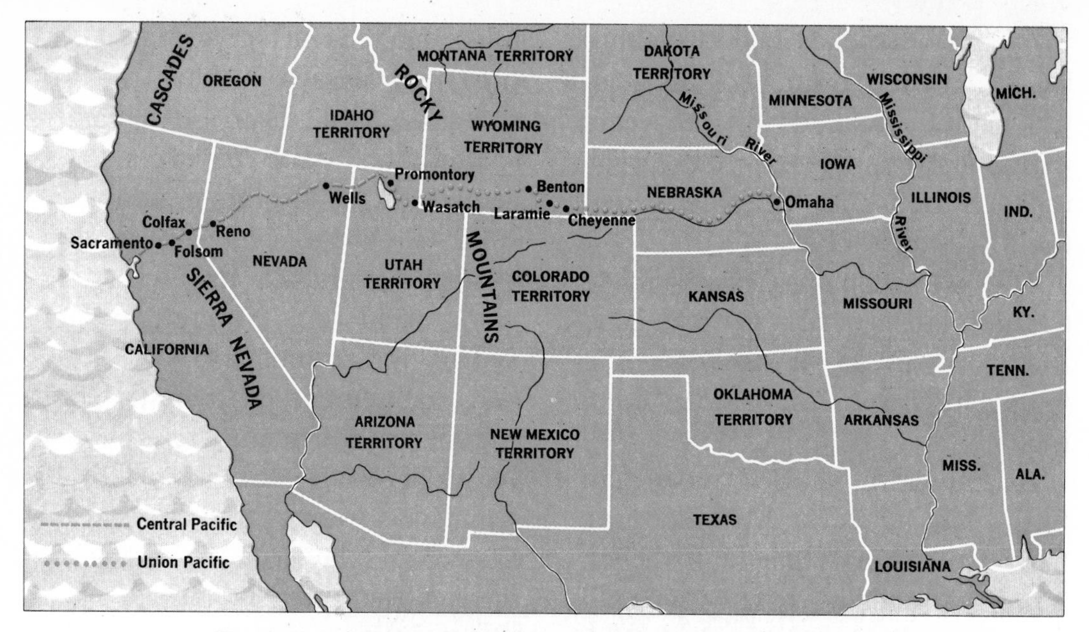

The map shows the route of the two railroads across the West.

and lassoed the tall smokestack of a passing locomotive. He went flying off his horse as the train charged on.

Another time a band of Indians tried stopping a train by holding a rope taut across the tracks. The train smashed into the rope and the Indians went sailing.

But as the railroad pushed ahead through Nebraska and into Wyoming, the Indian raids became more serious—and more deadly.

Led by chiefs named Spotted Tail and Turkey Leg, Indians of the Sioux and Cheyenne tribes raided railroad camps, where they stampeded horse and mule herds and stole guns, food, and clothing. They tore down telegraph wires and pried up tracks. They massacred surveying parties and scalped track-laying crews.

The Indians stepped up their raids, and General Dodge ordered every railroad worker to carry a gun. The crews' sleeping cars were turned into armed forts. Dodge asked for government troops from Washington, and soon they came.

Still the Union Pacific pushed on. By the end of 1867 it had moved ahead 240 miles to Cheyenne, Wyoming. There the crew set up camp for the winter.

THE RACE TO FINISH

With spring, the pace of the two railroads quickened. Surveyors for both roads worked far ahead of the other crews, staking out the routes east and west. Behind them, graders and bridge-building gangs made the road level and built wooden bridges across rivers and gullies. Then came the track-laying teams.

Horse or mule teams pulled the open supply trucks holding ties, rails, and spikes to the end of the track. They stopped. The animals were unhitched. Quickly, ties were dropped along the roadbed. When the foreman shouted "Down," rails were laid on the ties. They were "gauged" to be sure they were exactly four feet, eight and a half inches apart, and spiked down while a small horse pulled the supply truck ahead. When the truck was empty, it was tipped sideways off the tracks. Another truck with more ties and rails and spikes was whipped forward to take its place.

"Hurry!" was the word you heard most among the railroad crews now. Crocker's men had been making a steady mile a day ever since they had crossed the California state line and moved into Nevada. But messages from the Union Pacific said that General Dodge's men had laid three miles in a single day, then four.

Crocker's men stepped up their work and put down a record seven miles in a day. The Union Pacific raised it to seven and a half.

The Union Pacific's construction boss said his men could lay eight miles of track in a single day. He challenged Crocker to do as well. Crocker laughed and said his men could do ten.

The Union Pacific's vice president, Thomas C. Durant, sent Crocker a message: "Ten thousand dollars if you can do it before witnesses."

"We'll notify you," Crocker replied.

The two railroads edged closer and closer. By the spring of 1868 the Central Pacific had passed through a little wagon stop called Reno and moved into the Nevada desert lands.

The Union Pacific rushed ahead through Wyoming—past Laramie and into Benton. The Central Pacific snaked its way across the Nevada desert and along the Humboldt River.

By September, General Dodge's ten thousand laborers and five hundred horse and mule teams had passed through the burning Red Desert and the waterless country of the Bitter Creek Basin. By the end of 1868, they had laid another 425 miles of rails and were camped in Wasatch, Utah.

The Central Pacific was pressing on through Wells, Nevada, then crossing the state border into Utah. The railroads were forty miles apart, thirty miles apart, twenty. The transcontinental railroad was almost joined. And then, on April 28, 1869, Crocker announced, "Tomorrow we'll lay those ten miles." He invited doubters to come see for themselves.

The following day Crocker's men were up at dawn. Their hammers were ringing on the rails by seven in the morning. Six miles of rail had been laid by one-thirty in the afternoon, and still the workers sweated on. Tie after tie was dropped in place. Rail after rail was set and spiked. Froth-covered mule and horse teams galloped up and down the ever longer line of track. Crocker rushed this way and that urging his men on, yelling, threatening.

At last, as the sun went down and the day's-end whistle blew, the workers dropped their hammers and slumped to the ground. They had laid ten miles of track, and several hundred feet more for good measure. Crocker had won his ten-thousand-dollar bet. The tracks of the two railroads were now less than ten miles apart, and there was no possibility of the Union Pacific matching the Central's feat.

Three days later the gap between the two railroads had narrowed to a single rail's length. The Union Pacific had laid 1,086 miles of track. The Central Pacific Railroad had laid 690.

THE MEETING OF THE RAILS

Early on the morning of May 10, 1869, a nine-year-old boy climbed up to the top of a telegraph pole in Promontory, Utah. This is what he saw:

Promontory itself was a jumble of tents and wooden shacks. The main street was a muddy pathway. Only the shining twin sets of railroad tracks, entering the town from east and west, seemed permanent.

Facing each other across the gap in the rails were two steam locomotives—the Central Pacific's *Jupiter* and the Union Pacific's unnamed *Number 119*. Their steel-plated sides gleamed with polishing. Their smokestacks sparked and billowed smoke with a full head of steam.

Promontory was jammed and noisy. Close to fifteen hundred sightseers milled around the hooting locomotives. Four companies of infantry soldiers drilled. Two brass bands played patriotic songs. Newspaper reporters from all over the United States were everywhere, asking questions and taking notes.

The two engineers shake hands. The Central Pacific is at the left. ►

At last the ceremonies began. The last tie—a block of polished California laurel wood—was put in place. Chinese laborers carried the last rail to the roadbed and laid it down. The Reverend John Todd of Pittsfield, Massachusetts, led a prayer.

Speeches were made. "The Star-Spangled Banner" was sung. A railroad spike of solid gold was set into a hole especially drilled for it. Now everything was ready. When the golden spike was driven, the two roads would become one.

Leland Stanford stepped forward to represent the Central Pacific Railroad of California. He raised the silver-headed sledgehammer which had been made especially for the occasion. He took a deep breath, swung the hammer—and missed! The crowd cheered anyway.

Now Thomas C. Durant of the Union Pacific Railroad and Telegraph Company seized the hammer. He swung—and he missed too! The crowd cheered again, and guests of the two railroads stepped up to the golden spike and drove it home. The cheers became a deafening roar as the two locomotives—the Central's *Jupiter* and the Union's *Number 119*—first one, then the other, chugged forward and back across the last rail.

And so the railroads finally met. It was a time for cheering, that early spring afternoon in Promontory, Utah, where the Union Pacific and the Central Pacific were joined a century ago. And it was a time for hope for the future of our young country, a hope expressed in a prayer engraved along one side of the railroad's last, golden spike. It read:

May God continue the unity of our Country as this Railroad unites the two great Oceans of the world.

Using Glossaries

You have found that many new words in your textbook are explained in the context. But sometimes you find new words that are not explained. In such cases, you need to turn either to a dictionary or to the list of words in the back of the book. This list is called a *glossary.* A glossary is similar to a dictionary. It includes the special words of the book with their meanings. Some glossaries tell how to pronounce words, too.

A Glossary in Mathematics

Here are several entries from a mathematics glossary. Notice that the entry words are in **boldface** type. They are listed in alphabetical order. Notice also that the entries are explained in different ways. Some entries have definitions, some have definitions and pictures. In other entries, equations and mathematical terms help to make the meaning clear.

Glossary

angle. A set of points, consisting of two rays with a common endpoint.

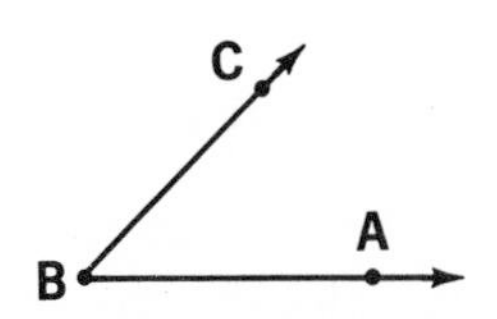

arc. A part of a circle—for example, arc *AC* or arc *ABC*.

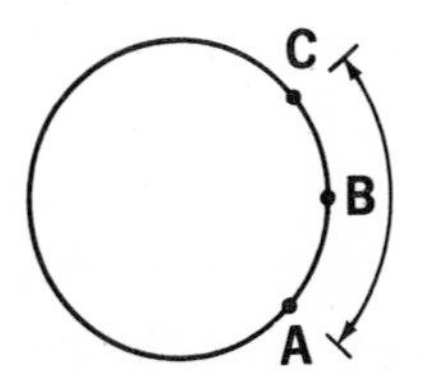

arc degree. A unit that is used to measure arcs. One arc degree is $\frac{1}{360}$ of a circle.

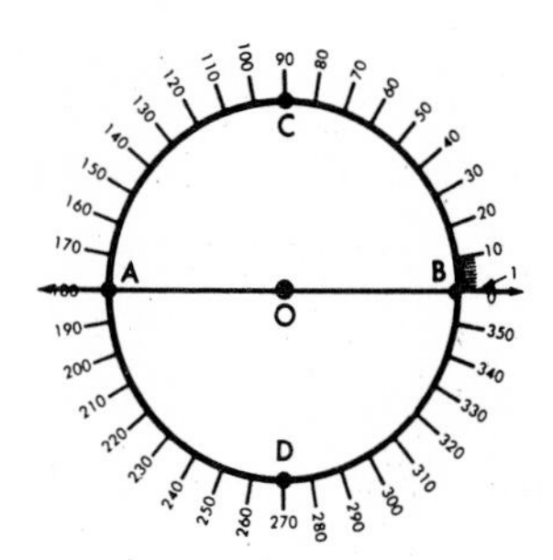

area. The measure of a region.

cardinal number. A number that tells how many members there are in a set.

commutative property. In addition, if □ and △ represent any numbers, then □ + △ = △ + □. In multiplication, if □ and △ represent any numbers, then □ × △ = △ × □.

curve. In geometry, a path that can be drawn without lifting the pencil. A curve that can be drawn by starting at one point and ending at the same point is a *closed curve*, or a *closed figure*. A *simple closed curve* is a closed curve that does not intersect itself.

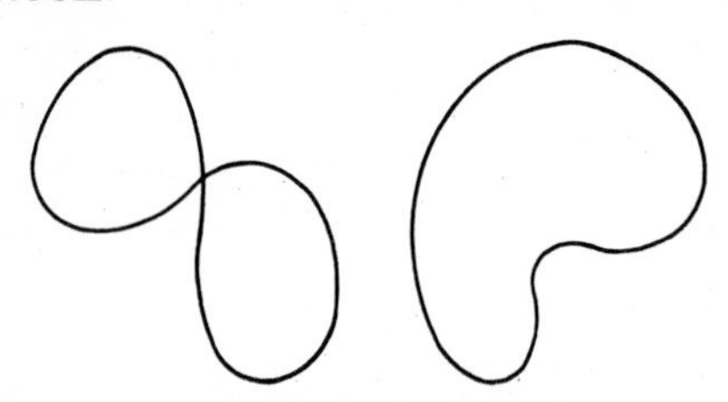

Closed curve **Simple closed curve**

distributive property. If N, □, and △ represent any numbers, then N × (□ + △) = (N × □) + (N × △).

edge. A line segment formed by the intersection of two faces of a space figure such as a prism—for example, $\overline{AB}$.

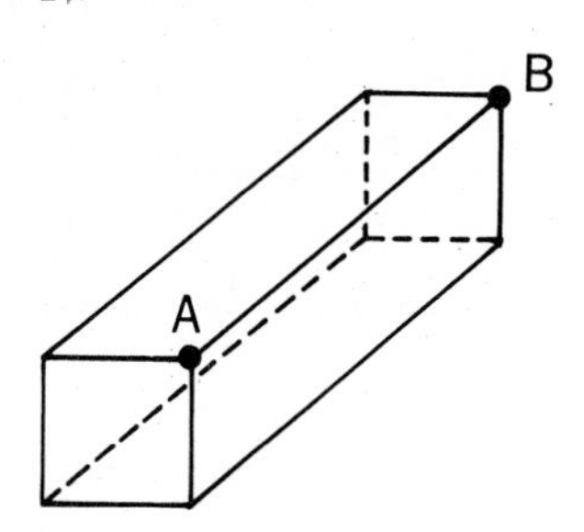

fraction. A numeral such as $\frac{1}{2}$, $\frac{3}{4}$, $\frac{6}{6}$, $\frac{8}{7}$. The digit below the fraction bar names the *denominator*. The digit above the fraction bar names the *numerator*. The numerator and denominator are the *terms* of a fraction.

line segment, or **segment.** A part of a line, consisting of two points—called *endpoints*—and all the points of the line between these two points.

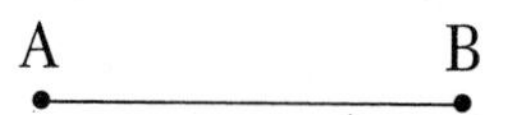

negative numbers. Numbers that are less than 0—for example, −3, $-\frac{2}{3}$, and −150.

ordinal number. The number that tells the position of a member in a set.

—from *Modern Mathematics Through Discovery*

Building Skills

To Write

1. Write the entries that include equations to help you understand the meaning.
2. Write the examples of negative numbers that are given in the entry.
3. What two kinds of curves are explained?
4. Write the entry word that means "a figure made up of two rays with the same endpoint."

To Discuss

1. Look at the entry for each of these words: *arc, arc degree, curve, edge, line segment.* Tell what each entry includes, besides the definition, to help you understand the meaning.
2. What mathematical terms are used to help you understand the meaning of fractions?
3. Explain the difference between *cardinal number* and *ordinal number.*

A List of Key Words in Science

A word list or a glossary usually begins with a paragraph that explains its use. Such a paragraph tells you exactly what help you can find in that particular word list. You should read the paragraph before you begin to use the list.

Some word lists and glossaries also include aids to pronunciation.

The following page is from a science glossary. Study the introductory paragraph. Then answer the questions on pages 101–02.

Key Concept Words: A Beginning Vocabulary for Science

To record what they have learned from their investigations, scientists use words that have the same meaning to every other scientist; that is, scientists try to use words accurately. You are building up a vocabulary of key concept terms of science during this year. You will, of course, want to use them properly. The first time a term is used with a special meaning for scientific communication, it is in boldface type in your textbook. In this vocabulary of key concept terms, a page reference is given to refer to if you need more information or examples of the meaning than are given here. In other words, the definition given may need filling out. As you study science, the terms you use will take on fuller meaning. A few terms you probably know from earlier work in science do not have a page reference; you should already know how to use these terms in their correct meaning. The index gives other page references.

Pronunciation Key

This key is the same as that used in *The Harcourt Brace School Dictionary, Second Edition.*

SYMBOL	KEY WORDS	SYMBOL	KEY WORDS
a	*a*dd, m*a*p	o͞o	p*oo*l, f*oo*d
ā	*a*ce, r*a*te	o͝o	t*oo*k, f*u*ll
ä	p*a*lm, f*a*ther	th	*th*in, bo*th*
e	*e*nd, p*e*t	u	*u*p, d*o*ne
ē	*e*ven, tr*ee*	y	*y*et, *y*earn
i	*i*t, g*i*ve	zh	vi*s*ion, plea*s*ure
ī	*i*ce, wr*i*te	ə	an unstressed vowel as in the words *a*bove, sick*e*n, clar*i*ty, mel*o*n, foc*u*s
o	*o*dd, h*o*t		
ō	*o*pen, s*o*		
ô	*o*rder, j*aw*		
oi	*oi*l, b*oy*		

acid, a compound whose water solution turns blue litmus pink, 132

action, a thrust or force acting in one direction that is equal to a thrust or force (reaction) acting in the opposite direction, 15

[Part of the list is omitted here.]

cambium (kam′bē·əm), layer of living cells beneath the bark of a tree, 227

capillary (kap′ə·ler′ē), the smallest and narrowest of the blood vessels, 284

carbohydrate (kär′bō·hī′drāt), a compound of carbon, hydrogen, and oxygen, produced by living things; it has about twice as many hydrogen atoms as oxygen atoms; any sugar or starch found in living cells, 248

cartilage (kar′tə·lij), a substance made by cells that gives certain parts of the body support and flexibility, 271

cell, the smallest living part of a living thing, 202

cell division, method by which a cell divides to produce two similar cells, 226

cell membrane, the outer boundary of the living cell of an animal, 153; the inner boundary of a plant cell, 211

cellulose (sel′yə·lōs), substance that makes up the walls of plant cells, 223

cell wall, the outer nonliving boundary of a plant cell, 223

cerebellum (ser′ə·bel′əm), the part of the brain that is the center for control of the movement of muscles, 292

cerebrum (ser′ə·brəm), the part of the brain which is the center of thinking, imagining, 292

–from *Concepts in Science 5*

Building Skills

To Discuss

1. Answer each of the following:
   a. What are "key concept" words?
   b. In this textbook, how do you know which words have special meanings in science?
   c. What do the numerals after the explanations stand for?
   d. If you want more information about an entry, where can you look?

2. Look at the list of words—**acid** through **cerebrum.** Why do you think some of the words in the list are not respelled for pronunciation?
3. Which words in the list have two accent marks? Which syllable in those words gets the stronger stress?
4. Find and pronounce the words from the list that have schwa in them.
5. In the definition of **action,** what does *reaction* mean?

To Write

1. Look at the Pronunciation Key. The key words illustrate the sounds the symbols stand for. What key words illustrate the sounds that the following symbols stand for?

ä   o͝o   u   ə
ō   a   th

2. What is the difference between **cerebellum** and **cerebrum**?

Summary

Context helps you to discover the meanings of many words. But sometimes you need more help than the context gives. Then you must turn to a dictionary or to the list of words in the back of your book. In using a glossary, or list of key words, you have learned to:

—Read the introductory paragraph.
—Study the meanings of words.
—Study any illustrations that are given.
—Study any additional helps that are given for the entry word, such as formulas, other terms, and so on.
—Use the pronunciation key.

In Chains to Louisiana: Solomon Northup's Story by Michael Knight.

Solomon Northup, freeman, son of a freed slave, spent his early life in upper New York State. In 1841, at the age of thirty-three, Northup was kidnapped and sold into slavery in Washington, D.C. For twelve years he remained a slave, and this book tells of his life during that time.

Land of the Free by Enid Meadowcroft.

This book recounts the important events in our country's growth from the voyages of Columbus to the founding of the United Nations.

The Negro Cowboys by Philip Durham and Everett L. Jones.

Ride along the cattle trails, through the snowy mountain passes, and into the great West with some of the men who paved the way for America to grow. Maps and photographs are included.

Red Hawk's Account of Custer's Last Battle by Paul and Dorothy Goble.

We have all read the settlers' and the soldiers' version of Custer's Last Stand. This account follows the Indians' descriptions of the battle. Even the illustrations are in the Indian style.

The Alaska Gold Rush by May Y. McNeer.

When gold was discovered in Alaska, the stampede began. Prospectors, swindlers, and adventurers came from all over the world to seek their fortunes.

Homesteaders and Indians by Dorothy Levenson.

As the settlers moved west into Indian lands, trouble erupted. This book tells of those troubles but also describes the sod houses and claim shanties, the buffalo, and the crops of the old West. Dorothy Levenson also provides many interesting details about the life of pioneer women.

Unit 3

Communicating with Others

A film crew on location in the Mojave Desert.

SKILLS LESSON

RELATING IDEAS IN SENTENCES

What is the meaning of this "sentence"?

The swing would mailbags the his rider saddle to the leather.

You don't know? Try reading the same words below:

The rider would swing his leather mailbags to the saddle.

Why could you understand the second sentence? In the second example, the words are arranged to show clearly how they are related.

Sentence Meaning

Reading is largely a matter of understanding the relationships among words. In most sentences the relationships are clear. You readily see what the writer means because he puts his words in sentence patterns that you use all the time in speaking and writing.

Sometimes, however, a writer varies the usual order. Perhaps he does so to keep you interested! Or he may need to

write a very long sentence because his ideas are complicated. Short sentences can show relationships only among a few ideas. Long sentences can include many ideas.

Let's look at some ways of understanding the ideas in long sentences.

Do you remember how a qualifying word or phrase changes the meaning of a sentence? Here is an example:

The younger men had gone to war.
Many of the younger men had gone to war.

In the same way, **qualifying ideas add to, or alter, the meaning of the main thought of a sentence.** To understand how the main thought may be qualified, consider these sentences:

The newspapers will be delivered by six o'clock if the roads are clear.

The newspapers will be delivered by six o'clock even though the delivery men are on strike.

The newspapers will be delivered by six o'clock because the delivery truck got an early start.

The main thought of every sentence is the same, but how different the whole meaning of each sentence is! Do you see how important it is to keep in mind the meaning of the words that come after the main thought?

Sometimes the qualifying idea comes before the main part of the sentence. You must hold that idea in mind until you have read the whole sentence. Then you must relate the ideas.

When telegraph lines were built all the way to California, the Pony Express was no longer needed.

What do the words before the comma tell you about the Pony Express?

Qualifying ideas often express time relationships. In the next sentence, the words before the comma tell when the rider quit. They also tell how far he rode before quitting.

After he had ridden about seventy-five miles, the Pony Express rider passed his mailbags to a fresh rider.

Sometimes the qualifying idea and the main thought interrupt each other.

In South America, Inca couriers, in the days before horses were brought to the Western Hemisphere, carried messages on foot.

What information would you miss if you read only the main thought of the sentence? Does the qualifying idea suggest one reason *why* the Incas used runners?

What is the main thought in the sentence below?

Inca couriers, running short relays of about 3 miles each, could send a message 150 miles in a day.

What idea is expressed by the words that interrupt the main thought? Does this qualifying idea explain *how* the message was delivered so speedily?

When you read a long sentence, your aim is to see how *all* the parts are related. Long sentences need not be difficult sentences.

TRY THIS

Here are groups of sentences that are rather long and may seem puzzling. Answering the questions that follow should help you see how qualifying ideas are related to the main thought.

[1] Modern technology produces many materials that are hard to dispose of after they have been used. [2] Metal, plastics, and glass cannot be burned or dissolved. [3] Because these materials are hard to dispose of and our resources are limited, scientists are trying to find new ways to **recycle** [use again] our trash and garbage.

Sentence 1: What kind of materials?
When are they hard to dispose of?
Sentence 3: What are two reasons scientists are trying to recycle?

[1] If it were not for the warmth carried across the sea by this ocean river [the Gulf Stream], northern Europe might be as bitterly cold as Greenland, England might be covered with snow and ice most of the year, and part of Norway which is within the Arctic Circle might be hemmed in by icebergs.

Sentence 1: What keeps northern Europe from being as bitterly cold as Greenland?
Would England be covered with ice and snow all the time?

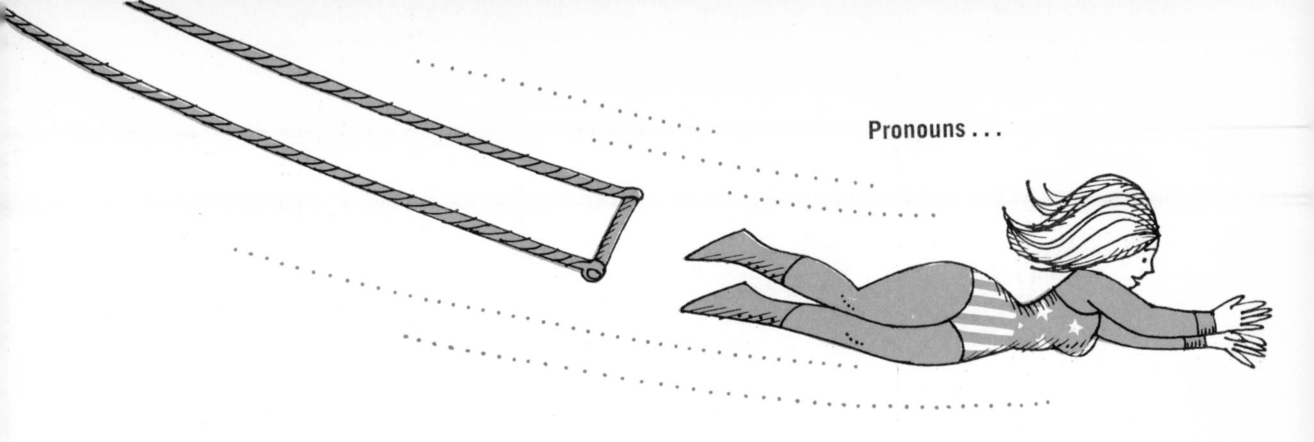

SKILLS LESSON

THE PART THAT PRONOUNS PLAY

Pronouns are words like *they, it, her, them,* and *what, who which.* They stand for the names of people and things. Pronouns are useful words to a writer because they make it possible to write without repeating the same name over and over. Pronouns are also useful to a reader so long as he knows what each pronoun stands for.

One group of pronouns is especially useful in relating ideas to each other. For this reason, they are called **relative pronouns.** Examples are: *who, which, that, whoever, whom.* Notice how helpful the pronoun in the next sentence is in tying together the main thought and the qualifying idea.

There was a stationkeeper at each station along the two-thousand-mile route **who** always had a fresh horse ready as the Express rider galloped up.

What did the stationkeeper do? You can answer this question because you know that **who** refers to stationkeeper. It ties the parts of the sentence together. Relative pronouns always relate. When you see one, be sure to think *back* to the person or thing or idea it stands for.

Because pronouns always stand for something else, every pronoun helps the reader to relate ideas. In the following sentence, the relationship between the main thought and the qualifying idea is carried by that small word, **it.**

Although the Pony Express did not last long, **it** is remembered as one of the exciting parts of our country's history.

Pronouns also relate ideas expressed in separate sentences.

A Roman emperor in the first century, Caesar Augustus, started the first real postal system. **He** needed a good communications system to hold **his** empire together.

You know that the second sentence is closely related to the first. **He** and **his** in the second sentence refer to Caesar Augustus in the first sentence. You can see still another relationship between the second sentence and the first. The second sentence tells *why* Caesar Augustus needed a postal system.

Pronouns do not always refer to persons or objects. Sometimes a pronoun is used to stand for an idea that is expressed by a group of words, by a whole sentence, or by a whole paragraph. The following paragraph contains an illustration:

In England, in 1836, a man named Hill proposed that the people sending the message should pay for it. He suggested

postage stamps and envelopes and a uniform rate for letters. **That** was the beginning of cheap, efficient postal service.

What does the pronoun **that** stand for? You cannot answer the question with any one word. **That** stands for the whole proposal made by Hill—the ideas expressed in the first and second sentences.

Frequently, *that* or *this* serves as a bridge from one idea to another. Here is another example:

Each stopping place for changing horses was called a post. **This** is why we have "post offices" today.

If you learn to keep alert for the words and ideas represented by pronouns, you'll find these small words are big helps in seeing relationships.

TRY THIS

For the sentences below, write what each pronoun in boldface type stands for. You may need to write one word or several.

1. ZIP code numbers stand for postal regions, cities, and zones. **They** enable postal clerks to sort mail faster.

2. Samuel F. B. Morse in the 1840's made one of the important advances in communication. **He** built a successful telegraph.
3. The boy spoke very rapidly and excitedly in French. **This** made his message impossible for us to understand.
4. The two groups of settlers who first came to Virginia and Massachusetts left their native country for different reasons. They found different climates in their new land. But **both** shared the experience of carving a home out of wilderness.
5. The Pilgrims allowed only those who attended their church to help make the laws. **That** was true in the Puritan colony, too.
6. The planets close to the sun move more rapidly in their orbits than **those** farther from the sun.
7. Plants in the Arctic have several ways of adapting to the cold climate. **They** need only a short growing season.
8. Have you ever played the game Gossip? **It** starts with one person whispering to another.
9. All forms of art, including music and painting, express ideas, but **they** are not always expressed in words.
10. One student wanted to spend money for a class trip, but a group of girls suggested buying a present for the school. There were other proposals and **each** was discussed at the meeting.

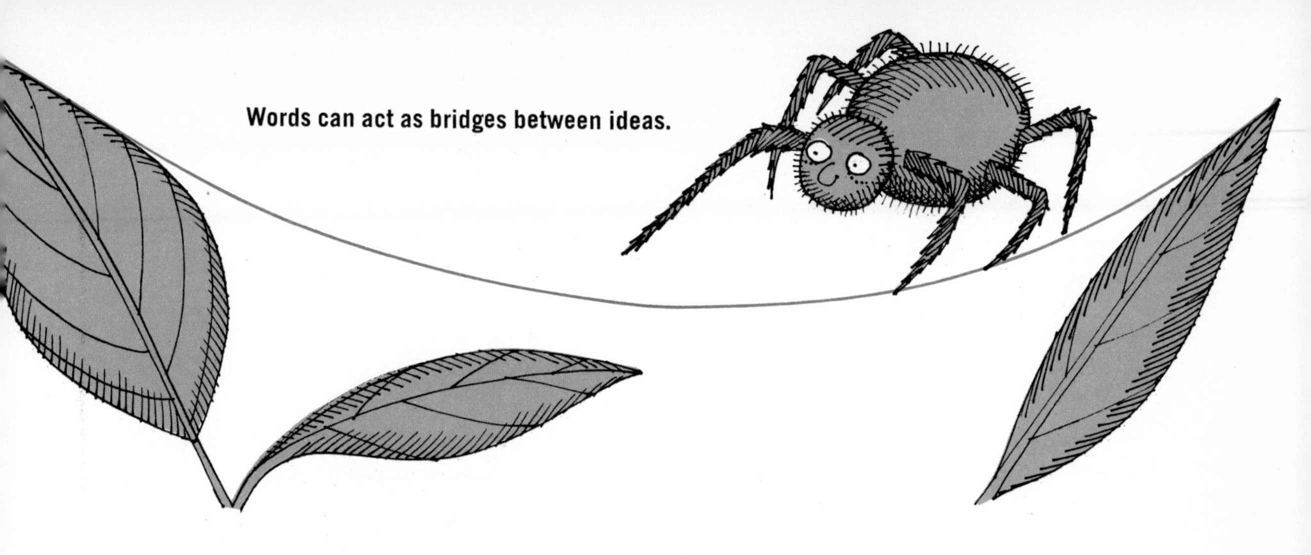

SKILLS LESSON

SEEING RELATIONSHIPS BETWEEN SENTENCES

In order to see relationships *between* sentences, you sometimes have to think of words and phrases that act as bridges between the ideas. As you read the next two sentences, think of how the ideas in both of them are related:

There was no demand for a general postal system. Few people could read or write.

The second sentence tells why there was no demand for a general postal system. The writer depended on you to supply a linking word like *because.* Perhaps you weren't aware of supplying that word. But if you really grasped the relationship of ideas, you did.

Here is another example:

By then telegraph lines had been built all the way to California. The Pony Express was no longer needed.

What words between those sentences would show how the ideas are related? You might thing of: *so, that's why, therefore, as a result, for that reason.*

Between what happened in the first sentence and what happened in the second, some time passed. So you may have thought of *then* or *later* or *after that.*

Not all sentences require connecting words, but many do.

TRY THIS

In the following paragraphs, the connections between sentences are not stated. Usually, as you read, you supply these connections in your mind. This time write them down. Copy the numerals and supply a connecting word or phrase to go in the place of each one.

Alexander Graham Bell was a teacher of the deaf in Boston when he became interested in sending human speech over telegraph wires. (1) He quit teaching and began to experiment. (2) He found he lacked the skill to make the parts he needed. (3) He went to an electrical shop for help. (4) Thomas A. Watson began to assist Bell.

In 1875, Bell wrote the specifications for his first telephone patent. (5) Watson started to build a telephone to these specifications. The two men worked for forty weeks. One night in March, 1876, Watson was working in one room. (6) Bell was at work in another room. They were about to try a new transmitter. (7) Over the wire Watson heard Bell's voice saying, "Mr. Watson, come here. I want you."

WHAT DID YOU LEARN?

1. If, in your reading, you come to a sentence you do not understand, how can you try to get the meaning?
2. How do pronouns help to show relationships between ideas?
3. Why is it sometimes important to supply connections between ideas in two sentences?

The Beginnings of Printing

by ALBERT BARKER

Use the illustrations to help you understand the text.

Suppose you woke up one morning and discovered that there were no newspapers nor a single book nor magazine, no shopping bags, no tickets, no labels, no cardboard boxes, no paper money–nothing made of paper!

A stage in the papermaking process–pulp taken from a vat and dried on a screen.

A CHINESE INVENTION

If you had lived two thousand years ago in China, the lack of paper wouldn't have bothered you. You would have written your lessons on strips of bamboo or blocks of wood. Sometimes, you might write a letter on silk. But silk was expensive and wood was too heavy.

One day in the year A.D. 105, a Chinese named Ts'ai Lun got tired of carrying his master's heavy wooden blocks. He thought, "If only I make something that is light and strong and cheap my master can write on, it will make my burden easier."

Ts'ai Lun noticed that old rags and fish nets were made out of tiny fibers–thousands of fine thread-like strings. Looking closely at the bark of mulberry trees and hemp plants, he could see more fibers. These tiny fibers gave him an idea.

Taking the rags, nets, bark, and hemp, he dumped them into a kettle of boiling water. As they boiled, he pounded them to separate the fibers. When nothing remained but a thick soupy liquid, he poured it onto a flat screen. The thousands of fibers spread out across the top of the screen. When the fibers had dried, they formed a thick rough sheet that could be written on.

At last, Ts'ai Lun had found a way to make his burden lighter! This was the first step in China's papermaking process. For many years, the Chinese were able to keep papermaking a secret.

The Chinese, however, were not satisfied just to write on their paper; they wanted to find a way to *print* on it.

The need for printing arose because hand-lettering was a slow, tiresome, and costly process. Printing would be faster and cheaper. Mainly, it would be a way to make many copies from one original piece of writing. To make copies from an original is to reproduce the original. Printing, therefore, is a method of reproduction. Making copies, or reproductions, is the main purpose of printing.

The Chinese carved designs on one side of small wooden blocks. In order for the blocks to print, only the raised surface of the designs would be inked; the cut-away areas would not. A black pastelike ink was smeared on the raised surface of the design which was carved out of the wood block. Then the block was pressed down on the paper.

Printing with blocks was clumsy and slow, so the Chinese looked for a faster way to print. They took soft clay and carved a letter, or symbol, on it. Then they baked the clay until it was hard. They made hundreds of these clay letters, which could be arranged to form a word or a sentence. After these clay letters were inked, paper was pressed down on them. These letters are called *type,* a word meaning "impression." Because this type could be rearranged and used over and over again it is called *movable type.* However, the Chinese language is made up of over forty thousand different letters, or signs. Even though the clay type could be moved, the work of printing a single book often took many months to complete.

Of course, these two secrets—papermaking and movable type—could not remain hidden forever. By the sixth century A.D., Arab traders were able to smuggle samples of paper and type into other Asian countries. Eventually, in the year 1150, these Chinese secrets reached Europe by way of Spain.

In Europe, only churchmen, royal families, and a few rich merchants could read or write. Now, with the two Chinese inventions at hand, it was possible to print books that would teach many people to read. They could learn from books about new things in the world. But paper was very expensive and there were almost no printers. So only the very rich could afford to buy books.

What was needed was a quicker, cheaper way to print so that more people could have books. But that quicker, cheaper way was a long time in coming.

JOHANN GUTENBERG'S SECRET

Some short documents were being printed in Europe before Johann Gutenberg was born in Mainz, Germany, in 1398. After his father died, young Johann went to work for a goldsmith. He soon learned to carve and stamp designs on metal. In his spare time, he would go to a nearby papermaking factory and watch the men at work. He was fascinated with the idea of printing.

Knowing how to melt gold, silver, lead, and copper started him thinking about making single metal letters and placing them side by side to form words. He knew, of course, that wooden block prints had been used for centuries. Whole documents were printed from blocks—a separate block for each page. An entire page was carved on a single solid block of wood.

What Gutenberg wanted to make was *movable* type. Only one letter would be carved on each tiny block.

An entire page printed in the Middle Ages from a single block of wood.

Moreover, Gutenberg wanted to make *metal* type with each piece exactly the same height. This type could be used over and over again in printing many different books.

Carving the blocks for block prints took a very long time. Gutenberg wanted a quick way to make type. That is one reason he decided to make his type of metal. Metal can be melted and molded; wood must be carefully carved. Besides, metal would last longer than wood.

How was Gutenberg going to make the tiny pieces of type? How was he going to make all the letters of the alphabet so that each tiny letter would fit evenly against the next letter?

Here is what Gutenberg did: He took two L-shaped pieces of iron shaped like this. These would slide together like this 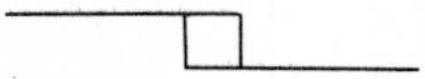 to form a hollow square called a mold. The bottom of the mold was made of soft metal. Then he took a tiny square of metal. With small steel tools, he carefully tapped and cut the shape of the letter into the metal. Next, he pressed the shape of this letter into the soft metal part of the mold. Now he poured molten lead into the mold. The hot lead filled the letter-shaped hole Gutenberg had formed in the soft metal. In fact, the lead filled the square mold up to the top. When the lead had cooled and hardened, he opened the mold. Gutenberg held in his hand a small square block with a raised letter on one end. This is a piece of type.

Sounds simple, doesn't it? The L-shaped pieces with which Gutenberg made his type are called *adjustable type molds,* because they can be fitted to letters of different widths, such as an *I* and an *M*. One of the best features of this kind of mold was that Gutenberg did not have to press and cut the same letter over and over again. He simply filled the mold with more molten lead to make another piece of type. This *cast* type was harder and stronger than any carved letters could be.

After he had made all the type he needed, Gutenberg arranged the type to spell out words and sentences. He used a plain block of metal with no raised letter to separate words. Soon Gutenberg had an entire page of type. He fastened the pieces of type together tightly and spread ink over the letters. Then he pressed a sheet of paper down on the inked letters. This kind of raised-type printing is called *letterpress* today.

GUTENBERG'S BOOKS

Now that Gutenberg had the movable metal type, he was ready to print his first book. But he needed some kind of machine that would press the paper firmly and evenly on the inked type, so that he would get a good black impression.

Gutenberg was able to buy a winepress for his shop. A winepress is used to squeeze the juice out of grapes. Gutenberg used it to press the paper against the type. Soon his hand-operated press began to turn out printed pages, one sheet at a time.

His great ambition was to print copies of the Bible in Latin. He knew this work would cost more money than he had, so Gutenberg borrowed the money he needed. A wealthy goldsmith named Fust loaned him the money, but made him sign several legal papers. When Gutenberg was unable to pay his debt, Fust took over the shop and equipment.

Johann Gutenberg was not a good businessman. He lost everything except some copies of his Bible. He sold these precious Bibles for whatever he could get. Today only twenty-one perfect copies of the Bibles remain. One of them is in the Library of Congress in Washington.

When a new ruler came to Mainz, he granted Johann Gutenberg a small pension. It was a reward for "the grateful and willing service rendered, and that he may still render in the future."

Johann Gutenberg never did any more printing. He did not realize that his simple little invention—the adjustable type mold, and his use of a press for bringing the inked metal and paper firmly together—would have a great effect on printing throughout Europe.

When Gutenberg died at the age of seventy-one, printing shops had opened in Italy, Holland, Belgium, and France. Many printers journeyed across Europe. Some carried their type and equipment on their back. In every village they found the people eager to read.

By the time Columbus discovered America in 1492, almost forty thousand different kinds of books had been printed in Europe.

The printed word began to change people's lives. The word of mouth and storytelling that formed the oral tradition of learning was no longer necessary. It was replaced by a body of *recorded* knowledge that grew with each printed book. As long as these printed books are preserved, the wisdom and knowledge of poets, historians, and scientists of the past are available to men of the future.

A page from the Gutenberg Bible printed on a press with movable type.

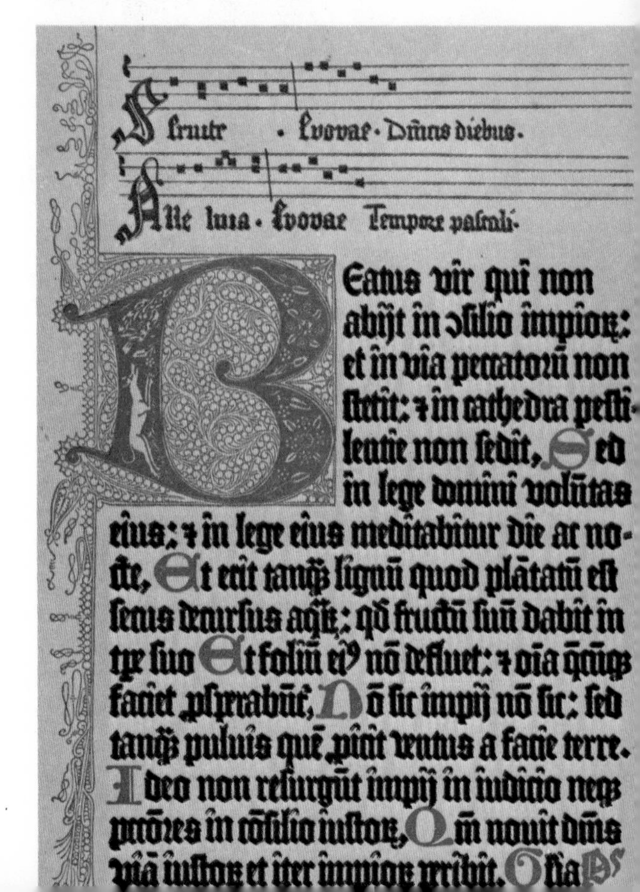

Seruite · Euouae · Dñius diebus ·

Alle luia · Euouae Tempore paschali·

Beatus vir qui non
abiit in consilio impioꝝ:
et in via peccatorū non
stetit: ⁊ in cathedra pesti-
lentie non sedit, Sed
in lege domini volūtas
eius: ⁊ in lege eius meditabitur die ac no-
cte, Et erit tanq̄ lignū quod plātatū est
secus decursus aquaꝝ: qd fructū suū dabit in
tpe suo Et foliū ei⁹ nō defluet: ⁊ oīa q̄cūq̄
faciet pspabūt, Non sic impij nō sic: sed
tanq̄ puluis quē picit ventus a facie terre.
Ideo non resurgūt impij in iudicio neq̄
pctores in cōsilio iustoꝝ, Qm̄ nouit dn̄s
viā iustoꝝ et iter impioꝝ peribit. Gl̄ia

■ You might call a greeting and wave your hand to a stranger in your own country. He would wave back. But suppose you did the same thing in another country, and the stranger threw rocks at you! What has gone wrong with your communication?

Communication Is More than Words

by FRED WEST

There are many pronouns in this selection. As you read, notice that sometimes they stand for people and sometimes they stand for ideas.

Early in 1943 an American plane carrying a crew without an interpreter was shot down over Tunisia. The crew bailed out in parachutes and landed in the middle of a desert. An Arab appeared. He addressed them in Arabic, then in French. None of the Americans understood either one.

By sign language they showed they wanted him to guide them across the desert to their own lines. He agreed. Or so they thought. A day and a half later they wound up behind the German lines, prisoners.

If they had understood the Arab's language, they would have known that he was asking them for a reward. Not understanding, they failed to offer one. So he led them to the Germans, some of whom spoke Arabic. They paid him.

Not long after the war, another American had an opposite experience. John Camp not only spoke Arabic but also understood Arab ways of thinking and acting. He went to Saudi Arabia as a medical missionary. Then he became one of the first Americans to join the desert hunt for oil.

One evening he was alone in a desolate part of the desert called Rub Al Khali. He had been making a map of the area. As the sun went down behind the endless sand dunes, a dozen or so Arabs appeared out of nowhere. Camp recognized them as a group of religious fanatics.

He stood quietly as they came closer and surrounded him. *"Nasrayny!"* they exclaimed. "A Christian!" Although the American wore Bedouin robes and headdress, they could see that his beard was brown, not black like theirs. His eyes were gray; theirs were deep brown.

Camp saw their teeth gleaming, but there were no smiles. Their fingers played with the daggers at their belts.

"Dakhil," said Camp. This is a magic word in the desert. It is a courteous demand for protection, and among the Bedouins it is always respected. These Arabs, though, were not ordinary Bedouins; they hated all non-Moslems.

A long-bearded fellow stepped forward, his dagger in his hand. "Repeat the Moslem creed!" he snarled in Arabic.

Camp knew the creed: *La ilaha Allah, wa Mohammed rasul Allah.* (There is no God but Allah, and Mohammed is his prophet.) He also knew that repeating the creed would not necessarily mean they would spare his life. Another thing he knew: An Arab respects courage and truthfulness. They have a proverb that says, "He who is true to his God is true to his fellow men."

So Camp answered them boldly in their own dialect: "You can kill

me and bury me in the sand and nobody but Allah will know. But before you do, answer me this question: If you were in my country where there are only a few Moslems, and I threatened to kill you unless you recited the Christian creed, what would you do?"

At first the Arabs stood speechless. Who was this man who answered them so bravely in their own language? They considered his words. Then they broke into shouts of approval. Bringing out food, they sat down on the spot and had a small feast in honor of the American.

Camp's secret was not as simple as merely knowing what collections of sounds stood for what words in Arabic. To communicate with another person in a way that will interest and convince him, you need to know something about him. Camp knew Arab attitudes as well as dialects.

Some language experts insist that different languages represent different ways of looking at life. The same words may have different meanings to people with different attitudes. The science of meaning is called "semantics," and to understand it, one must understand people.

The expression "thank you" is a good example of how people feel about gratitude in different parts of the world.

The original meaning in English was "I think of you with gratitude."

A Japanese says *arigato,* which translates "It is difficult." He means "It is difficult for me to express gratitude sufficiently." The Malays suggest that a good deed carries its own reward. They say *trima kasi,* "To give is to receive."

An Arab considers it sacrilegious to thank any human being. All good things come from Allah, so he gives thanks to God for others' kindness. *Al-hamdu lil-laah,* he says, "Praise be to God." This was also the original meaning of the Russian "thank you." *Spasibo bog* means "thanks to God." Today most citizens of the Soviet Union just say *Spasibo,* because their government does not encourage religious expressions.

Besides acknowledging a kindness, "thank you" can mean "no" to a Latin American or European. To North Americans, it can also mean "yes."

"Would you like a cup of coffee?" asks the hostess on an intercontinental plane. The North American answers, "Thank you, I would" or simply "Thank you."

"Voce quer um cafezino?"—"Would you like coffee?" the hostess asks the Brazilian. *"Muito obregado"*—"Many thanks," he replies, meaning "no."

¿"Desea usted café?"—"Would you like coffee?" she asks the Colombian. *"Muchas gracias"*—"Many thanks," he responds. "No."

She turns to the Frenchman. *"Désirez-vous du café?" "Merci,"* he replies, with a downward inflection. Again, "no." If his voice had risen, he would have meant "yes."

"Hello" is another word which reflects attitudes. Its meaning shows what people consider most important when they greet each other.

The English word came from an old Anglo-Saxon expression *Hal beo thu* which means "Be thou whole." A modern version would be "Health to you."

That's exactly what the modern Greek hello means: *hygeia su,* "health to you." The Russians say practically the same thing: *"zdravstvuite,"* or "Be in health."

Hello to a Hebrew is *shalom*—"peace." Hebrew is a Semitic language; so is Arabic. The two hello's are similar. Arabs say *salaam alaikum,* "Peace be upon you." The Chinese, too, say "peace"—*Tsǎo ān.*

All these greetings are concerned with the well-being of the other person. The English, Greeks, and Russians put the other person's health first. Arabs, Jews, and

Chinese think peace is more important.

To the Vietnamese, well-being is directly concerned with food. One villager greets another, *"An com chua,"* "Have you eaten rice?" The mountain aborigine says, *"Nam lu,"* "Let us feast together."

To a Zuni Indian, life itself is of greatest concern. His expression of greeting is *kesh to iya,* which means roughly, "Already you are coming." With this, two Zunis will clasp hands, and each in turn raises the other's hand to his lips. According to ancient belief, each thus inhales life from the other. The Korean says *"any-angha simnika,"* "I hope all is well." This can include everything!

In understanding another people, rules of politeness are as important as rules of grammar. What is polite in one language may be insulting in another.

For instance, few American women care to be called "old woman." Most would be insulted. Yet in China, Vietnam, and other Far Eastern countries where age is greatly revered, it is a sign of respect to call a woman "old woman."

In Mexico, where life moves less hurriedly than in the United States, the attitude toward time is different. When a Mexican makes an appointment for four o'clock *(a las cuatro)*, he may show up at four-thirty or even five.

A North American who doesn't understand the Mexican tempo is apt to say the Mexican is always late. The Mexican, on the other hand, says the North American is *agitado*—in a big rush. The result is two new phrases in Mexico. It is becoming usual, when making a date, to specify *hora mexicana* (Mexican time) or *hora americana* (American time).

Customs can affect the meaning not only of spoken but also of sign language. One American learned this in Greece. One day he was driving toward Athens. It was a beautiful day, and he had the top of his Volkswagen rolled back.

The road was narrow and so he drove slowly as he wound down out of the hills. As he made a turn in the road, he saw ahead a milling flock of sheep, herded by several shepherds and their dogs. He slowed down even more to let the shepherds move the flock out of the road. Then as he drove by them, he shouted a friendly greeting in English. At the same time he waved.

To his complete surprise, one of the shepherds grabbed a rock from the ground and threw it at him. He ducked and stepped hard on the accelerator. Another rock flew

past him, and all the shepherds shouted angrily.

That evening an English-speaking Greek explained the reason for what had happened. "You'll notice," the Greek told him, "that here in Greece we always wave hello or good-by by waving toward ourselves. Your way is considered very unfriendly. According to an old belief, you put a curse on anyone to whom you wave with your palm outward."

What would you think of a Soviet representative at an international conference who joined in clapping for himself after a speech? If you thought he was acting pretty stuck up, you'd be wrong. In his country, it's considered polite to acknowledge applause from an audience by joining them in it. If his audience booed and he shook his fist back, you might think him violent, unless you knew that this response, too, is traditional in the Soviet Union. While getting all stirred up over this fist-shaking, you might overlook the speaker's pause for a sip of water. That sip is a Soviet sign of true intention to be insulting.

Whether by gesture or word, communication isn't always what it seems. Meaning can be taken for granted only by those who are at home with the other fellow's language and his way of life.

As a little girl, Helen Keller could not see, could not hear, could not talk. She lived in a world of darkness and silence. When she was nine years old, a teacher helped her to discover language.

Helen Keller —Conqueror of Darkness

by ARNOLD DOLIN

If you have difficulty in understanding the meaning of a long sentence, look for the main thought.

Could you imagine living in a world that was pitch dark and absolutely silent? You would not know what your father or mother looked like, or even how you looked yourself! You would never have heard a dog bark, or any other sound. You would not know how to talk, because you would have never heard a word spoken. In fact, you would not know that there were such things as words!

You would have no idea of sunshine, except to feel its warmth. You would have no idea of right and wrong, because no one would have even been able to explain that to

◄ **Helen Keller at the age of seven.**

you. You would not understand that something was yours, or that it belonged to someone else, because no one would have any means of communicating with you except to touch you.

This was the kind of world in which Helen Keller lived.

When Helen was born, she was a normal, beautiful baby who could see and hear. But at nineteen months of age, she became very ill, and her sickness left her blind and entirely deaf.

She had just begun to talk before the illness struck, but soon, in the darkness that enclosed her, she forgot the few words she had known. Except for a dim memory of sky and trees, she might as well have never seen anything.

"My poor baby," sobbed Mrs. Keller, "it's as if she were lost to us."

"We must spend our lives trying to make her happy," Mr. Keller replied, as he attempted to comfort his wife.

"But what can we do?" Mrs. Keller argued. "She can't see us. She can't speak to us. She can't hear us. We're helpless – helpless!"

As time passed, Helen did learn a few things. By the time she was five, she could recognize her own clothes and would put them away in her own bureau drawers. She had made up a sort of sign language, and her family could tell when she meant *Come, Go, Yes,* and *No.* When she touched her own cheek, it meant that she was referring to her mother. If she wanted something small, but a large object was given her, she would make her sign for *No.* Then she would take a tiny bit of the skin of one hand by the thumb and a finger of the other. Spreading her fingers wide and bringing her hands together meant she wanted the object – a piece of cake or whatever else – to be large.

And she was becoming a very naughty girl. Since no one could teach her anything, she became spoiled. Her father and mother, in efforts to make her happy, tried to think of everything she could want. Whenever she could make herself understood, her demands were instantly fulfilled.

You know how it is on a gloomy, rainy day, when you've read and played games until you're tired and bored and have nothing to do.

"What shall I do, Mother?" you say. "Think of something for me to do."

Now suppose you were enclosed in complete darkness and silence and you couldn't think of anything to do, but you couldn't even ask your mother to help you. You would be shut in, and there would be no way to get out.

Helen was indeed shut in. She had no possible way to get out, so she began to have temper tantrums. The few signs she had used became more and more inadequate. Every time she failed in expressing her wants, she became angry. Her father and mother knew that something must be done, for Helen was terribly unhappy and was making their life wretched as well.

Doctors had decided long ago that Helen's sight could never be restored. Finally, Helen's father wrote to Boston to the Perkins Institute for the Blind.

One day, when Helen was not quite seven years old, a teacher came to help her, Her name was Anne Sullivan. She was not much more than a girl herself. She, too, had been almost totally blind, although now she could see quite well.

She set to work to try to release Helen from the darkness and silence in which she lived.

Anne began by spelling the word *doll* into Helen's hand when she gave her doll to the little girl. In this kind of talking, the speaker uses the single-hand alphabet generally used by the deaf. The blind listener lightly places her hand over that of the speaker and feels the words as they are spelled.

Helen didn't know what the finger movements meant, but it was something new, and she quickly imitated it. Soon she realized that if she made those particular motions, the doll was put in her arms. But she didn't know that the movements meant the name doll. In fact, she didn't know that things even had names!

Helen was a very bright little girl, and she quickly learned to make a good many words. But still she didn't know that they meant anything except a way to get something she wanted.

And she continued to be very naughty, for she had never been taught to obey.

Anne decided that the very next thing she must teach Helen was obedience.

But how do you teach someone to mind when you can't talk to her or show her anything? There was only one way, and that was force. When Helen kicked and screamed and bit, Anne held her until she stopped. Helen was a healthy, strong girl, and sometimes these tussles lasted an hour or two. Anne would be exhausted, but she would not give up.

Gradually, Helen learned discipline. At the same time, she was learning more and more combinations of finger movements. But she still didn't know that they meant the names of things.

She had learned the combinations for *mug* and for *water,* but she kept getting them mixed up. One day Anne took her into the garden. She had Helen hold her hand under the spout of the pump in the well house. As the cold water gushed out over Helen's right hand, Anne spelled the word *water* into Helen's other hand.

Helen stood stock-still, while an expression of delight came over her face. At last she had understood. She spelled water several times. Then she dropped to the ground and made it plain that she wanted to know the name of that. Anne spelled it for her.

Helen had found the way out, and, once given the key to understanding, nothing could stop her. In a few hours she learned thirty new words! She knew, at last, that they were the names of things.

From that day on she progressed rapidly. Just as a baby learns to

speak, Helen learned to make words. Then she began to make sentences. Soon the sentences became longer and more complicated.

Now she could actually talk with anyone who understood finger spelling. Helen's father and mother learned it so that they could talk with her.

The next step was to teach her to read. She already liked stories, for Anne would read to her by the hour, translating into finger spelling the words that she read from books.

Helen was given books in Braille – the system of raised dots in which most books for the blind are printed. She soon learned to read them by passing her fingers over the letters. Helen's hands were to her what eyes and ears are to everyone else.

Of course, she could not speak, because she could not remember ever having heard speech. But the impulse to utter sounds was strong. She liked to feel the cat purr and the dog bark. She could "listen" to her pet rooster crow when he perched on her knee and she put her hand on his throat. She liked to put her hand on a singer's throat or on the piano when it was being played.

She liked to feel her mother's lips move, and she moved her own; although she couldn't talk, she made sounds. There was just one word that she remembered from the time before she was ill, and that was *wa-wa*. This, to her, meant she wanted a drink of water.

One day a visitor told Helen by finger movements about a deaf girl who had learned to talk, and at once Helen was wild to learn. She was taken to the Horace Mann School for the Deaf in Boston. There she got her first lessons in positioning her tongue and lips to make the sounds of speech.

Now another door was unlocked.

But there were still new fields to conquer. Helen wanted to go to school. This was felt to be quite impossible, but Helen persisted.

Anne went to all her classes with her. Patiently, as the teacher spoke, Anne spelled everything into Helen's hand. Helen learned to use the typewriter so that she could prepare her lessons. She read books printed in Braille. She learned to swim, and to row, and to ride a bicycle.

In 1904 she was graduated from college with honors. Her life entered a new phase. Helen wanted to be more than an unusual example of a handicapped person. To most people, she had always been a pitiful girl they read about

Helen Keller as a young girl with her teacher, Anne Sullivan.

in newspapers and magazines. Now she was no longer a child, loved by the whole country. She was a woman, ready to rely upon her own abilities.

Helen now became a living legend. She was a great American success story. After her book, *The Story of My Life,* was published, she began writing on behalf of those still shut off from a normal life. Her articles reached many people and brought her tremendous support.

Later, Helen realized that she could help the blind and deaf most by meeting the public face to face. She had to mingle with people. She had to become a real flesh-and-blood person to win her fight for the handicapped.

Helen's greatest ordeal was her first appearance before an audience. She was very shy and quite frightened, but her determination carried her through.

With Anne, she went on speaking tours all over the United States and Europe. Everywhere she went, she tried to get help for the blind and deaf.

Helen Keller's great courage made it possible for her to conquer a world of darkness. She lived to make an honored place in the world she once feared.

Studying Sentences

Like other books, textbooks sometimes have long sentences that can be difficult to understand, even when you know all the words. When you find a sentence that is not clear to you, look for the main idea. Then read again for the qualifying ideas. Try to see how these ideas are related to each other. Seeing how ideas are related helps you to unlock the basic meaning.

Understanding pronouns also helps to unlock sentence meaning. Make sure you know what all the pronouns stand for. They may help you see the relationship between parts of the sentence.

Sentences in a Social Studies Selection

In this selection several pronouns are encircled. Some pronouns stand for persons. Some stand for ideas. As you read the selection, be sure that you understand what each pronoun stands for. If you need to, go back and reread until you are sure.

As the years passed, more French colonists settled along the St. Lawrence. There were fur traders and trappers, of course, but farmers also came. (They) laid out long, narrow "strip" farms that faced the St. Lawrence. On such farms, neighbors could live close together and help each other in time of danger. Also, each strip farm had its own piece of river front. (This) was important, for the St.

What does **this** stand for? Why was this important?

Lawrence was the main "highway" in those early days.

At first, life was hard and discouraging, as it was for all pioneers about whom you have read. Families had to provide nearly everything for themselves or do without. So they worked from sunrise until dark, or later, day after day.

The worst problem of all, though, was how to get along with unfriendly Indians. There was always fear of dreadful Indian attacks.

Gradually conditions improved. The settlers learned how to manage on the frontier. They were able to raise more food and build more comfortable homes. There was less worry now, too, for French soldiers had forced the Indians to make peace.

Still, there were quarrels with the English. Some had started over the rich fur trade.

—from *Your Country and Mine*

Building Skills

To Write

Five pronouns besides the pronoun *this* are marked in the selection. Tell what each one stands for. Write each pronoun on your paper, and write your answer beside it.

To Discuss

In what way was the St. Lawrence River like a highway for the early settlers?

Sentences from Various Textbooks

Read the short selections below. They are from several kinds of textbooks. Show your understanding of the sentences by answering the questions at the side.

A

Besides the Congress to make laws, the Convention decided to have a President. It also agreed to have a *Vice-President,* who would direct the government if anything happened to the President. Both he and the President would be elected and would serve for four years.

What does this pronoun stand for?

What does the pronoun **he** stand for?

Finally, the Convention made plans for a *Supreme Court* of the United States, which would explain the laws that Congress made and be sure that they agreed with the Constitution.

—from *Basic Social Studies* 5

Finally is a time word. What is the main thought? What two other ideas about the Supreme Court are given?

B

Some places on the earth's surface receive practically none of this rain, while other places have as much as 400 inches of rain in one year.

—from *Science: A Modern Approach* 5

What word in this sentence connects two main thoughts?

C

There are many ways to make the characters in a story real to the reader. Their conversation shows what kind of people they are. The way they accept success and failure, their kindness to others, or lack of it, their courage or cowardice in danger—

What do these pronouns stand for?

these are some of the ways we get to know the people in books.

—from *The Roberts English Series: Fifth Book*, Second Edition

What does this pronoun stand for?

D

The astronauts are comfortable in the cone-shaped command module as they await the end of countdown. At lift-off, the rocket rises smoothly. First and second stages of the Saturn rocket are fired, one by one. When their fuel is used up, their job is done and they fall away. The third rocket stage is then fired, taking the Apollo spacecraft into Earth orbit.

—from *Concepts in Science: Purple*, Third Edition

Can you think of a connecting word with the same meaning?

To what does each of these three pronouns refer?

E

But the time came when there was very little level or rolling land left to clear. People began to farm on steep hillsides. They cut down trees, plowed the land, and planted crops. This, too, caused a big problem.

—from *In All Our States*

What time word could you supply to show the relationship between these two sentences?

What does each pronoun stand for?

F

Submarines are used mainly for military purposes, but from their travels under the seas much knowledge of water currents and temperatures has been gathered.

—from *Science: A Modern Approach 5*

What does this pronoun stand for?

G

Your cells are grouped in tissues, tissues are grouped in organs, organs are grouped in organ systems.

—from *Concepts in Science: Purple*, Third Edition

How many main thoughts does this sentence contain?

Building Skills

To Discuss

Paragraph F contains only one long sentence. It contains two main thoughts.

1. Read the first main thought in the sentence.
2. Read the rest of the sentence after the connecting word *but*. What is the main thought in this part?

Sentences in a Social Studies Selection

The paragraphs below are about the Middle Atlantic colonies before the American Revolution. The sentences are long and packed with meaning. Read them carefully so you will understand all the ideas. Then answer the questions that follow.

The sentences are numbered so that you can refer to them to complete the exercises that follow. Pay no attention to the numbers as you read.

[1]In Delaware, the farmers grew wheat and other foods that were sold in Wilmington to merchants who shipped them to England. [2]There was also trade between Delaware and Pennsylvania, and some Delaware farmers came into Pennsylvania to sell their products in the fresh food markets of Philadelphia.

[3]Across the Delaware River from Pennsylvania, the Colony of New Jersey also grew in population and in wealth from the crops of its rich farms. [4]Farmers in New Jersey grew wheat as well as other foods, which they sold to merchants in Philadelphia and New York. [5]From these American seaports, products were shipped to England.

[6]At the mouth of the Hudson River, the small city of New York began to grow, much like Philadelphia. [7]New York was an excellent seaport. [8]In later years, as the colony grew and more farm crops and other products were sold in the city, it became larger than Philadelphia.

—from *Basic Social Studies* 5

Building Skills

To Write

1. To be sure that you understand the first sentence, answer these questions:

   a. Where did the farmers live?
   b. What did the farmers grow?
   c. What was sold in Wilmington?
   d. What did the merchants send to England?

2. In Sentence 5, to what do the words "these American seaports" refer?
3. In the last sentence, the main thought comes at the end of the sentence. What does the pronoun **it** refer to in the main thought?

To Discuss

1. Read the two main thoughts in the second sentence.
2. The basic framework of Sentence 3 is *Colony grew.* What information do the other words add to that sentence framework?
3. Several of the sentences contain groups of words that could be moved within the sentence without changing the meaning. Find some of those sentences and read them aloud. Then reread them in another way. Do the sentences still mean the same thing?

Summary

In this unit you have been practicing these skills:

– Finding the main thought and related ideas in long sentences.
– Seeing how groups of words are put together to carry meaning.
– Recognizing what words or ideas pronouns stand for.

Books About Communication

The Magic of Words by Arthur Alexander.

Here is a simple book about something we use every day—language. Many kinds of communication, including small messages with big meanings, are discussed.

The First Transatlantic Cable by Adele G. Nathan.

They said it was impossible. Imagine stringing a copper wire across the bottom of the ocean to carry messages! In the 1850's, the idea seemed fantastic. But after months of backbreaking work, the job was done, and the first telegraph message crossed the ocean between Europe and the United States.

Signs and Symbols Around the World by Elizabeth S. Helfman.

How can people communicate even though they speak different languages? One way is by signs. This lively book has hundreds of illustrations.

All About Language by Mario Pei.

What *is* language, exactly? When men in the Canary Islands whistle messages to each other, are they using language? How do Boy Scouts talk at an International Jamboree? This book is full of information and ideas.

The First Book of News by Samuel and Beryl Epstein.

News is printed, spoken, tapped out on telegraph keys, photographed, relayed by satellite—in fact, communicated in every way possible. Read all about it here.

Flashes and Flags: The Story of Signaling by Jack Coggins.

Here are many forms of communication: hand signals, flag systems, the Morse Code, traffic signals used on sea, land, and in the air, and signals used in sports.

Talking With the Animals by Daniel Cohen.

People have always tried to talk to animals. Today, scientists understand many of the signals of bees, birds, whales, and apes.

Unit 4

Man Meets Beast

A Yasu boy of the Ivory Coast, Africa, feeding his pet monkey.

SKILLS LESSON

FINDING TOPICS AND MAIN IDEAS

Ever since you learned to read, you have been reading to get information. Of course, that is not the only reason you read. But much of your school reading is directed toward understanding ideas and learning facts. You get information from several kinds of books, including textbooks. The more you know about how to find the important ideas in what you read, the more you will get from your reading.

Do you recall how to find the topic of a paragraph? You ask, "What are the sentences in this paragraph about?" The answer to that question tells the topic of the paragraph. When you know the topic of the paragraph, you can find the main idea by asking, "What is the most important thing the sentences say about the topic?" The main idea is often stated at the beginning of a paragraph, but not always.

TRY THIS

Read Paragraphs A, B, and C. Find the main idea in each paragraph, and write it on your paper after the letter of the paragraph.

A. When compared to a shark, a piranha fish is very small. But this little saber-toothed fish is one of the most bloodthirsty and fearless fishes in the world. When hundreds of ferocious piranhas start tearing away bits of skin and flesh with their sharklike teeth, a large animal is reduced to a skeleton in a matter of minutes.

B. It would be tempting to say that an animal returns to the region of its birth because it wants to go back home again. But if animals do not think as we do, we cannot expect them to be as homesick as we sometimes are away from home. Scientists, therefore, seek to discover animal, rather than human, causes for migration.

C. There are different viewpoints on cats, but there is general agreement that cats have strong personalities. Ask a cat-lover what he likes about his pet, and he will mention its intelligence, independence, ability to get along by itself—in a word, its self-confidence. "That cat *knows* it is a superior animal," he may say. Ask a person who dislikes cats to explain his feeling, and he will point to the same traits. "Cats are too independent," he may say. "A cat always thinks it's better than a dog."

SKILLS LESSON

LOOKING FOR UNSTATED MAIN IDEAS

In some paragraphs, the main idea is not stated. You must first find the topic, and then you must think what each sentence says about the topic. By thinking about each statement, you find the main idea about the topic. Then you can express that main idea in your own words.

The paragraph below is an example. What is the main idea? First, read the paragraph and look for its topic. Then ask yourself, "What is the most important idea about the topic?"

What guides migrating birds and animals? Some animals seem to use landmarks and objects in the sky to tell direction. It may be that birds "feel" things that we cannot feel. For example, waterfowl have been known to fly in a strange way when they enter beams of radar waves. Some scientists think that birds may be able to sense differences according to what they are flying over. But more experiments are needed, for so far there is no proof that migrating animals can sense such things.

All of the sentences in the paragraph you have just read tell how animals, including birds, find their way in their migrations. But the writer did not state the most important idea about the topic in any one sentence. The reader might state it in these two ways.

We can make some guesses about what guides animals during migration, but we don't really know.

Some migrating animals seem to use guideposts on the land and in the sky, but there is no evidence to support this.

You can see that the main idea can be expressed in several different ways. The important thing to remember is that all the sentences in the paragraph help you to decide what the main idea is. Learning to find the main idea is one of the skills you use most often in reading.

TRY THIS

Here are two more paragraphs in which the main idea is not stated. Write the main idea of each paragraph in your own words.

A. Giraffes are generally considered to be voiceless. Hunters have said that they do not make a sound even when wounded. For years, biologists believed that giraffes were mute, or voiceless. Recently, however, female giraffes have been heard to make certain types of noises when their offspring were in danger.

B. After a day of sleep, all animals are hungry. In early evening they begin to move about in search of food. Smaller animals wait for the darkness to provide them with protection. Larger animals sleep during the day and stalk the smaller, more timid animals in the darkness. In the damp night air, odors stay close to the ground, and small animals are able to smell the odors that they have learned to fear.

Which details are important?

SKILLS LESSON

WHICH DETAILS ARE IMPORTANT?

Look back at the paragraph on page 145 about the piranha fish. If you said that the second sentence states the main idea of that paragraph, you were right. That sentence gives the most important information about the piranha fish. But probably you were interested in the last sentence, too, which tells how the piranhas attack a victim. That sentence contains interesting details.

When you are reading for information, you always meet main ideas and details. The details may make the main ideas clear, or give examples, or supply additional information, or give evidence to prove a point. Often the details are interesting and colorful. But of course a reader cannot remember everything that he reads. His job is to find the main ideas and the important details and to concentrate his attention on them. Some details are more important than others. How do you decide which are the important ones?

Reading with a Purpose

When you read a book or an article, a good guide for deciding which details are important is this question: "What is my pur-

pose in reading?" Think of the different reasons you have for reading for information:

– You may be reading for the pleasure of learning new ideas.
– You may be reading to find the answer to a certain question.
– You may be reading an assignment for your homework.
– You may be reviewing for a test.

Once you know what you want to get out of your reading, you will be better able to judge which details are important and which ones you can safely forget. Ask yourself, "Does this detail add anything to my understanding of the main idea? How much do I need to know about this subject?"

Suppose you are learning about animals that live in swamps. You come to this paragraph, in which the writer tells about a swamp animal.

A. One of my first discoveries was a little water shrew. No larger than a mouse, and sometimes smaller, these tiny creatures are among the world's smallest mammals. I recall measuring an adult shrew years later; its body was just over two inches long, plus a one-inch tail. It weighed less than half an ounce.

It is easy to see that the topic of this paragraph is the water

shrew. The main idea is stated in the second sentence. What are the details?

– The writer measured an adult shrew years later.
– It was just over two inches long, with a one-inch tail.
– It weighed less than half an ounce.

Are these details important? The main idea of the paragraph is that a shrew is no larger than a mouse. If you know the size of a mouse, you know about how big a shrew is. You can see that the details, interesting as they are, do not add anything important to the main idea. If your purpose is to get general information about swamp animals, you should remember the main idea about the water shrew, but you need not remember the details.

Here is another parapraph. It tells some things people in India believe about tigers. Suppose you were reading to learn what these beliefs are.

B. Although tigers are not worshiped, the Indian people have a great deal of respect for this Lord of the Jungle even when a man-eater has killed a number of people from one village. They have developed some strange beliefs connected with this animal. Oil made from tiger fat is supposed to have healing properties for rheumatism. When a tiger is killed on a shoot, there is rivalry among the men for the lucky bones, which are found at the point

of the shoulder. Special good fortune is supposed to come to anyone carrying these bones about on his person.

Do you agree that the second sentence tells the main idea of the paragraph? All of the other sentences contain details. Which of these details are important for you to remember?

1. Tigers are not worshiped, but they are respected.
2. The tiger is the Lord of the Jungle.
3. A man-eating tiger may kill several people from one village.
4. Oil made from tiger fat is supposed to be good for rheumatism.
5. When a tiger is killed, there is rivalry for the lucky bones.
6. The lucky bones are the ones at the point of the shoulder.
7. These bones are supposed to bring good fortune to anyone who carries them.

Since your purpose is to learn what the Indian people believe about tigers, of course the first detail is important. The second and third details are not concerned with beliefs about the tiger, so you will not need to remember them. The fourth detail states another belief that you will want to remember. Details five, six, and seven are all connected. What do they tell you about Indian beliefs?

You can see whether a detail is important or not depends on your purpose in reading. As always, you must be thinking while you are reading.

TRY THIS

The paragraphs below contain main ideas and details. Follow the directions for each paragraph. The sentences are numbered to help you in answering the questions.

Read Paragraphs A and B to learn all you can about family life in India.

A. [1] The work of looking after a house in India is much harder than it is in America. [2] The mother of a family has to send the father off to his work in the morning. [3] She, or another woman in the family, prepares breakfast and looks after the children. [4] She keeps busy at something all day long. [5] All these things the American mother does, but not at all in the same ways.

B. [1] Ninety percent of the children of India live in the villages. [2] Their fathers are farmers. [3] Their way of life is the difficult one of constant work, little play, no school. [4] There are some exceptions, but that is the rule. [5] They have a responsibility to the family as soon as they are able to work. [6] There is something to

be busy with all the time, even if it is no more than attending the family baby while following a herd of cows sent out to graze.

1. In paragraph A, what sentence contains the main idea?
2. What other sentences add important details?
3. Write a sentence expressing the main idea of Paragraph B.
4. List the important details in Paragraph B.

Suppose that you are about to take your first flight in a jet airliner. Read Paragraph C with that thought in mind.

C. [1] A jet plane gets a complete overhaul—of the engines, cabin, everything—after six thousand hours in the air. [2] It takes fifteen workdays to overhaul a jet engine. [3] Each part is X-rayed for cracks and wear. [4] Hundreds of rotor blades are cleaned, inspected, and replaced if necessary. [5] The electrical wiring, forty miles of it, is checked. [6] Instruments are tested for accuracy. [7] In the passengers' cabin, carpets and seats are taken out and cleaned. [8] The galley, where the food is stored and prepared for serving, is scrubbed until it shines like new.

5. What is the main idea of Paragraph C?
6. Write two details from the paragraph that you think you would remember during your flight.

Read Paragraph D to learn as much as you can about life on the early farms in Vermont.

D. [1] When the early settlers came to Vermont, they brought only those things which they might carry on a sled or rude cart, selecting the barest necessities for both home and farm. [2] On arrival they made whatever else was needed from the wood that grew everywhere on their new land. [3] The farming tools were primitive—not very different from those which men had used in ancient times. [4] The trees were cut and burned, and the dry, upland soil beneath them was planted to grains.

7. Which of these sentences best expresses the main idea of Paragraph D?
   a. Early settlers in Vermont had to work hard with only the primitive equipment that they brought with them.
   b. Vermont's early settlers arrived with some of the things they needed and used the resources of their new land for other things that they needed.
   c. The forests in Vermont were the best source of wood

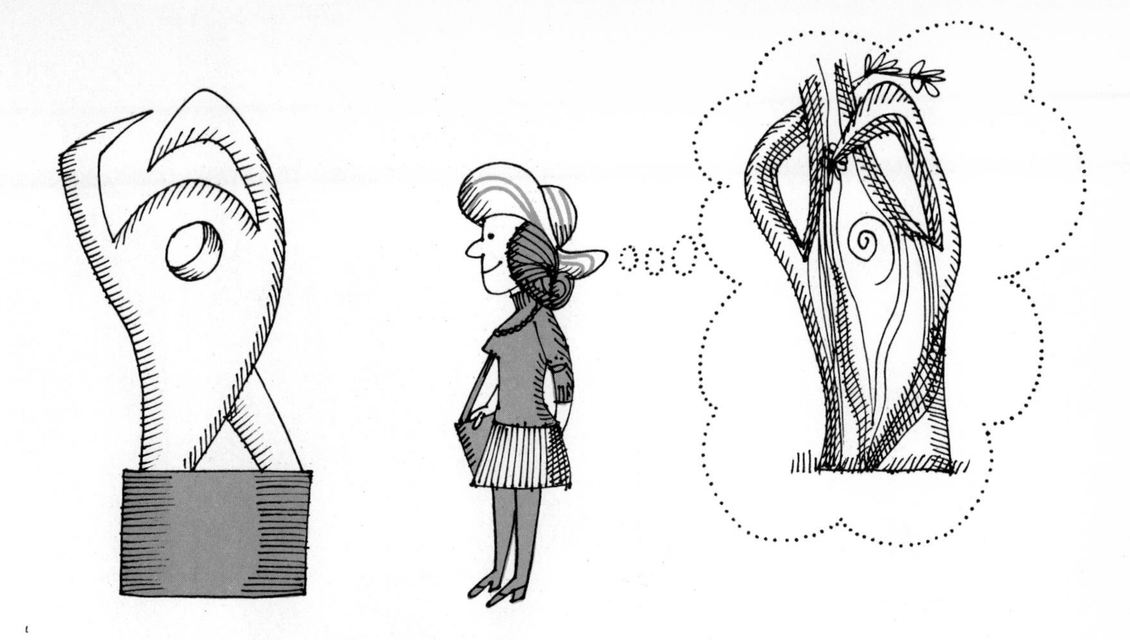

for early farmers, and they quickly made the tools they needed for logging and lumbering.

8. Write three details from Paragraph D that are important for understanding the settlers' way of life.

You can see that thinking about main ideas and important details is not always easy. Sometimes two readers understand ideas a little differently, even if they have both read carefully. One reader may think a certain detail is not important, while another reader thinks it is. Both may be right according to their own understanding of the question. There are always such differences when reading and thinking are involved. The important point is that reading does involve thinking.

WHAT DID YOU LEARN?

1. How do you find the main idea of a paragraph?
2. Why is it important to know the main idea?
3. How do details add to the meaning of a paragraph?
4. How can you tell which details are important and which are not?

How did the dog become man's first friend among the animals?

Man's First Dog

by CARL BURGER

Preview the headings in this selection. They will help you to know what main ideas to look for as you read.

A blind man confidently follows his guide dog along a crowded sidewalk. He holds a bar attached to the dog's harness. Coming to a street crossing, the guide stops for a moment, warning its master that he must step off a curb. Down the street it leads him, carefully avoiding a place where the sidewalk is being repaired. With the aid of his dog, the man goes on his way almost as freely as if he could see.

At a lonely farmhouse, a dog stands guard over a baby. The child's father is at work in the fields. The mother has gone to carry food to a sick neighbor. She can safely leave home for a time, confident that the dog will guard the baby, with its life if need be.

A boy and his dog set out on an adventure. A homemade raft carries them across a quiet pond. The dog is just as excited as the boy. The two are fast friends and playmates.

These are only a few examples of the many ways in which the life of the dog is interwoven with the life of man. This animal, more than any other in the world, has become man's partner and companion.

The partnership between man and dog began long ago, long before any other animal had been domesticated. Wherever traces of prehistoric man have been found, the bones of dogs usually lie among the primitive tools and weapons.

IN THE DAYS OF CAVE MEN

Let us imagine that we are sharing the daily life of a Stone Age family. Our story will tell how prehistoric men probably began to tame and make use of dogs. In order to make it clearer, we shall tell the story as if it had happened in the life of one man. Probably, though, it took a much longer time for the dog to become man's partner.

Our family lived in a small cave, dark and gloomy except near the entrance. Well back inside the cave was a pile of boughs on which they slept. Dried pelts of animals served to keep them warm on cold nights. A few crude spears stood against the walls. These and a blunt stone ax and some sharp-edged flints used as knives were all the tools the family had. Wild forest, in which many animals made their home, surrounded the cave.

In the family were a father, mother, and several children. Their clothing was made of animal skins. Squatting about an open fire on which chunks of meat were roasting, they took pieces of it in their hands and ate greedily. There were no refined table manners here. The bones and scraps were thrown on the ground or into the nearby bushes. The place was by no means neat.

In time the odor of garbage became too much even for these rugged people. But a ready-made garbage-disposal was at hand. After the family had gone to bed, jackals lurked about the cave kitchen, attracted by the odors.

They finally plucked up enough courage to come near and eat the scraps.

JACKALS BECOME PETS

Little by little, the family got used to having the jackals about. They saw how useful the animals could be. The jackals, in turn, began to lose some of their fear of man. The animals had found a ready supply of food, and the family was no longer bothered by odors. From being a danger that lurked in the forest, the animals had become useful neighbors.

One day when the man was out hunting, he found a female jackal that had been killed by some other animal. Her two pups, their eyes only recently opened, crouched whimpering beside their mother's torn body. Thinking that his youngsters might be pleased with the tiny balls of fur, he carried them home. Both children and pups took kindly to the arrangement. Growing up together, neither had any fear of the other, and they became fast friends. Playing together at the cave's mouth, they amused the mother as well as the children. The pups helped keep the children clean by licking them.

At length the pets became fully grown jackals. They were well fed and slept near the fire, quite content with their changed way of life. They had become members of the family.

JACKALS PROTECT THE FAMILY

There came a day when the children and their pets wandered too far away from home and were attacked by a bear. Their mother, hearing their screams, ran up just in time to see the two jackals attack the beast and put it to flight. Here was a new service that the pets had performed. In addition to their kitchen cleaning, they had become protectors of the family. Their sense of loyalty to the pack had prompted them to guard its members. The cave family had become their pack; the father was now their "boss dog."

At another time, the jackals warned the sleeping family of the approach of a thief, intent on stealing one of the father's spears. Now the man began to take more interest in his children's pets. He realized that they were useful as protectors of his family and possessions.

The life led by these people was a rugged one. Danger lurked on every side. The forest sheltered fierce beasts, always on the prowl for food. It was comforting to have the tame jackals always on watch to warn of approaching danger.

JACKALS GO HUNTING WITH MAN

This family kept no domestic animals as a food supply and grew no crops. The few vegetables that they ate were gathered from the woods. Since meat was their chief food, the very life of the family depended entirely on success in hunting.

The father of our family had only one hunting weapon, a roughly pointed piece of flint lashed to the end of a straight stick. One day with this spear he wounded a large deer. It did not fall but dashed off through the forest. Recovering his weapon, he followed the animal for a mile or so but finally lost the trail. Tired out from forcing his way through the tangled bushes, he sat down on a rock to rest. Soon he heard the yelping of a pack of wild dogs ahead of him, following the trail of the wounded deer. Ordinarily, they would not have followed such a large animal, for they could not hope to overtake it. But this one, being wounded, offered a chance for a meal.

Soon the sounds told him that the deer was no longer fleeing but had turned to face the wild dogs. At his approach, the pack disappeared among the trees. But the deer was too far spent to run, and the hunter was able to kill it with his spear. With a piece of sharpened flint, he skinned and cut it up, taking the best meat home to his family. After he had gone, the wild dogs returned and ate the meat he had not taken.

The hunter saw that here was another way in which dogs could be useful. Their sense of smell

Jackal

Wolf

was far keener than his own. They could trail an animal he was hunting and hold it at bay till he came up. They could not overcome a large animal when it stopped and faced them, but he, with his spear, could do so easily.

Why, thought the man, should he not take along his two tame jackals when he went hunting? Then he would always have helpers at hand when he needed them. Perhaps he could teach them to obey his commands and so be of greater use than the wild dogs. His children's pets had learned to come running when they were called for feeding. Perhaps they would learn to obey other commands.

At first, he had some difficulty in making this plan work. After long and patient effort, however, he taught the tame jackals to obey him some of the time. They would follow at his heels till he reached a likely spot for finding game. Then, at his command, they would roam through the nearby forest until they picked up a scent. Following it, they would find the animal and chase it, yelping loudly. The man could follow the sound of the chase till he came up to where the animal stood at bay. After the kill, he always rewarded the jackals with the leftover meat.

Here was another link in the chain of partnership. The man found the jackals a great help in

Egyptian Greyhound

Collie

finding and running down game. The animals came dimly to sense what was expected of them and to know that a reward would come at the end. This is the way man first learned to train a dog to do what he wanted.

One morning the man had followed an unusually loud clamor of his hunting jackals. When he came up, he found them in a desperate fight with a saber-toothed tiger. The catlike beast was heavier than both the jackals, and they were no match for its terrible teeth and claws. Just as the man arrived, the savage beast suddenly lunged at the smaller jackal, seized it by the neck, and shook it until it dropped lifeless to the ground. The other jackal, having no heart for further battle, ran for safety. The man hurled his spear at the tiger and wounded it severely.

THE FATHER FINDS A NEW PET

The children were saddened by the loss of their pet, and their father missed its help in his hunting. So he began to look for another pup to replace it. He had seen that the two jackals were not strong or brave enough to stand up to the tiger. He was likely to need protection against such beasts at any moment. It would be good to know that he had hunting companions able to fight them off. He knew that there were larger, fiercer wild dogs in his neighborhood. These, he thought, would serve him better, both as protectors and as hunters.

As he walked one day along a rocky ridge, a she-wolf dashed out of a den among the rocks and attacked him. His jackal turned tail and fled. To save himself, he was forced to spear the wolf. He knew that her pups were nearby, or else she would not have attacked him. In the den he discovered a single young puppy, which he carried back to his cave. With generous feeding, it grew into a large, handsome wolf, friendly toward all the family. After much difficulty, he succeeded in teaching it to obey his commands well enough to help him hunt. It was stronger and more courageous than the jackal. On several occasions it defended its master when he was in danger.

A NEW BREED APPEARS

The wolf and the jackal, living together with the family, occasionally fought, but they were usually on friendly terms. As one was male and the other female, a litter of pups at length appeared. The man soon noticed that two of the pups were more alert than the others. They were always first to come when the man called them for feeding. In play, they showed that they could run faster than the others. Since the man did not want to feed so many dogs, he destroyed the three less alert pups. The two that he kept proved quick at finding game and swift in the chase. The man now had two wolf-jackal crossbreeds that were better hunters than either of their parents. He had developed a new breed of dog, better fitted for the use he wanted to make of them.

One of the crossbreeds, a female, was a wanderer. She would now and then disappear from the cave for several days, and finally deserted altogether. She had gone back to a wild life. But one day she returned, bringing with her two young ones quite different in appearance from the other dogs at the cave. The man knew that they had been fathered by a wild dog different from any of the others in his pack. Here was a new blood strain. The new pups, when they grew up, proved to be the best hunters of the lot. So the man decided to breed in future only from this strain.

His experience had shown him that he could breed dogs to suit his needs. He had only to select for breeding those pups that he judged to be the best hunters. Our cave man had discovered the process that has brought us many breeds of dogs.

Penguins playing games with sailors, penguins fighting with sled dogs, penguins outwitting their baby sitter—there were penguins everywhere when Richard E. Byrd explored the Antarctic.

Penguin Paradise

by EDNA M. ANDREAS

The title tells you the topic of this selection. Watch for details that give the important characteristics of penguins. What details show why the writer calls the setting of this selection a paradise for penguins?

When men first sailed far south, into Antarctica, they met a bird that walked like a man, swam like a fish, and acted like a busybody. It didn't seem to be a bird at all until it became sleepy. Then, like every other bird in the world, it tucked its bill under its wing.

This strange creature was the penguin, a bird found only in the southern half of the world. It shows no fear of man and sometimes is quite friendly toward him.

Though he was not the first to visit Antarctica, Rear Admiral

The largest of all penguins, the Emperor. ►

Richard E. Byrd made five trips there. The journals he wrote tell many fascinating stories about penguins.

Byrd made his first trip to Antarctica in 1928. Day by day he kept a record in his journal of all that happened. On December 17, he wrote the story of his first meeting with live penguins.

MEETING AN EMPEROR

The Admiral's ship was sailing through the ice pack—that ring of floating ice which circles Antarctica. Suddenly, on some ice near the ship, Admiral Byrd spied an emperor penguin. He knew that Antarctica couldn't be very far away now.

An emperor is the largest of all penguins, and this one was nearly four feet tall. It was a handsome bird. Its back was gleaming black and its chest feathers were the color of rich cream. On each side of its neck was a patch of golden yellow feathers, and on its beak were bright orange lines. The beak was so long and the body so large that the emperor's head looked very small indeed.

Straight and tall the bird stood on its two feet. It looked quietly at the men as if to say, "I own this great land of ice and snow!" And this is true, for the emperor spends more of its life on Antarctica's shores than any other living thing. In fact, before the coming of man to Antarctica, these birds had six million square miles of land all to themselves every winter. Other animals leave when winter and darkness come. But that is the time the emperors choose to raise their young!

Admiral Byrd was surprised to see how much the huge penguin looked like a man. In its fancy "coat" and "shirt," it seemed to be dressed for a grand party. Because the emperor looked so proud, the Admiral thought he must be careful how he spoke to it. But the real bird didn't want to speak to the man named Byrd. It just bowed a little, then turned and walked away.

Admiral Byrd soon had a better welcome to Antarctica. Later that same day he and his men met another kind of penguin, the Adélie. These birds are smaller than the emperors. They are more friendly, too. Whatever they do, they seem to have fun. At nesting time each year, thousands of Adélies visit the mainland of Antarctica.

Many of the birds came near the Admiral's ship. They waved their flippers at the men. Some came sliding down small hills of ice on their fat, round stomachs. As the

Penguins walk like men. Their strong flippers help them to balance.

ice was very close to the ship, some of the sailors jumped onto it and played with the penguins. No one knew who had more fun—the men, or the birds who looked like men.

These sea birds swam behind the boat like fish. The Admiral watched them dive under cakes of floating ice and was surprised to see them pop up on the other side. Now and then a bird would race across the ice on its stomach. By pushing with its flippers, the Admiral said, it could travel as fast as a man can walk.

A penguin's strong flippers are useful to him in many ways. They help to balance him when he walks. They can be used as clubs when he fights. As pushers they help him to glide over the snow like a fast sled. As paddles they make him one of the world's best swimmers. But a penguin's handy flippers are not like other birds' wings. They are not built to lift his plump body off the ground.

WHO'S AFRAID? NOT AN ADÉLIE!

As the men worked to unload the ships, they were never alone. The Adélies followed them everywhere. The birds came close and stared

This little Adélie shows its playful nature.

with their funny round eyes. The white rings around their eyes made them look wide-awake and very wise.

Admiral Byrd and his men soon learned that the Adélies were not as wise as they looked. The little birds were just too curious and too fearless for their own good. (Adélies are afraid of only three things in the world—the cruel leopard seal and the killer whale which gobble penguins in the sea, and the sly skua gull that steals eggs and eats baby penguins on land. Nothing else can frighten an Adélie.) The birds at the bay showed that they had no fear of the great ships nearby, the noisy men at work, or even the barking huskies who pulled the sleds.

The dogs in their coats of thick fur were a queer sight to the penguins. At times an Adélie busybody would insist on taking a better look at a husky. The men would try to frighten it away, but it isn't easy to chase an Adélie.

Some birds came quietly with their little heads cocked to one side. Others came squawking loudly and waving their flippers. Poor penguins! Such a visit was often their last, for the dogs struck hard. Admiral Byrd said that the Adélies just couldn't get it into their little pinheads that where the dogs were, there was danger!

In his book, *Little America,* Admiral Byrd told about one brave Adélie. It came squawking over the ice, heading straight toward a team of nine sled dogs. The Admiral knew that it took only one husky to kill an Adélie. This bird had no chance at all with nine of them!

There was no stopping the nosy penguin. On and on he came. When he reached the team, the brave little fellow started to fight with all nine dogs at once. Soon the whole bay rang with the noise. The nine huskies barked. The penguin squawked. The dogs tried to bite him with their sharp, strong teeth. The Adélie's squawks became louder, but he didn't run away.

Admiral Byrd went after the penguin quickly. He snatched him away from the dogs just in time. Then he carried the bird far away and put him down safely on the snow.

The huskies became quiet once more. But was the penguin quiet? No! Was he thankful to Admiral Byrd for saving his life? No, indeed! He was angry because the Admiral had not let him finish his fight.

The little Adélie was still squawking as he walked away. He held out his flippers and cocked his saucy head. Admiral Byrd thought the penguin seemed to say, "Well, I showed those animals a thing or two!"

THE BOY SCOUT AND HIS PENGUIN FARM

With the Admiral on his first trip to Antarctica was a boy named Paul A. Siple. The Boy Scouts of America held a contest in 1928 to choose a Scout who would go with Admiral Byrd on his trip. From the thousands of boys who wanted to go, Paul was chosen. He was then a nineteen-year-old Eagle Scout who had earned sixty merit badges.

Because the Scout was the youngest man in the Admiral's party, he was often given jobs which no one else wanted. He soon learned to unload ships, to drive a team of sled dogs, to skin seals, and to do many other things. Everything he was asked to do, he did cheerfully and well. Even when the older men teased him, Paul was a good sport.

One day in Little America the Admiral sent for the tall Boy Scout. "Paul," he said, "some zoos in America want penguins. I have given my word that we will bring back twenty of them. While you are here in Antarctica, one of your jobs will be to catch the penguins and take care of them. I'd like the birds to reach the United States alive and well."

"Yes, sir!" said Paul. "I'll do my best, sir!" Like a good Scout, Paul Siple did do his best. His new job wasn't an easy one, but he never gave up.

Catching twenty penguins wasn't hard to do, for the birds were always walking into camp. But *keeping* them was the problem. Paul had twenty of them on his "penguin farm," but they weren't always the same twenty. That was the trouble. One minute the penguins were there. The next minute they were gone. But how? Everyone knew they couldn't jump out. It seemed like magic.

The Boy Scout used a large pit to hold the birds. He always treated them kindly and fed them well. For food he cut up seal meat and hot dogs and fish. But the birds wouldn't eat. All they wanted was to be free.

Each time the Scout walked away from the pit, a few penguins got out. Paul put poles around the top to keep the rest in. But the birds just pushed the poles away with their bills, and soon they were free like the first ones.

Next Paul tried putting some large gasoline cans around the pit to make it deeper. Twenty more birds were caught. However, each day one or two of these were gone, also. No one knew how they got out. Every day Paul had to catch more.

Then, one day, someone told Paul that a few penguins were walking about the camp. The Scout thought he knew where they had come from. He ran straight to his penguin farm. Yes, he was right! Only half of the birds were left in the pit.

This time, at last, Paul learned the penguins' secret. He saw some of the birds making a ladder. Other penguins were climbing over the backs of the ones in the ladder. Out they climbed – all but two. The poor birds at the bottom of the ladder had no one to help them to get out.

Once more the Boy Scout had to start his penguin farm. When Admiral Byrd saw how hard Paul had to work, he was sorry he had given his word about bringing back the birds. But Paul Siple didn't mind. He loved penguins and everything else about Antarctica, and when the ship sailed for home, twenty penguins were on board.

On every other trip Admiral Byrd made to Antarctica, he took Paul Siple along. The young man began to call this land "my own country." Each time he returned he said that he was "going home."

Paul A. Siple, the Boy Scout, became Dr. Paul A. Siple. He has been called Mr. Antarctica, for the study of that wide, white land became his life work. He has spent more time in Antarctica than any other man. And it all started when he was baby-sitter to twenty penguins!

The Rood family had heard about the wild ponies of Chincoteague Island. Now they were on their way to watch the ponies swim across the channel.

A pony with her colt on the sand dunes of Assateague.

The Pony Auction

by RONALD ROOD

Important details may tell the place where something happens and why it happens there. Watch for such details in this selection.

The New Jersey flats stretched before us. The smell of salt marsh, factory smoke, and auto exhaust blew in the open windows of our microbus station wagon. The noise of passing cars and the singing of the tires beat constantly in our ears. But we didn't care. We were headed for the Chincoteague pony roundup.

"Chincoteague," the travel folder had read, "is Virginia's largest island. It is at the end of the Delmarva Peninsula. Each year it's the scene of the most famous wild-west show in the East—the wild pony roundup."

I had heard about the annual "pony swim" years ago. It seems that a ship carrying horses was once wrecked on an oversized sand dune called Assateague, which is located just offshore of Chincoteague. Or perhaps it merely let the horses off and never came back for them. At any rate, they were still there, apparently stunted in growth because of their harsh surroundings. They were supposed to be about midway in size between a Shetland pony and a small horse. However, they weren't as chunky as some ponies, but well formed, wiry, and tough.

Every year they round up the ponies on Assateague Island and swim them across the channel to Chincoteague, I had heard. So here we were to see for ourselves. We left the dog with neighbors and headed south from our home in Vermont.

Chincoteague proved to combine the gaiety of Coney Island with the charm of Cape Cod. We drove along the main street past camera shops, drugstores, and gift shops, all doing a whacking vacation business. Girls in shorts mingled with fishermen in rubber boots, and traffic crawled along in low gear.

Everywhere we saw Chincoteague ponies. Many were nearly as big as Chichi, our own little half-Morgan mare back in Vermont. They carried children and their parents up and down the street. Some of them were penned in front-yard corrals for the occasion. "For sale: Genuine Chincoteague Ponies," Alison read excitedly. "Oh, Daddy—couldn't we buy one and have it shipped back home?"

I was just about to answer her when Roger cut in at the top of his voice. "Stop, Daddy! Stop! I saw a sign about Misty!"

The children had read Marguerite Henry's charming book, *Misty of Chincoteague,* and knew every one of Wesley Dennis's illustrations by heart. They'd been looking for signs of the famous little pony ever since we had arrived. Now, as I stopped in the street, Roger craned his neck out the window.

I looked in the mirror. A line of cars a block long was behind me. "Better walk back and see what it says, Roger," I decided, pulling over to the curb. The words were scarcely out of my mouth before he and Alison had burst out of the door and gone running down the sidewalk.

They came back in an instant. "Beebe Ranch," Alison directed breathlessly. "Down this street and turn left."

In a few minutes we drew up to the Beebe Ranch. We parked in front of a little gift shop which fronted on a stable. The children took out their pocketbooks and counted out the necessary coins. Then, having paid their admission, they walked reverently into Misty's presence.

Peg and I took a brief look at the plucky little mare who'd once made the channel swim herself and, according to the story, had nearly drowned in the crossing. We admired her golden coat and silvery mane, and then went back outside.

We were joined shortly by our two starry-eyed youngsters. "Oh, Alison, isn't she pretty?" Roger asked.

"She's more than that, Roger. She's beautiful!"

The big morning of the pony swim came. Driven to a point of land on Assateague by "gumboot cowboys," the two hundred or so stallions, mares, and colts grazed with apparent calm on the salt grass. Opposite them, somewhat less than a quarter mile away on the Chincoteague shore, were several thousand tourists, vacationists, townspeople, photographers, writers, and reporters.

Between these two groups stretched the channel crammed with scores of boats. All morning the tide had been running in from the ocean like a river. Now, by about 11:00 A.M., it was almost at the flood. "Low tide is better," someone stated, "but it comes at the wrong time of day just now. So the boys are waiting for just the right moment at high tide. Then they'll swim the ponies across before the water turns and runs out again."

Suddenly there was a commotion on the opposite shore. The waiting cowboys spurred their horses. They shouted and whistled and drove the ponies to the water's edge. Here the herd hesitated, but the cowboys urged them on. They slapped the water with reins and ropes while the cowboys in the rear crowded the herd from behind.

Then the ponies took to the water. I had heard about the pony swim in several books, but the one thing that immediately impressed me had not been mentioned in any of them. This was the sound of some two hundred horses calling, neighing, whinnying to each other as they stretched their necks toward the opposite shore. It was a sound we shall never forget.

When the tide is just right in the channel, the ponies are driven into the water to swim to the opposite shore.

We watched the pony foals through our binoculars. Some of the little fellows laid their heads on their mothers' rumps to keep their noses out of the water. Their high-pitched little voices sounded over the calls of their parents as they flailed their tiny hoofs in the strange medium.

Finally, they made it to our shore. The tide was stronger than the cowboy-firemen had calculated, and the herd had drifted downstream a few hundred feet from where they were supposed to land. Men, women, and children melted away before them as the ponies found the ground and pulled themselves out of the water. Dripping and neighing, they were driven to a waiting corral. There they re-formed quickly into family groups, each stallion claiming his dozen or so mares and their foals.

The next day found us with thousands of others at the pony auction. The ponies, being wild creatures rounded up by the firemen, had become the latter's property. Now their colts were singled out and held in a little corral. Each colt came to the block in its turn. There husky firemen held the wild little creature as best they could while it was bid off. Apparently, even though they were only about two months old, they were old enough for instant weaning to grain and grass.

"Fifty-five, who'll make it sixty? Fifty-five, who'll make it sixty? . . . Sixty, who says sixty-five?" the auctioneer chanted as the colts were presented for sale.

Some of the buyers were obviously outfitted for just this occasion. There were horse trailers from Kentucky, and fancy vans from Pennsylvania. There were people in pick-up trailers and delivery wagons.

Other buyers were people who came to look and ended up owning one of the charming little colts. An auction will do that to you. A woman from Baltimore was among this group. "Eighty!" she shouted in a fit of enthusiasm at my side as a fine little brown-and-white colt kicked and struggled in his captor's arms.

The auctioneer waited for other bids. "Are you all done at eighty?" he called. Then he pointed to her. "Lady, you done bought yourself a hoss."

She clapped her hand to her forehead. "Oh no! Where will I put him when I get home?" Then, happily: "But won't my husband be surprised!"

There were plenty of other impulse buyers. And among them was a family in a microbus from Vermont.

Roger and Alison had watched one little colt after another come up for sale. Finally Roger came over to me and pressed his pocketbook into my hand.

"Alison's money is back in the car," he said. "But here's all my money. Dad, could you put enough with it to buy us a pony?"

At this moment, I knew there was nothing short of life itself that was more precious to my children. We didn't have a horse trailer, and we surely didn't have the money. But we were at Chincoteague and this was the pony auction.

"All right, Roger. Pick out the one you want."

"Golly, Dad. Golly. How much can we spend?"

"See if you can get one for about fifty-five dollars."

The colts had been going for

anywhere from fifty dollars up. I watched, happy as only a father can feel when he is able to give his son something he knows the youngster wants badly.

Carefully Roger made his choice. It was one of the smallest colts yet to be offered. Light brown with a straight little back and legs, he kicked and struggled in silence as the auctioneer's helper tried to keep him still.

"Who'll go fifty dollars to start it off?" the auctioneer asked.

"Forty!" shouted Roger.

"Forty I've got. Who'll make it forty-five?"

Someone on the other side of the crowd bid forty-five. Roger bid fifty. Then it went up in dollar amounts until the opposition had bid fifty-five.

Roger looked at me in despair. "Oh, Dad, what do I do now?"

A man at my side in a ten-gallon hat winked at me. "Surely you could spare the boy another dollar."

"All right, Roger. Tell him fifty-six."

"Fifty-six!" shouted Roger.

But the opposition was still with us. "Fifty-seven!"

My big-hatted friend turned to me again. "Now here's how to get your pony. Tell the boy to go all the way to sixty."

I nodded. Roger took a good hitch on his lungs. "Sixty!" he shouted in his best eleven-year-old, hoss-tradin' voice.

The auctioneer turned and looked full at my son. "Boy," he said gently, "this here's a fine hoss for a fella just your size. And he's yours for sixty dollars."

Alison had been watching, flabbergasted. Now she rushed over. "Daddy, is it true? Is it really true? Is he ours?"

Peg cleared her throat beside me. I'd almost forgotten her. "Yes, Alison, he's ours. Now all your father's got to do is get him back to Vermont."

We bought a little halter with our now sadly depleted cash, and managed to slip it over the tiny colt's nose. "What'll we call him, Dad?" asked Roger.

"I don't know. What's a good name?"

"How about 'Little Fellow'?"

And so Little Fellow joined our family.

The problem now was to see if we could get him from Virginia to Vermont. I measured him with my arms and then calculated how he'd fit in our bus-wagon. We'd already taken out the middle seat to make room for camping equipment, and just maybe . . .

We bought some packing lumber. In a couple of hours we had a sturdy stall built. It was four feet long, thirty inches wide, and three feet high—a perfect fit for our tiny guest. Finally came the time to put Little Fellow in the car. We'd fixed one end of his crate so it could be put up as a ramp for him. Roger went into the microbus coaxing and gently pulling the lead rope, and I urged him from the rear. Then, with a leap, he disdained the ramp and jumped into the car so fast he bumped his nose on the opposite window.

From the first, he was a perfect traveler. Newspapers and straw beneath him made a soft, absorbent bed. He tried to go to sleep, but with every jolt he'd wake up. Then he'd glance around at his new family with a little nicker of recognition and slowly doze off again.

All along the way we were the subject of much scrutiny, double takes and near collisions as drivers and passengers in other cars contemplated the unlikely spectacle of a horse in a station wagon. One car which passed us slowed down when it got in front until we were forced to pass it in turn. Then it pulled abreast of us on a straight stretch. In the car we could see a man and a woman. The woman was taking pictures of us with her home-movie camera. So somewhere, in somebody's collection, Little Fellow is in the movies.

We continued north with our pony. He occasioned a few raised eyebrows at toll bridges when the attendants tried to decide if he was a passenger or not. He panicked a little dog at a gas station when we suddenly let him out on a parking ramp. We discovered that he'd whinny if Roger left the car, so at more than one picnic area we'd have him whinny. Then we'd innocently stare into space while the other people at nearby tables would try to figure out where the horse must be.

We reached home. When we added up the miles we'd traveled with Little Fellow, we discovered he'd been with us in the car for five days and fifteen hundred miles.

At this writing in March, Little Fellow is about ten months old. Now he weighs perhaps a hundred fifty pounds and stands forty inches high. He grew a thick coat of hair to protect him against the Vermont winter, and spent half the time outdoors—though the barn door was open for shelter if he wanted it. Little Fellow had become a Vermonter.

This writer recalls one of the favorite pets of his boyhood and the adventures they had together.

A Boy and a Raccoon

by STERLING NORTH

The important details will be the ones that tell about the raccoon—what he looked like and how he behaved.

How do you feed a baby raccoon weighing less than one pound?

Some children feed them with a medicine dropper or a doll's nursing bottle. But I fed my tiny raccoon through a clean wheat straw. I took warm milk in my mouth, then tilted the hollow straw downward to his mouth and watched him suck eagerly.

I called my raccoon "Rascal" because he was such a mischief.

He had gleaming black eyes, a mask like a little bandit, and five black rings around his fluffy tail. His whispered trills were full of wonder and curiosity. In the wide-spreading oak tree behind our house there was a comfortable hole which made a good home for Rascal. Here he dreamed away his first two months, sleeping happily between feedings.

At the foot of this great tree lay my big Saint Bernard, Wowser. He was a dependable watchdog who protected all my pets:

My little woodchucks!

My good little black-and-white skunks in their cages!

My cats of many colors!

And even my wicked pet crow named Poe, who liked to steal every shining object he could find and hide these treasures in the belfry of the Methodist Church.

Wowser was a handsome animal weighing one hundred and seventy pounds. It would have been a brave dog or a foolish boy who tried to disturb Wowser's new friend, my little raccoon, Rascal.

One day in June, when cherries were ripe and the whole world cheerful with bird song, Wowser and I heard a quavering trill at the hole in the tree. A moment later we saw two bright eyes shining from a small black mask. Rascal was peering from the door of his home at the world below. Soon he began backing down the tree like a little bear, tail first.

Wowser was worried. He yelped a question or two and glanced up to see what I thought about this new problem. I told my dog not to worry, but to watch what happened.

I had a shallow minnow pool not far from the tree. Rascal hurried to the little pond and started fishing. His sensitive hands searched the shallows, while his eyes gazed far away as though he were thinking of something else entirely. Soon his clever little hands caught a minnow. He began washing it back and forth as raccoons do with almost everything they eat. Rascal carried his minnow to the edge of the pool, very pleased with himself, and began eating the small fish in polite little nibbles. Then he started exploring the back yard surrounding the oak tree. Once he pounced on a cricket. A moment later he lay very still while the dark shadow of Poe-the-Crow swept across the grass. When Rascal came too near to the edge of our green lawn, Wowser pushed him back, firmly but gently.

Having explored his little world, my raccoon climbed the tree and

disappeared into his safe home in the hollow of the oak. He seemed to be perfectly satisfied with his first trip abroad. Wowser sighed with relief. Rascal was again safely in his nest. He had not hurt himself nor run away. Perhaps he would not be the problem that Wowser had feared.

Being a Rascal-sitter was a twenty-four-hour-a-day job.

My father and I lived alone together in a ten-room house in the little town of Brailsford Junction in southern Wisconsin. My mother was dead, and my two older sisters, Theo and Jessica, were living elsewhere. My big brother, Herschel, was with the American Army in France, fighting against the Germans in World War I.

My father was very kind to me. He let me build my canoe in the living room, keep any number of pets, and wander as free as the wind over meadows and hills. I knew that he would not object to having Rascal eat with us at the table. From the attic I carried down the family high chair last used when I was a baby.

At breakfast next morning I put a shallow earthenware bowl of warm milk on the tray of the high chair. Rascal stood in the chair, placing his hands on the edge of the tray. He could reach the milk easily, and he chirred and trilled his satisfaction. He drank his milk, scarcely dribbling a drop. In fact, his table manners were better than those of many children. My father smiled fondly at our new breakfast companion, and I was delighted at Rascal's good behavior.

All went well until I offered the raccoon a lump of sugar. Rascal took it between his two hands and began washing it back and forth in his milk just as he had washed the minnow. In a moment or two, of course, it melted entirely away, and you could not imagine a more surprised little raccoon.

First he felt all over the bottom of the bowl to see if he had dropped it.

Then he looked in his right hand! No sugar lump!

Next he looked in his left hand! No sugar lump there either!

Finally he turned to me and shrilled a sharp question. Who had stolen his lump of sugar?

When I recovered from laughter, I gave him a second lump. He thought about washing it, but then a shrewd look came into his shining eyes. He took the sugar directly to his mouth and began munching it happily.

Rascal was a very bright raccoon. When he learned a lesson, he learned it for life. Never again did he try to wash a lump of sugar.

The kitchen screen door had a worn catch and weak spring. I did not repair them because I wanted my cats to be able to pull the door open to let themselves in, or push it from the inside to let themselves out. Rascal was certain he could do anything that a cat could do. Several times he watched them open the door. Obviously the trick was to hook your claws in the screen and pull. Feeling very proud of himself, he showed the cats that he was as smart as the oldest and wisest tom.

A few nights later I was surprised and delighted to hear Rascal's trill from the pillow beside me. Then I felt his little hands exploring my face. My raccoon baby had climbed down from his hole in the tree and had opened the back screen door. With eyes that could see in the dark, he had found his way to my downstairs bedroom. There were no very strict rules in our house, as both Rascal and I realized. My raccoon decided the most comfortable place to sleep was with me. He was as clean as any cat, and perfectly housebroken from the start. So for many months we slept together.

I felt less lonesome now when my father went away on business, leaving me all alone in that big ten-room house.

A boy, a bicycle, and a little raccoon! Imagine the adventures we had! Rascal had become a speed demon. He liked nothing better than whizzing down a steep hill. This lovable little creature had the heart of a lion. He liked to stand in the basket of my bicycle with his feet braced wide apart and his hands gripping the front rim of the basket. His natural goggles made him look like a racing driver. His small button of a nose pointed straight into the wind, and his whiskers blew back nearly to his ears, as his ring tail streamed out behind.

Sometimes he shared the bicycle basket with bunches of crimson white-tipped radishes which I raised in my war garden and sold to the grocery stores.

Once he shared the basket with blooming rose plants I had dug from the garden to transplant on my mother's grave. The white stone merely said:

In Memory of
SARAH ELIZABETH NELSON NORTH
1866–1914

Rascal could not understand why I felt so sad as I planted roses around that stone.

Sometimes Rascal shared the basket with my compact box of fishing tackle, when we went to the river to fish.

Often, after these rides, Rascal and I drank strawberry pop. He quickly learned how to lie on his back and hold the bottle in perfect position with all four feet while he drained the last sweet drop.

I had started to build my canoe in the living room during the previous winter when it was much too cold to work in the barn. The ribs that ran the length of the canoe were of clear white pine, fragrant and smooth to the touch. The circular ribs were cut from the tough water elm of several cheese-boxes which the storekeepers had given me. Naturally, all this canoe-building created some disorder and dust in the living room.

One day, when I was at work on the canoe, a big Stutz Bearcat automobile curved up our drive and out stepped my beautiful married sister Theodora. She had brought along one of her maids and enough luggage so that I knew she intended to stay for a while.

"Theo, Theo!" I shouted happily, running out to embrace her.

"Hello, sonny boy—my, you're all covered with sawdust."

"I'm building a canoe."

"Not in the living room!" Theo was already suspicious.

"Well, you see, Theo, it was too cold in the barn last winter . . ."

"Merciful heavens!" Theo said.

"Now help Jennie with the luggage and put it in the downstairs bedroom."

I loved this beautiful auburn-haired sister of mine, but I was a little afraid of her too. She had taught me to jump up like a jack-in-the-box whenever an older person entered the room, and for a time after my mother's death she had dressed me in such fashionable Norfolk jackets that the other boys had laughed at me. At the sight of the living room she threw up her hands in horror.

"I've never seen such a mess in my life," she said, "but we'll soon fix that. Jennie and I are going to clean this house from top to bottom. And out goes the canoe. We'll hire a full-time housekeeper, if we can find one."

"Can't you just leave us alone?" I asked mournfully. "Anyhow, you're not my mother."

"Oh, sonny boy," she said, fighting back the tears. She came around the end of the canoe and kissed me quite tenderly.

I didn't mind giving Theo my downstairs bedroom, but my little raccoon didn't understand the new arrangement. That evening, after Theo had gone to sleep, Rascal let himself in the back door and went confidently to our bed and crawled in with Theo.

My father and I, who were sleeping upstairs, heard a bloodcurdling yell. We rushed downstairs in our pajamas to find Theo standing on a chair, treed by my little raccoon, who blinked up at this crazy human being who was screeching like a fire siren.

"He always sleeps in this bed," I explained. "He's clean and perfectly harmless."

"You throw that animal right out of the house and hook the screen door so it can't possibly get back in."

"Well, OK," I said, "but you're sleeping in Rascal's bed."

"Don't be saucy," Theo said.

I kept the screen door hooked the next several nights, but one evening I forgot. Just before dawn Rascal opened the screen door, went cautiously to Theo's room, but decided not to crawl in with her. He did, however, prowl quietly around the bedroom and the adjoining bath. On the wide rim of the lavatory he found the most beautiful trinket he had ever stolen, my sister's diamond ring.

Raccoons and crows love shiny things, and Rascal and Poe-the-Crow often fought over treasures I gave to Rascal, such as bright new pennies. Just before dawn I heard a crow-raccoon fight on the back porch, so when Theo said she had lost her ring I had a theory about what might have happened.

After we had searched the house and yard and gardens, I decided to look in one more place—the belfry of the Methodist Church where Poe had his nest. I asked kindly Reverend Hooton, the Methodist minister, if I could climb the dark shaft to the belfry, and he said I might. The shaft was filled with cobwebs, and some of the cleats were loose. I was afraid that I might fall, but I could not turn back.

At last I reached the airy little room at the top, with its widely spaced shutters and its view of the town below. I touched the big deep-toned bell which had been tolled forty-seven times for my mother—once for each year of her short life—and which many years later would be tolled ninety-nine times for my father. I remembered the fragrance of hyacinths at my mother's funeral, and for a few minutes I forgot all about Theo's diamond ring.

Then, in a far corner of the belfry, I saw the circle of twigs, leaves, and black feathers that Poe-the-Crow called home. As some people keep their money in their mattress, Poe had made his bed even more uncomfortable with a pile of shining possessions that overran the nest and spilled across the floor.

Here were some of my best glass marbles, my football whistle, scraps of sheet copper, a second key to our Oldsmobile, and, wonder of wonders, Theo's diamond ring.

I put several of the valuable objects in my pocket, but left the worthless junk, knowing that Poe

couldn't tell sheet copper from a diamond ring. Poe dropped in at about this time. He cawed and cussed in crow language, acting as though I were the thief and he the honest householder. His angry voice followed me as I went down the shaft and out into the sunlight.

Theo was so happy to have her ring that she did not insist that I take my canoe to the barn. She even postponed the hiring of a full-time housekeeper. She merely fed us delightful meals, and, with Jennie's help, left the house shining clean. Then, with a good-bye kiss and a wave of the hand, she was off again, gallant, beautiful, and brave, her auburn hair shining in the sun.

Summer passes all too swiftly for an active boy of eleven. Rascal and I often went fishing below the dam in the river at Indian Ford. Sometimes I cast for bass and pickerel among the water lilies. More often I fished for big, fighting silver catfish in my favorite hole below a pleasant sandbar in the river. Rascal meanwhile fished in the shallows along the edge of the bar, often seizing a crayfish—those little monsters that look so much like small fresh-water lobsters. These he washed and ate, tail first, with obvious delight.

Despite mowing lawns and working in my war garden, I always found time to read, lying in the hammock and listening to all the sounds of summer—the clip-clop of horses' hoofs, the shrilling of the cicadas, and the murmuring of the birds.

On a few gala occasions, my father would hang a sign on the office door:

GONE FOR THE DAY

Then, with a picnic basket filled with sandwiches and a few bottles of cold root beer and pop, my father and Rascal and I would clamber happily into the front seat of the big seven-passenger Oldsmobile, with the top back and the windshield down. All three of us wore goggles—Rascal's being natural, of course. He liked to perch between us on the back of the seat, gazing joyfully ahead as my father shifted from low into second and from second into high, speeding up the river road toward Lake Koshkonong.

Here we hunted for Indian arrowheads, explored the little cave in the limestone at Taylor's Point, or swam in the cold water. Rascal, although only three months old, was an excellent swimmer, dog-paddling along beside us until he grew tired. He considered me his natural protector when we were in deep water, and would climb on my shoulder or my head for a rest. Often I would float on my back and arch my chest above the water to give him a better resting place. As soon as he had caught his breath, he would dive in again and paddle along bravely through the little waves, as we explored the coves and grassy points along the sandy shore.

Rascal had never been told about turtle eggs, but on our very first trip to the lake his keen nostrils told him that somewhere in this sand was a delightful form of food he had never before tasted. He dug furiously to bring up the eggs, nearly as large as golf balls. They had been laid by a big snapping turtle and left in the warm sand to hatch. Rascal tore the eggs open with his sharp little teeth and gorged until he could not eat another bite. Then for hours he slept blissfully on the back seat of the car as my father and I visited several of his farms to see how the crops were growing.

Finding Main Ideas and Important Details

Since textbooks are always written to give information, they are usually arranged to help you find easily the main ideas and the important details. Textbooks are often divided into short sections with headings that tell the topic of each section. The main ideas are usually stated clearly. Textbook writers try to make it easy for the reader to find the important details. Of course, when you read textbooks, as in all your reading, you must be thinking, too. No matter how clearly the writer presents the information, he cannot do your thinking for you.

Main Ideas in Science

Here is a section from a science book. "Mammals" is the topic. Look for main ideas about mammals. The paragraphs are numbered so that you can refer to them later.

Mammals

[1]Mammals are warm-blooded. Because of this adaptation, mammals can live practically anywhere on the earth.

If you don't know the meaning of **adaptation,** where should you look?

[2]The temperature of a mammal's blood does not usually change with the changes in the outside temperature. Whether it is very cold or very hot outside, the body temperature stays steady.

[3]Sometimes when a mammal is ill, its blood temperature may rise or fall just a few degrees, but not much. When some mammals sleep through the winter (hibernate), their temperature is much

Note that paragraphs 1–3 contain the first main idea: Mammals are warm-blooded and their body temperature does not change very much.

lower than when they are active. But most of the time the temperature of a mammal's body does not change.

[4]Mammals, and only mammals, have hair. Some mammals, such as bears, may be entirely covered with hair. Others, like the whale, have just a few bristly hairs.

Note the second main idea: Mammals have hair.

[5]A kitten's hair is soft and silky, a sheep's is thick and curly, while some of a porcupine's hair is in the form of thick, sharp quills. Hair can be different in many ways, but all mammals have some kind of hair.

[6]Mammals have lungs and breathe air. All mammals, even the ones that live in the sea, must have air to breathe. Air comes in through their nostrils and flows through a windpipe into two lungs. Here oxygen in the air passes into the blood. The blood carries the oxygen to all parts of the body.

What is the main idea of this paragraph?

[7]Mammal mothers can make milk. Mammals can feed their babies with milk from their bodies. While many other animal mothers take care of their young and feed them, only mammals can make milk.

Is there a main idea in this paragraph?

[8]Most mammals give birth to live young which are fully formed inside the mother's body.

Is this another main idea?

[9]Mammals are alike in these ways:

1. All mammals are vertebrates.
2. All mammals are warm-blooded.
3. All mammals have hair.
4. All mammal mothers can make milk to feed their young.

Here is a summary of the main ideas.

This idea was taught earlier in the book.

5. All mammals have lungs and breathe air.
6. Most mammals give birth to fully formed young.

[10]Are people mammals?

–from *Science in Our World* 5

Building Skills

To Write

1. The main ideas in this selection are listed below. After the letter for each main idea, write the numeral of the paragraph or paragraphs in which that main idea is presented.

    a. All mammals are warm-blooded.
    b. All mammals have hair.
    c. All mammals have lungs and breathe air.
    d. All mammal mothers can make milk to feed their young.
    e. Most mammals give birth to fully formed young.

2. List two examples of this main idea: All mammals have hair.
3. List two details that tell you more about this main idea: All mammals have lungs and breathe air.

Main Ideas in Social Studies

The selection you are going to read is taken from a chapter titled "Buffalo Hunters of the Great Plains." That title tells you that the chapter must be about the early days of our country, when there were great herds of buffalo. But you are going to read only a part of the chapter. This part has the heading "Horses on the plains." As you think about this title, ask yourself: (1) Where did the horses come from?

(2) Did anyone ride them? (3) What did they have to do with buffalo? Such questions will help you to find the main ideas.

Albert Bierstadt, *The Last of the Buffalo*, in the collection of The Corcoran Gallery of Art

[1]**Horses on the plains.** De Soto and Coronado had brought horses with them when they explored our country. The Spaniards in Mexico also had horses. Some ran away. Others were turned loose when they became sick or lame. Many of these horses wandered to the Great Plains. From the rich, short grass, the horses grew strong and tough. Soon, large herds of wild horses roamed the plains.

What use of horses is shown in the picture above?

The words in boldface type tell you the main topic of this section.

[2]We do not know exactly when the Plains Indians first learned to catch wild horses and ride them. We do know that when white men crossed the Great Plains to explore and settle the West, they met Indians on horseback.

[3]Horses did not really change the way of life of most Plains Indians. But they made life easier and enabled the Indians to hunt better.

In the next paragraphs you can expect some important details to tell how horses made the Indians' life easier and enabled them to hunt better.

[4]Horses can run faster than buffalo. Indians mounted on horses could ride close enough to shoot before the buffalo knew what was happening. On horses Indians could easily avoid stampeding herds. Horses could pull much larger loads on the travois than dogs.

Context tells you that **travois** must be something that could be pulled by dogs or horses.

[5]The Plains Indians were brave and daring, and they became expert riders. They became skillful at shooting arrows from galloping horses. This helped them greatly in hunting. And it made them the best warriors in the Red Man's America.

What does this paragraph tell you about horses helping the Indians?

—from *Knowing Our Neighbors in the United States*

Building Skills

To Write

1. Reread Paragraphs 1 and 3. Those paragraphs contain the two main ideas of this selection. Write those main ideas in your own words.
2. The details in Paragraph 1 tell how there came to be herds of wild horses on the plains. List these details.

To Discuss

1. Which paragraphs give details that support the second main idea? Tell what some of those details are.
2. Do you know who De Soto and Coronado were? What sentence gives you some information about them?

Details in Mathematics Problems

In order to solve a story problem in mathematics, you have to decide how the details, or facts, are related to each other and to the main idea. In most mathematics problems the details are given first. Then you read a question. Once you understand the question, you reread the details and decide how to use them to solve the problem.

Sometimes a story problem gives more information than you need. Then you must select only the details you need to answer the question. Other times a story problem may not give enough information. When that happens, you must decide what else you need to know in order to get the answer.

Pay close attention to the details as you read the problem.

1. Tammy's new TV set has a 21-inch screen. How much bigger is this screen than the screen on her old set?

   You see that this problem can't be solved until you have more information. What do you need to know?

2. Frank bought 5 comic books for 20¢ each and 5 packs of gum. How much did he spend?

   What detail do you need to know to solve this problem?

3. Laura went to the delicatessen to get what she needed for lunch. She bought one-half pound of salami for $.55, one-half pound of cheese for $.43, and a loaf of bread for $.31. How much change did she get?

   What detail is needed for this problem?

4. A bus driver collected $23.40 on Saturday, $10.60 on Sunday, and $18.20 on Monday. How much did he collect in the three days?

   Is there enough information in this problem?

5. Arrowhead School's baseball team purchased 9 uniforms at $15.00 each and 9 gloves at $8.00 each. What was the total amount of money spent outfitting the team?

   Do you have all the details you need to solve this problem?

6. Murray has 18 inches of rope. If he buys another 36 inches of rope at 60¢ per foot, how much rope will he have in all?

   What detail in this problem is not needed?

7. Six painters took four days to paint eleven rooms. If they used two gallons of paint to paint each room, how many gallons of paint were used in all?

   Which figure will you **not** use?

–from *Harbrace Mathematics, 5*

Building Skills

To Write

1. Rewrite Problems 1 and 2. Add the details which would allow you to find the answer to each of the problems.
2. Rewrite the question in Problem 3. Add a detail to the question which would allow you to find an answer to the problem.

To Discuss

Suggest an additional question for Problems 6 and 7 which will allow you to use all of the facts.

Summary

An important skill in reading is finding the main ideas and important details. To develop this skill, you learned to:

– Study headings as a guide to the topics you are going to read about.
– Use the topic as a guide to the main ideas you should look for.
– Note the details that explain or support main ideas.
– Study a summary of main ideas.
– Tell the difference between important and unimportant details.

Discovering What Gerbils Do by Seymour Simon.
Gerbils make excellent pets. This short book tells clearly how to make a gerbil happy in your home.

Animal Timekeepers by Navin Sullivan.
How do birds know when to migrate? How do groundhogs know when to awaken from their winter's sleep? This delightful book, illustrated with drawings, tells how the animal's inner clock affects his life and habits.

The Book of Ponies by Suzanne Wilding.
Did you know that there are twelve breeds of ponies, each slightly different in appearance? Each kind of pony also has its special abilities and uses. Sketches and paintings show the ponies in their natural surroundings.

Anna and Dula by Robert Vavra.
Anna's father is an animal collector in Africa. Anna's only playmates are jungle birds and animals until her father brings home Dula, a baby gorilla. Excellent photographs show Anna with all her friends.

Metamorphosis: The Magic Change by V. and A. Silverstein.
No one would ever mistake a baby kitten for an elephant. A kitten looks like a cat. But some young animals do not look like the adults they will become. A caterpillar does not look like the butterfly it will some day be. How does it happen?

Animal Astronauts: They Opened the Way to the Stars by Clyde R. Bergwin and William T. Coleman.
Monkeys, dogs, and bears have played a part in medical space research. This book tells of those experiments.

The Morgan Horse in Pictures by Margaret C. Self.
The author uses both text and photographs to show the character and the many uses of this breed of horse.

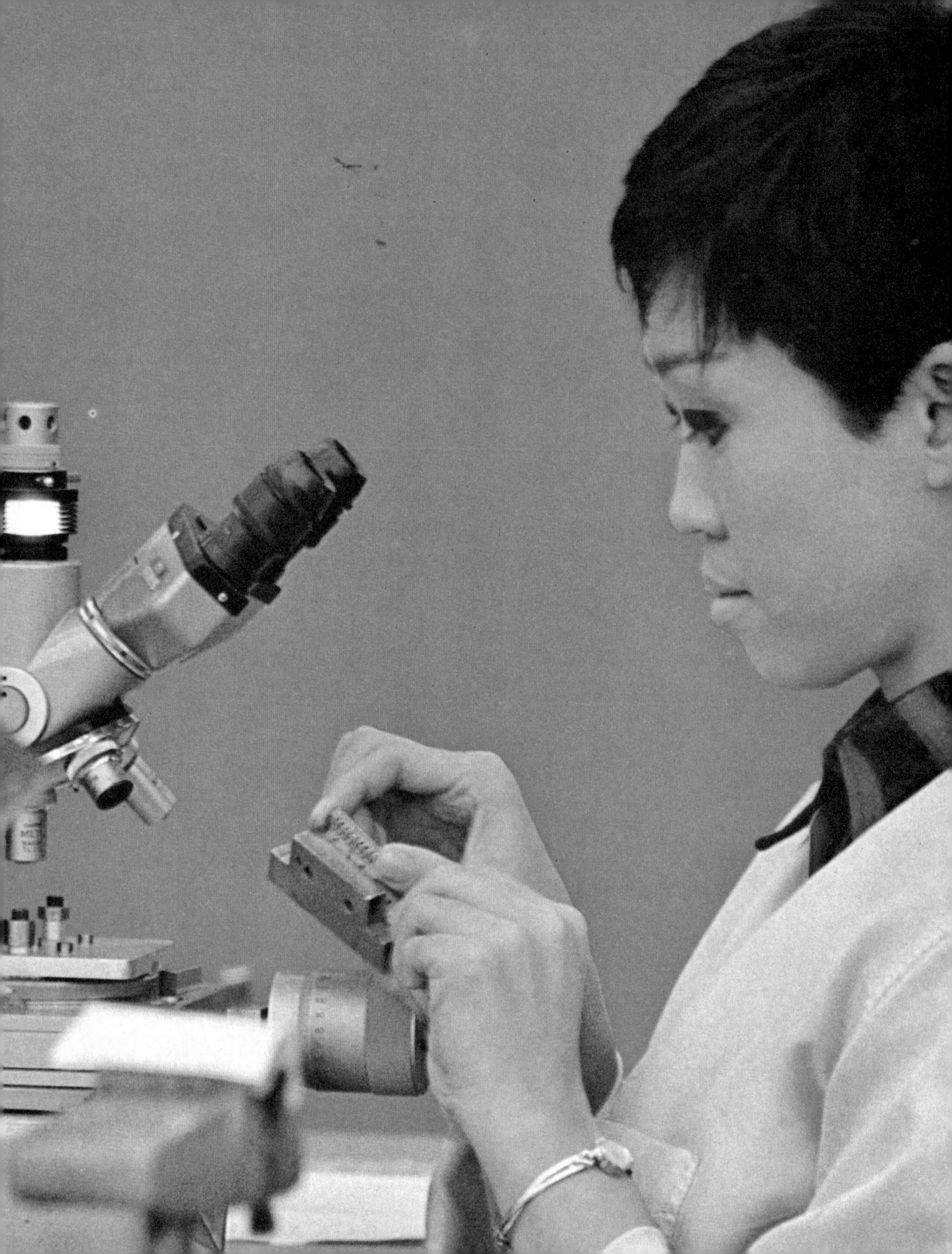

Unit 5

Putting Ideas to Work

A woman preparing slides for an electron microscope.

SKILLS LESSON

TOPICAL ORGANIZATION AND OUTLINES

Have you ever tried to put together something that has many parts, like a jigsaw puzzle? Perhaps you have noticed that, once you fit several pieces together, the other pieces are easier to put in place. Why? Because you begin to see the organization of the whole picture.

As a reader, you are often faced with a similar task: seeing how ideas go together. You have learned how details are related to main ideas. In these lessons you will study the organization of ideas in longer passages of writing—that is, in selections that contain several paragraphs.

One way of organizing ideas is by topics. We call this **topical organization.** In this kind of organization, the **major topics** follow one after the other. But each major topic may include several smaller topics (called **subtopics**). The writer may develop each subtopic by adding **details** about one.

We can picture the organization of a chapter, or an article,

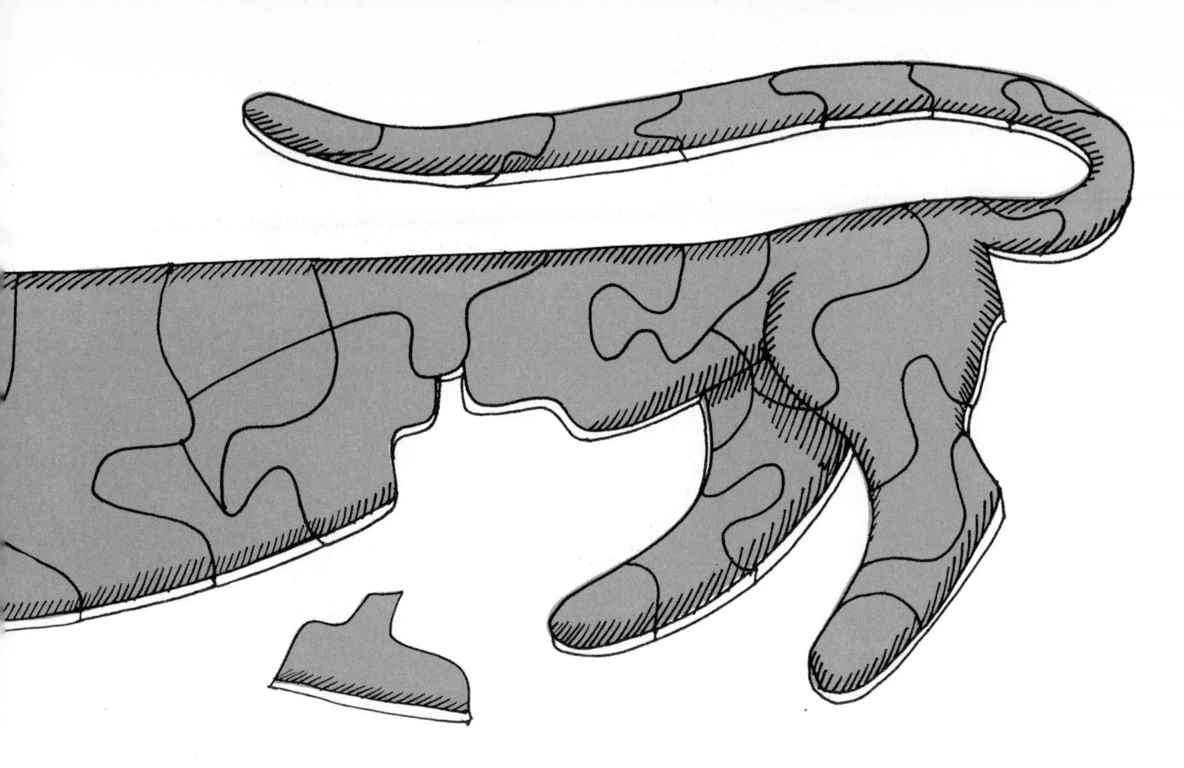

by means of an **outline.** Here is the framework for an outline that includes two major topics, several subtopics, and several details.

(Title)

I. (Major Topic)
   A. (Subtopic)
   B. (Subtopic)
      1. (Detail)
      2. (Detail)
II. (Major Topic)
   A. (Subtopic)
      1. (Detail)
      2. (Detail)
   B. (Subtopic)
   C. (Subtopic)

In topical organization, each major topic includes all of the subtopics that come under it, and each subtopic includes all the details related to it. The writer's thoughts move in an orderly way from a main idea to important details, and then to

less important details. Then he may introduce another main idea and the details that go with it.

Let's consider the relationship among these topics. Which is the major topic? Which are the subtopics?

The Gold Rush to California
The Discovery of Gold
New Gold Mines in the Klondike

It is clear that the major topic is "The Discovery of Gold." This major topic includes both subtopics, "The Gold Rush to California" and "New Gold Mines in the Klondike." Each of these subtopics tells something about the discovery of gold. Suppose the list included two more topics:

The Frozen North
Canadian Interests

These two ideas belong under "New Gold Mines in the Klondike." The beginning of the topical outline would look like this:

I. The Discovery of Gold
   A. The Gold Rush to California
   B. New Gold Mines in the Klondike
      1. The Frozen North
      2. Canadian Interests

TRY THIS

Read the list under A. On your paper arrange the list in outline form. Do the same with B and C. You will have a main topic, subtopics, and details.

A.

Continent	Sea	Lake
Ocean	Geography Terms	Temperate
Land Areas	Bodies of Water	Kinds of Climate
Tropical	Frigid	

B.

Rattlesnake	Plants	Cactus
Animals	Life in the Desert	Camel
Desert Rat	Sagebrush	Grasses

C.

Cricket	Scuba Diving
Water Sports	Horseback Riding
Swimming	Water Skiing
Land Sports	Kinds of Sports
Tennis	Running Races
Boating	Horseshoe Pitching

Previewing your assignment gives you an idea of the topic to be covere

SKILLS LESSON

FINDING THE TOPICS

Titles as Topics

In many books the units, chapters, and sections of chapters have titles. Usually those titles tell you the topics that are covered in that unit or chapter. Here are some titles from a book about American Indians. You can see that they show the topical organization of the chapter.

Chapter 2: The Aztecs
Their Way of Life
Growing Up in Aztec Society
Trading and Other Business
Religion
  Belief in the Gods
  Priests and Temples
Law and Justice

When you are studying, it is a good idea to turn the pages and look at the titles in your reading assignment *before* you begin to read. This is called **previewing.** Previewing your assignment gives you an idea of the topics to be covered and of how they relate to one another. Then, as you read, you can organize your ideas.

As you read, you can organize your ideas.

TRY THIS

The following titles appear in a chapter on modern transportation. Find the three major topics. Each major topic has two or three subtopics. One subtopic has two details. Make an outline. Use "Modern Transportation" as the title.

Travel on the Ground	Big Jets for Speed
Millions of Automobiles	Diesel Trains
Boats for Fun	Travel in the Water
Travel in the Air	Freighters
Sailboats	Propeller Planes
Passenger Ships	Helicopters
Propjets	Motor Boats

When No Topics Are Stated

It is helpful to have titles that suggest the topics for you, but this help is not always given. In much of your reading, you have to look for the topics and subtopics yourself.

When you are reading material in which the topics are not stated, it is helpful to take notes in the form of an outline. An outline helps you to

—understand how one idea relates to another;
—remember important ideas.

Let's examine the organization of the following paragraphs:

Early man found several very important uses for fire in his home. The first was as heat. Not being equipped with protective fur, man found fire extremely useful during the long, cold winter nights. Built under the shelter of a rock overhang or inside a cave, a fire gave a cozy warmth.

Fire also produced light, and light gave more meaning to the long, dark nights. It was probably by firelight that the first artists in history painted the wonderful pictures which have been found in prehistoric caves. This light also enabled the women to make clothes and the men to chip weapons.

Fire performed another valuable function, as well. All wild animals were deathly afraid of the blazing heat which singed fur and caused pain and death. So fire was perhaps man's first defensive weapon. But there were other and more important uses of fire yet to come.

It seems quite natural today to use fire for heat to cook food, but it undoubtedly took a great many years before early man learned to use fire in that way. Perhaps it came about accidentally when some raw meat fell into a fire. Or maybe hunters

found the burned bodies of animals after a forest fire. However it was discovered, the use of fire for cooking was extremely important in the history of man.

All of these paragraphs tell something about the uses that prehistoric man had for fire. Therefore, a good title for this short article would be "Early Man's Uses of Fire." That would be a good title, too, for the outline of this article.

What four uses of fire did the writer tell about? He described one use in each paragraph, so you know your outline will have four major topics. You may wish to note subtopics in your outline, too. For example, the second paragraph tells three things that light made possible. The outline will look like this:

Early Man's Use of Fire

1. For heat
II. For light
    A. For painting
    B. For making clothes
    C. For making weapons
III. As a defense against animals
IV. For cooking

TRY THIS

Read the following article about Malaya. Make an outline showing its topical organization. The title of your outline should tell what the whole article is about.

As a newly independent nation, Malaya faced several problems. More than half of the Malayans were able to read and write, but the government wanted a higher standard of education than that. How could the adults be educated further? Children also needed education. They were crowding the schools. The country must find money for building new schools and for training teachers.

The new government also knew that the people's health should be improved. Smallpox, malaria, and other diseases were widespread. Health workers were needed throughout the country. But much of Malaya is jungle, and travel is difficilt. Airplanes, trucks, and boats were found to carry doctors and nurses to the people who needed them.

An important food in the diet of Malayans is rice. But the country grows only about half of the rice it needs. Agricultural experts were called on to improve methods of farming. Help was needed, too, for increasing the catch of fish and for raising more livestock.

Some paragraphs give examples.

Different Kinds of Paragraphs

In the article about Malaya, each paragraph was about a major topic. There were three paragraphs in the article, and three Roman numerals in your outline.

But you should not expect that every paragraph in an article will give you a major topic for an outline. Writers use paragraphs for different purposes. Let's look at different kinds of paragraphs.

Some paragraphs give examples. To give information to the reader, a writer presents many ideas and facts. He may give several examples to help the reader understand one main idea.

Paragraphs that give examples usually do not state a new main idea. Their purpose is to explain or to illustrate an idea that has been stated in another paragraph. It is usually easy to tell when you come to an **example paragraph.** It may contain such words as "for example," or "as an illustration," or "for instance."

The next two paragraphs show how an example paragraph is related to the paragraph before it. The first one states a main idea and the second one gives examples that explain the main idea.

About a hundred years ago seven eighths of the American people lived on farms or in small villages. Today less than one third live there. The great majority of Americans today live in cities or in suburbs of cities. The rapid growth of cities brought new problems, some of which are yet to be solved.

For example, there are problems of health protection. A city needs an adequate supply of pure water. Garbage and sewage must be disposed of. Pure, clean air is needed; this is a problem in many modern cities. Other examples are the problems of handling traffic, of crime prevention, of fighting fire, and of providing for play and recreation.

Some paragraphs make transitions. Sometimes writers use a paragraph to move from one idea to another. Such a paragraph is called a **transition paragraph,** because *transition* means getting from one place to another or from one idea to another. A transition paragraph is a kind of bridge. It reminds the reader of what has gone before and gives him a hint of what is coming. A transition paragraph may introduce a new topic, but usually it does not contain an important statement about the new topic. Often a transition paragraph contains ques-

tions to start the reader thinking about the new topic to come.

Notice how the paragraph below serves as a transition between two topics.

You can see that taking care of an ordinary kind of pet is not very difficult if one has the right information. But what if your pet is an unusual one? Let's consider the problems that would face the owner of an antelope.

The topic of the paragraph that came before this one must have been "The care of common pets." What will the next paragraph be about?

Some paragraphs summarize. Another kind of paragraph that may not introduce a new main idea is the **summary paragraph.** As the name suggests, this paragraph brings together the main ideas of several previous paragraphs. The summary paragraph is often at the end of a section or a chapter.

A good reader always notices a summary paragraph. He knows that the paragraph will not express new ideas or give new information. But he knows that it is an important paragraph because it will help him to organize and remember the important ideas he has just read.

Usually you can identify the summary paragraph by recognizing the main ideas presented in earlier paragraphs.

Summary paragraphs may begin with phrases like "In summary," "To review," "As we have noted," or "Considering all our earlier points."

Study this paragraph:

We have now seen how lions obtain their food at night and how big-game hunters beat the bushes to drive out the fierce beasts. We have learned how tigers kill large numbers of cattle every year. Stories about man-eating tigers have also shown us that tigers will kill men if they become extremely hungry. The tiger is one of the most challenging of all hunted beasts.

Several phrases hint that this paragraph is a summary paragraph. Can you find them? Which statements in this paragraph could have been main ideas of earlier paragraphs?

TRY THIS

Decide what purpose each paragraph serves. Then write the kind of paragraph you think each is – **example, transition,** or **summary.**

A. There are certain trees and shrubs that will help to attract birds to your yard. You can make your own plan and do the planting yourself. But before we get into details, let's consider some of the basic questions you should ask yourself.

B. Most magnets we use today are man-made, but there are natural magnets, too. One natural magnet is the lodestone, a particularly interesting kind of rock. Let us see where the lodestone gets its magnetic force.

C. William Beebe was a pioneer in exploring the ocean world. His early dives opened the way to an unknown region. To the deep-sea divers of today his equipment may seem crude. But they owe a debt to that crude equipment and to the courage of the man who used it to descend to record depths in the ocean.

D. As an illustration of how sound travels through hard conductors, try listening through some hard sound-conductors. Put an alarm clock at one end of a wooden bench; or put it at one end of a board five feet long. Place your ear at the opposite end. You will hear the ticking through the wood.

WHAT DID YOU LEARN?

1. What is an outline?
2. How can titles be a help in reading?
3. How can you find the topic of a paragraph if it is not stated?
4. Some paragraphs do not introduce a major topic. Tell what these paragraphs do.

■ A sharp-edged stone, a stick, and long, tough vines—how could these three things have kept man from perishing hundreds of thousands of years ago?

Man's First Inventions

by SAMUEL EPSTEIN *and* BERYL WILLIAMS

Before beginning to read, preview the topics in the selection by reading the headings. This will help you to see how the ideas are organized.

The next time the alarm clock wakes us early in the morning, we might pretend we are prehistoric man waking up 500,000 years ago. Of course, there are no written records of life in that ancient time. That's why we call it prehistoric—meaning *before history.* But we have a rough idea of the kind of life he woke up to. It wasn't an easy one.

In the first place there was no alarm clock to wake him. How could there be? Metals were unknown and no one had even thought to invent a wheel. And what kind of an alarm clock can you build without wheels and steel springs?

So we'll have to imagine that he's been awakened by the roaring of some ferocious beast outside the house. But wait—there weren't any houses yet. He's living in a cave.

Very well then: he hears a roaring outside the cave and, being a brave hero, throws back his warm blanket and . . .

But no! There is no blanket. No one yet knows about wool or cotton or how to weave them into cloth, so there are no blankets, and no clothes either.

Not having to dress saves him a lot of time. He reaches for his gun . . . Impossible! No one has yet invented guns. It is with only his bare hands for weapons that he leaps to his feet and heads for the mouth of the cave. And there in the darkness, only a short distance away, he sees two evil, gleaming eyes. He hears the savage growl in the beast's throat. He faces the enemy, hands clenched, muscles tensed for the leap.

But just before he hurls himself forward, a sharp pain reminds him that he hurt his hand the day before, trying to smash a nut. He realizes that with only one good hand he is no match for this beast.

A STONE TO STRIKE WITH

Suddenly he has an idea. If he could use something instead of that bruised and aching hand . . .

He gropes on the ground. His fingers close over a rock that fits neatly into his palm. It is much harder than a fist. He leaps forward, the rock held high. It comes down hard. It strikes squarely. He has vanquished the enemy. And he has become a hero.

Not for killing the beast—many beasts have been killed before. He is a hero because he is the first person to have used something other than his own body to do his work.

That stone in his hand is much more than a stone. It is the forerunner of the hammer, and of all the tools man's ingenuity has devised since that dim day so long ago. He has started civilization on its way.

DISCOVERIES COME FIRST

The prehistoric man who first used a rock as a weapon didn't really invent anything; he made a discovery. He discovered that a stone held in the hand did more than protect his hand from injury;

it also increased the power of his blow. A stone is harder and heavier than a hand. Therefore it could strike harder and more heavily.

Prehistoric man was strong—stronger than the man of today. He had to be strong in order to survive in his wild and dangerous world.

But some of his enemies—the saber-toothed tiger, the huge woolly rhinoceros, the great elephant-like creature called a mammoth—were even stronger. Any of them could kill a man with a single blow or tear him apart with fierce claws or tusks. Yet man had to compete with these enemies for food and had to protect himself from their attack.

Two important things gave man an advantage over his enemies. First, he stood upright, while his enemies walked on four feet. Thus man could use his hands—his "forefeet"—to protect himself and to perform many tasks.

Second, he had a better brain than his enemies had. He could think better than they could. It was his brain that discovered how a stone could be used instead of a fist.

A SHARP EDGE AND A SHARP POINT

His brain led him to two more very important discoveries.

He discovered that a sharp-edged stone could serve him as well as sharp claws served his enemies. With a sharp stone he could cut up the animals he killed for food. With a sharp stone he could even scrape the hide clean and use an animal skin as a protection from the cold. His simple sharp-edged stone was the beginning of the tool we call a knife.

He also discovered that he could use a stick in the same way his enemies used their tusks—to dig up roots that were good to eat. He learned that the best stick for digging was one that had a pointed end like a mammoth's tusk. Often he looked for a long time to find a stick that had a sharp point. And finally he learned how to point the tip of a stick with his sharp stone.

Now he had three important discoveries: a stone to strike with, a sharp-edged stone, and a pointed stick. He would eventually do a great many things with these simple objects.

THE FIRST INVENTION

And one day man made a real invention.

He had been using his heavy stone for a long time—for hundreds, perhaps thousands of years. But he was still in great danger. He had to come very close to an enemy in order to strike it with a stone. He had to come so close that often the enemy struck him before his stone could do its work.

Suppose—man's brain suggested one day—suppose he fastened the rock to a stick. Then he could stand some distance away from an enemy and still strike at it.

With strips torn from one of his animal hides, he clumsily tied a stone to a stout branch. When it was well fastened, he tried swinging the stick over his head and letting the stone strike against a tree. It made a good, solid thump. It was safer to use than a stone alone. And it struck much harder than a stone held in the hand, because a stone at the end of a stick moved faster.

He struck the tree again and felt very proud of himself. And he should have been proud. He had taken two natural objects—a stone and a stick—and had combined them to form something which never existed before. He had made the first hammer.

Man had become a true inventor!

But it is important to remember how this invention came about. First, the stones and sticks had to exist so they could be discovered and made use of. Second, there had to be a need. Man's brain went to work because man needed help in his fight for survival. And third, the inventor had to know what others before him had done—how they had used stones in order to strike heavy blows.

Man's brain—man's ingenuity—invented the hammer. But the invention could not have happened without those other three things: the raw material, the need, and the work of earlier men. All inventions, even today, depend on those same three things. They are very important to remember.

HOW THE AX CAME ABOUT

We can see, for example, how all three were necessary to bring about the invention of the ax.

Sharp stones existed, and man discovered their usefulness.

Then there came a time when man needed to do something which his sharpest stone could not do. Perhaps he needed to cut down a tree, and he found that no matter how hard he struck it with his stone, he could make only scratches in the tree's bark.

But suddenly he remembered that tying a stick to a stone increased the strength of the stone's blow. And so he tied a stick to his sharp stone and was able to chop the tree down with little difficulty.

He had made another important invention.

The materials, the need, the work that has gone before—they all appear in the story of every invention.

The materials have always existed.

The metals, the chemicals—all the vast number of things which go into our most complex inventions today—have always been a part of the earth.

Some of these materials were hidden so well that it took man a very long time to find them. Some, like iron, were so mixed up with other things that it took man many years to learn how to separate them. Some lay deep beneath the surface of the earth, where early man could not reach them. Today we are able to sift through tons of crushed rock to obtain a tiny pinch of uranium, and we dig thousands of feet into the earth to find minerals or oil.

Still other things—like fire and electricity—were so terrifying in their natural state that it took man many years to learn to tame and control them for his own use. To early man, lightning was a danger; today we know lightning is a form of electricity—and electricity is one of our most valuable possessions. Fire, which can destroy vast forests, is usually our faithful servant. We can summon it today simply by striking a match.

All things, in one form or another, were here from the very beginning. Slowly man learned to make use of them, as his needs increased.

WHAT DID EARLY MAN NEED?

What kind of things did man need in those days?

Five hundred thousand years ago—even as recently as thirty thousand years ago—man was what we call a forager; he searched for his food. He searched for animals and killed them for meat. He searched for fish and caught them with his bare hands. He searched for berries and other fruits and wild vegetables. And he discovered that seeds of wild grasses were also good for food. These were the ancestors of today's grains.

Of course, it wasn't always easy to catch and kill animals for food. The bison and the small horse that roamed the world then could both run very fast, and it was difficult to catch them. Man could seldom get close enough to strike at either a horse or a bison with a stone or a hammer.

He tried to throw stones at them, and sometimes he was lucky—but not very often. A light stone, which he could throw a long distance, was not heavy enough to kill. And a heavy stone couldn't be thrown very far.

THE SPEAR

Perhaps, one day, a man sat at the edge of a clearing looking at the herd of bison feeding some distance away. The man was hungry. If he could kill one of those bison, he would have enough for a great feast. But if he ventured into the clearing, they would see him and run off.

Perhaps he sat for a long time, growing more and more hungry. He *needed* food. He began to think of all the ways man had already invented to kill animals. And suddenly he thought of a new way, based on those old ones.

He looked around until he found a stone with a sharp point. Next he pulled a branch from a tree—a long straight branch—and trimmed off the twigs. Then, with some long, tough vines, he fastened the pointed stone to the very end of the branch.

Holding his new weapon in his hand, he advanced to the edge of the clearing. He raised the long, stone-tipped shaft aloft and hurled it at the nearest animal. To his great delight it flew straight to its target, point first. The stone buried itself in the bison's flesh, and the animal fell.

Man had a new source of food. He had a new weapon. He had invented the spear.

MAN LEARNS TO PLANT

His need led him to invent other uses for that sharp point.

Sometimes, when he walked long weary miles to the place where he had once before found berries or grains, he discovered that wandering animals had already eaten them all. Man wished there were more of those berries and grains, and that they were nearer the stream where he lived in his cave. He knew that there would be more next year, of course. New plants came up each spring from seeds that dropped in the fall, and new berries appeared every summer.

Suddenly the idea came to him. Why couldn't he carry seeds home and put them in the ground close to his cave? Why couldn't he make a small hole in the ground with a sharpened stick and drop the seeds in? This is just what he did.

The first seeds he planted with his sharp stick were the beginning of today's great farms.

Today those first simple tools—the hammer, the sharp edge, the sharp point—seem too simple to be worth remembering. But without them man would probably have perished long ago, destroyed by his enemies.

With them he created the world we know.

Without modern tools or machines, the Indians of Central and South America built tremendous walls, forts, columns, and bridges. How did they do it?

America's Earliest Engineers

by MARY ELTING *and* FRANKLIN FOLSOM

The title tells the topic. The second paragraph asks a question that suggests what will be said about the topic. Watch for other questions that suggest what is to come. Look also for paragraphs that give examples.

How in the world did they do it?

How did Indians, long ago, manage to accomplish some of the tremendous things they did? Archeologists are not always sure, but they have worked out some theories.

How did ancient builders cut and shape huge blocks of stone? An abandoned quarry in Maya country gives one answer. For some reason, men stopped work in this quarry and went away, leaving their stone chisels and hammers and an example of every stage in their work.

First the stonecutters chiseled into solid rock until they had almost a whole block of it cut out. Then they used big wooden crowbars to break the block loose.

Quarry workers in Peru left unfinished jobs that reveal another ancient engineering trick. First they drilled a row of holes in the rock. Next they pounded dry wooden wedges into the holes. Then they drenched the wedges with water. The wood absorbed water, swelled up, and cracked the stone block free.

How did they move a huge block for miles and miles?

Often they used logs as rollers. Men pushed and pulled, the logs turned, and the block would slide forward. In at least one place, the Mayas may have slid big rocks along a road that was greased with slippery fresh mud.

The Incas built tremendous stone walls without the help of any machinery. Archeologists figure that thirty thousand men must have labored for eighty years on the great fortress called Sacsahuaman (SAHK-sah-wah-MAHN) near Cuzco, the Inca capital. Many of the stones they

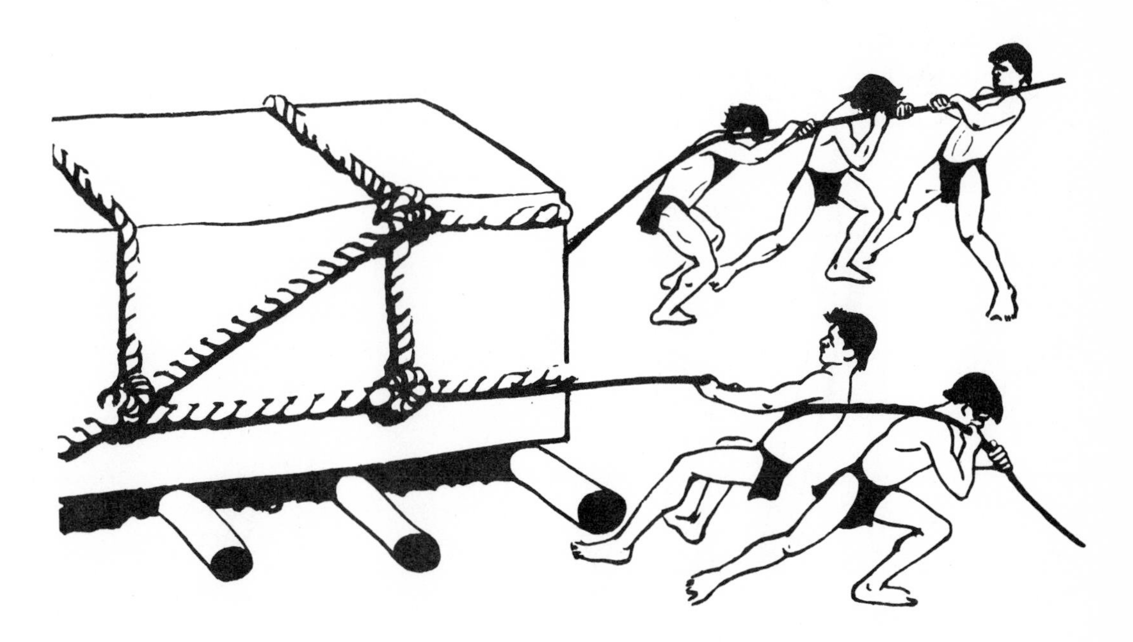

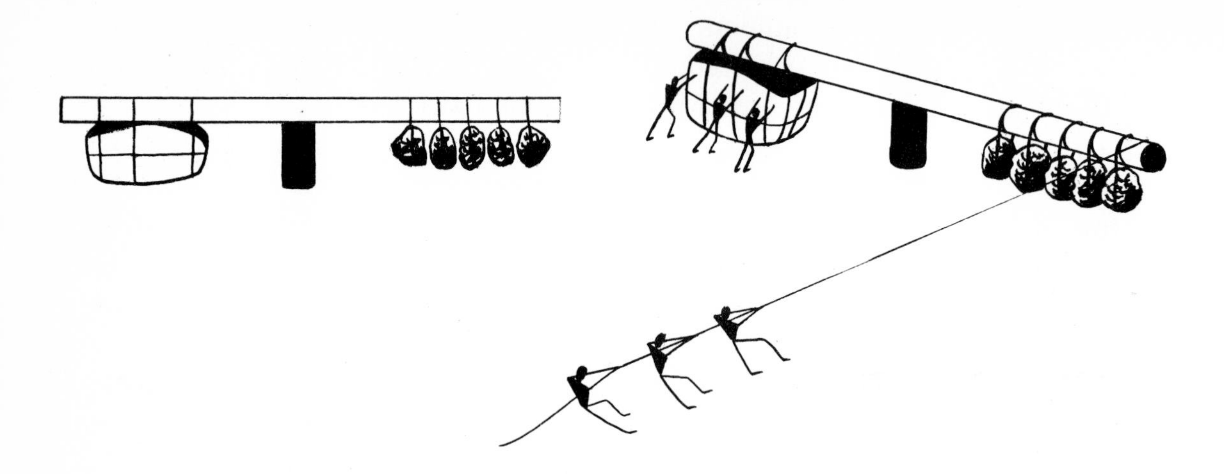

used weighed twenty tons or more. The pictures show the way in which one expert thinks they may have moved some of the huge blocks:

(1) They set a post in the ground, then balanced a strong log on top of it so that the log could swing around without falling off. Next they tied the big stone to one end of the log. On the other end of the log they tied bags. Into these they put stones that were small enough to be easily handled.

(2) The bags full of small stones at one end of the log finally balanced the big stone on the other end and lifted it off the ground—just the way several small girls on one end of a see-saw can lift up a large man on the other end.

(3) When the big block was off the ground, men pulled on ropes and swung the log halfway around a circle. The big block had now changed places with the bags of

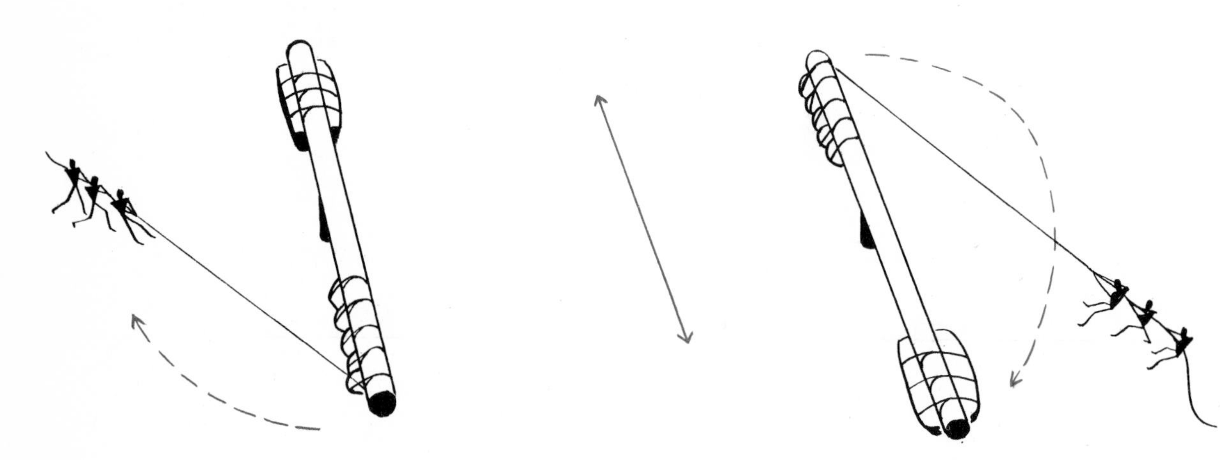

little stones. The big block had been moved a whole log-length closer to the building site.

(4) Now the men untied the stones and let them rest on the ground. A new post was set up farther down the road. Again the men balanced the log on the post and repeated the whole process.

How did Indian builders manage to raise a big stone into position high above the ground?

They made a sloping roadway of earth up to the level where they wanted to put the stone. Then they hauled the stone up on rollers. When it was in position they removed the road! Archeologists know that this method was used in Peru because they found there an unfinished building with the sloping road still in position.

How did the Mayas set up a heavy stone column? Look at the pictures below.

To make the column stand perfectly straight, they used a plumb bob, just as a modern builder does.

How did the Mayas build a roof over a room, using pieces of stone that were too small to reach from wall to wall?

On top of one wall they laid a

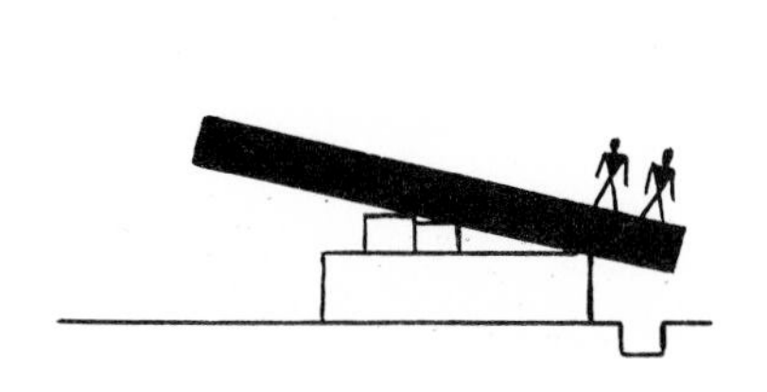

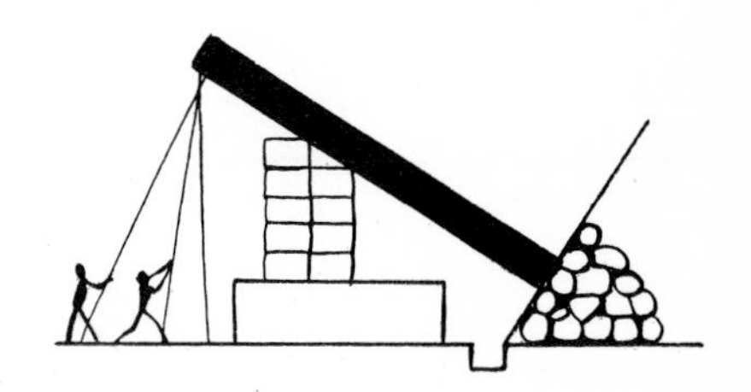

row of stones which jutted out into the room. On top of the opposite wall they did the same thing. Then on these stones they kept laying row after row of stones which jutted out farther and farther until the front ends met over the center of the room.

A great deal of weight pressed down on the stones where they stuck out over empty space. To keep them from falling into the room, equal weight had to push down on the other ends of the stones. The builders piled up more masonry to do the balancing.

Engineers say a roof like this is built in the form of a *corbeled arch.* The Mayas also used this kind of arch in constructing stone bridges. So did the Incas.

The corbeled arch was a clever invention, but it had its disadvantages, too. A Mayan stone roof was tremendously heavy. In order to hold it up, the Mayas built thick walls. Thick walls meant small rooms. A Mayan temple, which was huge on the outside, had surprisingly little space inside. Nevertheless, simply by using small stones in a new way, people had learned how to do big things they could not do before.

What could you do with hot water coming from the ground? A young man in Iceland answers this question.

Grapes grow in Iceland's greenhouse gardens.

Hot Springs in Iceland

by STURGES F. CARY

As you read, notice which paragraphs explain or illustrate the author's main ideas. Watch, too, for transition paragraphs that move from one main idea to another.

"Yes, bananas grow in Iceland," said Gudjon, "though you might not believe it on a day like this."

It was a wet, raw afternoon. The outside temperature hadn't risen above a bone-chilling 40 degrees.

Inside the glass-enclosed garden, though, it was a steamy 80 degrees. And on a ten-foot-tall plant hung bunches of small, green, but genuine bananas. Nearby, other tropical plants flaunted their lush green leaves.

Stepping into this jungle from the bleak and treeless Icelandic plain was like entering another world.

The director of the greenhouse pointed to a plant in one corner. "The day before yesterday, this pineapple was growing in Nigeria. It arrived by air just this morning. Here's an orange tree from California. We have fig trees and coffee bushes, too, all growing in the warm climate they like.

"How do we do it? On most days we don't get enough sunshine to keep a greenhouse warm, and we can't afford to heat greenhouses with expensive imported fuel. So we use something that's almost as cheap as sunlight, cleaner than any fuel, and absolutely constant in temperature—hot water from underground."

The director pointed to rows of bare metal pipes that ran around the inside walls and across the underside of the roof.

"Hot water is flowing through these pipes, water that we pump from hot springs right beside this building. Like radiators, the pipes give off heat and keep the air in here as warm as the tropics."

In greenhouses, and in many homes too, Icelanders overcome the chill of their subarctic climate by tapping water heated by the fires of the earth. The water comes from more than a thousand hot springs. They well up in all parts of the country—on the plains, in the hills, beside the sea; they occur even under the sea, bubbling up in plain sight at low tide. In several places where hot springs come in groups, Icelanders have built acres of greenhouses. The biggest ones are at Hveragerdi. One of the few inland towns of Iceland, it draws the traveler's alarmed attention from miles away. The whole place seems to be on fire. Clouds of what seems to be smoke billow around the houses. But a closer look shows the "smoke" is steam from dozens of hot springs.

Hveragerdi's banana garden always astonishes visitors from abroad.

"We aren't in the banana business," the director said with a smile. "This particular greenhouse is run by the Icelandic government for experiments with tropical plants. The greenhouses next door, however, raise plants to sell. Flowers grow in a good many of them, because green plants and blossoms mean a lot to us in our bleak land.

"More important, our gardens-under-glass produce food—grapes, for example, and our total supply of cucumbers and tomatoes. I

Iceland has more than a thousand hot springs. Here is one.

don't believe any other country raises its entire commercial supply of a vegetable in greenhouses. In this way we can have fresh vegetables seven or eight months a year. We can't operate the greenhouse gardens the year round because, here at the edge of the Arctic, the winter daylight is too short. Plants need light as well as heat in order to grow."

While the big commercial greenhouses produce for the market, many farmers raise food and flowers for themselves in hothouse gardens warmed by hot springs on their own land.

Iceland's hot springs are the warmed-up leftovers from dying volcanoes. After a volcano stops

A few hot springs are spouters. A fountain of steam jets up to seventy feet in this spouter.

erupting, hot rocks below ground take a long time to cool. Rain water works its way into the earth, percolates among the hot rocks, and seeps back to the surface as a hot spring.

A few of these springs are spouters. Every so often they empty their basins by tossing out the water in a hot shower bath. These spouting springs draw their water from cracks that run deep into the earth. The pressure of the water at the top of the "pipe" and the heat of volcanic rocks at the bottom raise the temperature of the water at the bottom far above the boiling point. Finally the temperature rises so high that water at the bottom flashes into steam and blows out the hole.

Hveragerdi has a spouter. Every hour it heaves several bathtubfuls of water about forty feet into the air. That's a puny effort compared to what goes on at another spouter an hour's ride away. There, on a lava slope, clouds of steam boil up from dozens of pools and rivulets of hot water. A little way up the slope lies a saucer-shaped pool about thirty feet across. The smell of sulfur hangs over it. This spot is Iceland's number one tourist attraction, "Great Geysir." The word comes from the Icelandic verb *geysan* (to rush forth furiously). Geysir had given its name to all other spouting springs. (The biggest are in New Zealand and in the United States at Yellowstone Park.)

When Geysir is getting ready for its act, it gives a warning rumble. The earth quivers, and then a dome of water rises like a bell. With a whoosh of steam, a fountain of near-boiling water jets up 100 feet, sometimes 200 feet. The spray rises and falls, drenching everything around the pool. One

Scottish sea captain, watching in awe, remarked, "There's power enough to sail half a dozen Queen Marys right across the Atlantic."

At last the spout droops and falls back. Then one can walk right into the empty basin and look down the narrow throat to the water bubbling far below.

While Geysir attracts the tourists, less spectacular hot springs are working hard, too. Some have served for centuries as preheated laundry tubs.

Missionaries long ago baptized converts in certain warm springs, because Icelanders refused to be dunked in cold arctic water. Snorri Sturluson, greatest genius of early times in Iceland, thought of original ways to use a hot spring beside his house. He made himself an outdoor bathtub. And he piped hot water into the house to heat the rooms.

It took seven hundred years for Snorri's ideas to catch on, and then it was a British traveler who saw the possibilities. About fifty years ago Sir William Craigie suggested, "Why not pipe hot springs into Reykjavik and heat the houses? You Icelanders could save a lot of fuel that way."

Nobody had ever tried heating a town with volcanic hot water. Engineers had no experience to guide them. Cautiously the city of Reykjavik went ahead. It bought from private owners the right to use hot springs near town. Engineers discovered that, by boring through solid rock at the right spots, they could tap streams of hot water that never varied in volume or temperature.

In a test project, engineers piped hot water to a hospital, two schools, and about sixty homes. Everything worked fine. Planning began for a bigger plant. Wells were drilled at Reykir, about ten miles outside Reykjavik.

Then World War II broke out. Germans occupied Denmark, and this cut off the supply of materials Iceland had ordered. Fortunately the United States provided materials to finish the job. By 1943 an artificial river of hot water was on its way to Reykjavik. It runs inside a boxlike concrete casing that winds like a great gray snake alongside the road from Reykir. The conduit ends at a cluster of huge tanks on a hillside above Reykjavik.

"Those tanks are the hot-water reservoir," Gudjon explained. He pointed out that 150 miles of piping carry a million gallons of water a day under the streets and into the houses. After being used, the water runs off through the sewers to the ocean.

About two out of every three houses in the city use the natural hot water for heating. New wells are being developed to serve more homes.

Under the windows in Gudjon's apartment stand metal radiators. On a cool day he turns a knob, and the volcanic hot water flows through the radiator, warming the room.

Each house has a meter, and the householder pays the city of Reykjavik for the hot water he uses. Natural hot water not only gives the city government an income, but saves the cost of buying many shiploads of fuel. Every pound of coal and every gallon of oil must come from abroad. Iceland has no fuel of her own except peat and a little brushwood.

Though Reykjavik's name means "smoky bay," smoke never clouds the air because so little fuel is burned. Reykjavik calls itself "the smokeless city at the gate of the Arctic Circle." Lucky people! Those who use the hot water have no furnaces to tend. Shirts stay clean for days, and laundering in the soft, volcanic hot water keeps them snow-white.

New schools are usually built near hot springs. The water heats the school and also fills the swimming pool, for dozens of schools have their own pool. Reykjavik also has two big public pools, one indoors and one outdoors. They open early in the morning and don't close until well into the evening. Winter and summer, many boys and girls take a dip in the outdoor pool on their way to or from school, or both. If it weren't for the natural warm water, Iceland couldn't afford the luxury of swimming pools.

"But they aren't really luxuries," argued Gudjon. "In our island country many men are fishermen or sailors. More people die from drowning than from any other kind of accident. That's why our government insists that every boy and girl learn to swim."

Some farmers are experimenting with yet another use of the natural hot water. They have cut irrigation channels to their fields from nearby hot springs. This warm-water irrigation, it is claimed, permits fields in sheltered spots to produce almost any kind of vegetable.

Besides using the warmth of the natural hot water, Icelanders are trying to harness the fires of the earth in another way—for electric power. Engineers hope to tap mighty steam jets deep in the earth and then use this steam to produce electric power. This plan is still a dream of the future, but some day Iceland's hot springs may light homes as well as warming them.

Farmer, inventor, mathematician, astronomer—Benjamin Banneker was one of the most remarkable men in the colony of Maryland. He lived in the time of George Washington, and, like Washington, made a lasting contribution to the young United States.

He Reached for the Stars

by LAVINIA DOBLER *and* EDGAR A. TOPPIN

There are many details in this selection. By noting how they are related, you can find the important topics—the kinds of work that Benjamin Banneker did.

Young Benjamin Banneker sat on the doorstep of his grandmother's house in Maryland, looking at the night sky with all its stars. His grandmother sat beside him. Suddenly a sparkling white object shot across the heavens. Seconds later it disappeared.

"Where did it go?" he asked, puzzled. The boy leaned his head back as far as he could, searching eagerly for the mysterious star. But his sharp black eyes could not find it.

"Grandma, where *did* the star go?" he asked. Benjamin often asked his grandmother questions about things he did not understand.

"I do not know," she answered, shaking her head. Her straight brown hair, streaked with white, was drawn severely back from her face. "Maybe the Book can tell us," she added, as she got up from the wooden step.

Together they went inside the weather-beaten cabin. His grandmother lighted a candle, and Benjamin, standing on his bare toes, reached for the Bible on the shelf. He carried the heavy book to the crudely hewn table.

Mrs. Banneker had taught Benjamin his letters. On Sunday mornings Benjamin used to read the Bible to her. She hoped he would grow up to be a religious man.

His grandmother, who had learned to read as a girl growing up in England, turned the pages

and searched for passages about the stars and the heavens. But she could not find the answer about the shooting star.

"You are a bright boy and you can read," she said proudly. "Someday you will find the answer," she prophesied. "Then you can explain why a star falls."

"I will find the answer," Benjamin said, looking out the doorway at the mysterious black sky. There was a look of determination in his eyes.

Benjamin's grandmother had taught him many wonderful things about nature. He knew where to find roots, grasses, fruits, nuts, and gay-colored berries that were good to eat. His sensitive nose quivered like a rabbit's at sounds and smells. He knew when the howling wind changed its course. He knew when a deer or fox had been in their fields or orchards. He knew how to tell the age of a tree.

But he could not understand what had happened to the star, and why his grandmother could not tell him. It remained a puzzle to bother him for a long time.

When Benjamin Banneker was growing up, Maryland was a colony belonging to England. Benjamin was born on November 9, 1731, three and one-half months before George Washington. His birthplace was his grandparents' farm near the Patapsco River, about ten miles from Baltimore. He had three sisters, Mollie, Minta, and Tillie.

One brisk spring morning in 1737, five-year-old Benjamin woke up and scrambled into his clothes. All he could think of was "This is the day!" Today his parents and his grandparents were going to deliver several thousand pounds of fine tobacco to Richard Gist. The tobacco had been grown on his grandparents' farm.

At the breakfast table, the family was unusually quiet. Benjamin was bursting with eagerness. He couldn't sit quietly in his chair and eat. Finally he said, "This *is* the day, Mama, isn't it?"

She smiled and said, "Yes, Benjamin, this is the day!"

His parents, Robert and Mary Banneker, had waited many years for this chance. Now, with the earnings from the tobacco, they were going to buy land. They were well aware that they were assuming a big responsibility. It would mean putting in longer hours each day than they were now doing. But both were hard workers and liked to be outdoors, and their children were old enough to help them.

The purchase of this land proved to be a good investment. People often talked about the fine crops

this family produced, even when there was no rain and other farmers had poor crops.

Benjamin's father had grown crops in Africa and perhaps felt closer to the soil than his neighbors. So he had dug ditches. Then when the soil was dry, the water from the deep springs located on the hill irrigated the parched land. He and his wife Mary had also built gates and locks to control the flow of the spring water. These same springs, known as the Bannaky springs, also supplied water to the land owned by Benjamin's grandparents.

Benjamin also started to school that year. He could hardly wait for the Monday morning in September. At last he would have many books to read. Then, too, he had so many questions he wanted to ask. If the teacher didn't know all the answers, then he surely could find them in the books.

"You will like school," his grandmother told him. "Mind what your teacher tells you and be respectful." She patted his head. "Soon you will be at the head of your class."

"I'll try, Grandma," Benjamin said, as he started out the door.

The school was a short way from the farm, and Benjamin ran all the way, clutching the slate in his hand. But when he reached the schoolhouse, he straightened his tie and brushed his white shirt and walked slowly up the steps. The Quaker schoolmaster was at the desk talking to several children.

Until he was sent to school, the only book Benjamin knew was the large Bible he read at his grandmother's house. But now that he was going to school, he was fascinated by the books his teacher showed him.

Every school day was a new adventure for Benjamin. He listened carefully to every word the teacher said. Benjamin repeated the words to himself, so that his way of saying them would be the way his teacher spoke.

But it was arithmetic that he liked best of all. He quickly learned how to add and subtract, and he liked multiplication and division.

The first time the teacher gave the students problems to solve, Benjamin had the answers in no time at all. He raised his hand to let the teacher know that he was finished with his work.

"Have you worked all the problems?" the teacher asked, as he peered over his eyeglasses.

"Yes, sir," Benjamin answered.

"Have you checked them? You know you must prove them."

Benjamin nodded.

"Bring your slate to my desk," the teacher said.

Benjamin walked proudly to the front of the room and placed the slate on the big oak desk.

"The answers are correct," the teacher said a few minutes later. "I shall have to assign you much more difficult problems."

In 1746, when he was fifteen, his nine years of schooling were over. Benjamin missed going to school, especially because there were so few books at home. He continued to be a careful observer of nature and listened intently to anyone who could give him information.

As a young man, Benjamin Banneker did not have any desire to leave his family or the farm. He seemed to prefer to remain at home, for there was a close family tie. His parents' farm was one of the best kept in that part of Maryland. The Bannekers had fine horses and cows, healthy fruit trees, and many hives of bees.

Benjamin was twenty-eight when his father died. Seventy-two acres of farmland were left to the only son, Benjamin, and his mother, as joint heirs. The remainder was left to Benjamin's three sisters.

Since Benjamin had worked with his father, he was able to continue living comfortably from the produce grown on the farm, including the fruit, vegetables, and honey from the apiary. His mother, Mary, who like his grandmother knew about the herbs that grew wild in that section, did most of the selling of the farm products.

Benjamin plowed and hoed the fields, planted crops and cared for the bees, but he also found time to study mathematics.

People who knew Benjamin Banneker were impressed with his ability. They often commented on his keen mind, and the ease with which he solved difficult mathematical problems. When, in 1761, he built a wooden clock, his fame spread far beyond Baltimore County. At that time Benjamin was thirty years old.

Banneker had never seen a clock, but he had seen a pocket watch which served as his model. Probably there was not a clock within fifty miles of the farm. He worked a long time on the clock. He had few of the right tools that would have made the work easier, but he did have the watch, which he took apart. The clock he made was many times larger than the watch.

A century later, an article in The Atlantic Monthly described the wooden clock: ". . . this was the first clock of which every portion was made in America. It is certain that it was as purely his own invention as if none had ever been made before."

When word got around that a comparatively uneducated person had made a clock with wooden parts that worked, visitors came for miles around to the Banneker farm.

One person declared that the clock was "perfect in every detail, for years it struck the hours with faultless precision, and was considered a mechanical masterpiece by all who saw it."

As the days went by, people became more aware of Banneker's remarkable memory, his mathematical ability, and his excellent English. He was now recognized as one of the best mathematicians in that area, for he was astonishingly rapid in solving problems. Scholars from other sections of the thirteen colonies sent him puzzles to test him. As soon as he received them, he would sit down at his table in his scantily furnished house and start figuring them out. With his quick mind, he would have the correct answers in no time at all.

Banneker found that he much preferred solving and making up problems to working on the farm. But his livelihood was the farm. In order to have food, he had to plant crops and hoe the fields. But this was not as exciting as working out a problem.

Even though Banneker was receiving recognition, he was actually very lonely. He had never married so he did not have a wife or children to talk to. There was no one in his neighborhood who could discuss mathematical and scientific problems with him.

Then something wonderful happened.

In 1772 Banneker was forty-one. That year the three Ellicott brothers—George, Joseph, and Andrew—moved to Patapsco Valley. They were millers. Joseph, like Banneker, had made a clock that had received considerable attention.

The Ellicotts became lifelong friends of Banneker and helped him in many ways. Indeed, their arrival marked the turning point in his career.

While the Ellicott mills were

being built and the machinery brought from Pennsylvania, the Ellicotts bought provisions for their workmen from the Banneker farm. Banneker's mother always selected for them the largest and freshest vegetables and fruits, the fattest chickens and the best grade of honey. She packed them carefully and walked to the mills which were several miles away. This she did almost daily.

Although most farmers in that part of Maryland grew tobacco, the Ellicott brothers encouraged the farmers to grow wheat. They claimed that there was a bigger market for grain. The Ellicott flour mills thrived. A prosperous community, called Ellicott Mills, developed.

What interested Banneker most about the mills was the machinery that ground the wheat into flour. He studied the big rollers, fascinated. The Ellicotts were impressed with this fine man who came often to the mills. They entertained him in their home and visited him at his farm. The Ellicotts were also mechanically and scientifically inclined.

One day, in 1787, when Banneker was visiting at his friend's home, George Ellicott offered to lend him some books on astronomy.

Banneker was delighted. When he was ready to return to his farm with the books, George Ellicott said, "I'll be over soon to help you with the tables and instruments."

"I shall appreciate that very much," Banneker said.

But George Ellicott was called away unexpectedly on business. When he returned, he went over to see Banneker, expecting to explain certain principles. To his amazement, he found that Banneker had already mastered them and was absorbed in studying them. At this time Banneker was about fifty-six years old.

From that time on, astronomy became almost an obsession with Benjamin Banneker. As a boy, he had been fascinated with the stars that shone so brightly, but up to now he had never had the good fortune to see books on the subject. The last twenty years of his life, Banneker devoted most of his time to scientific studies.

Every night as soon as it was dark, Banneker would leave his log cabin. A blanket over his arm, he would walk over to a certain tree. He carefully spread the blanket on the ground, and then he made himself comfortable on his back, so that he could watch the stars. Until they disappeared in the early dawn, Banneker was still there, his hands under his head, his eyes concentrating on the heavens. As one writer has said: "His favorite time for study was night, when he could look out on the planets, whose story he was reading, and whose laws he was gradually but surely watching."

As soon as the sun rose, reluctantly, he got up, stretched, and went inside his house to sleep.

His neighbors, who did not understand Banneker's peculiar habits, shook their heads.

"He is a lazy old man," they said. "When he was young he was a hard worker and was proud of his fine crops."

What his neighbors said about him did not seem to bother Banneker. He was too busy with his scientific observations. Through his study of astronomy, Banneker predicted a solar eclipse in 1789.

Banneker also was keenly aware of nature. He noted that locusts seem to recur in seventeen-year cycles, and then explained how they lay eggs.

He observed that a stronger hive of bees seemed to have taken the honey of a weaker hive and killed the bees when they tried to recover their honey.

On August 27, 1797, he wrote the following: "Standing at my door I heard the discharge of a gun, and in four or five seconds after

the discharge, the small shot came rattling around me, one or two of which struck the house; which plainly demonstrates that the velocity of sound is greater than that of a cannon bullet."

Until the 1790's, Banneker's fame was still essentially local. Then in the next decade he received national and world recognition in two ways.

The Congress of the United States, in July 1790, passed a law to establish a permanent capital on the Potomac River. The President, George Washington, was authorized to pick the site and to name the three commissioners to survey and plan the location of the buildings.

Seven months later, in February 1791, President Washington sent Andrew Ellicott III to survey the general site, under the direction of the three commissioners. The actual plan for the city was to be made by the Frenchman, Pierre Charles L'Enfant.

At the request of Mr. Ellicott and Thomas Jefferson, then Secretary of State, Benjamin Banneker was appointed to assist Ellicott in surveying the land. This was the first presidential appointment of a Negro and the first national recognition of Banneker's abilities.

The commissioners were impressed with this distinguished man. His suit was of fine broadcloth, made in the old style of a plain coat, with straight collar and long waistcoat. He wore a broad-brimmed hat.

It is believed that Banneker had learned surveying from the Ellicotts. He worked ably on the survey, impressing his colleagues. He served from 1791 to 1793.

L'Enfant, who was extremely temperamental, got into a dispute with the commissioners and left. Ellicott, probably assisted by Banneker, reproduced from memory the plan that L'Enfant refused to turn over on leaving. In 1792 Andrew Ellicott III became the first Surveyor-General of the United States.

George Ellicott encouraged Banneker to compile some of his mathematical and astronomical calculations into an almanac. This was to be Banneker's second widely known accomplishment. Almanacs then were one of the highest examples of scientific achievement. They were popular and served as an essential source for weather and tide news and entertainment.

While helping to lay out the nation's capital, Banneker worked on his *Almanac.* He finished the manuscript during the summer of 1791.

Banneker was sixty years old when his first *Almanac* was published. It undoubtedly helped to change the prevailing image of the Negro. Banneker continued to publish *Almanacs* regularly until 1802.

In his *Almanac* for 1793, Banneker proposed a remarkable Plan for Peace. He suggested that a Secretary of Peace be appointed to the President's cabinet. While much of this Peace Plan was impractical, it did contain far-sighted demands for free universal schooling, abolition of capital punishment, and disarmament. The plan, too, was a great tribute to Banneker's independent thinking.

The years passed by. On Sunday, October 19, 1806, Banneker took a walk. He admired the beauty of the gold, bronze, and red leaves that covered the ground. Suddenly he collapsed. Friends carried him into the log cabin where his wooden clock still ticked rhythmically. There he died. He was almost seventy-five years old.

Understanding Organization of Ideas

In textbooks the headings nearly always state the topics. Usually there are many headings, so that it will be easy for you to follow the organization of the ideas. Frequently the writer also helps you to follow the organization of ideas within a section. He writes a sentence like "There are four important food groups" or "Three main reasons explain this fact." Such a sentence tells you what to look for in the paragraph or paragraphs that follow.

When you read your assignments, look for clues that tell you in advance the important ideas to be presented. Watch, too, for paragraphs that give examples, make transitions, or summarize the main ideas.

This section will give you practice in the efficient use of textbooks.

Organization of Ideas in a Science Lesson

The title of this selection is "The Bottom of the Ocean." What topic do you expect to read about? The first sentence gives you a clue to the organization.

The Bottom of the Ocean

[1]The ocean bottom is divided into three parts. The **continental shelves** are the parts nearest the continents. It is believed that continental shelves were once above the water. They are the shallowest parts of the ocean. Sunlight can get

The first part.

through the water to almost all parts of the shelves. Plant life grows well in the water above the shelves. This is where most fish live. Can you see why?

[2]The shelves drop suddenly into steeper hills, called **slopes.** At the bottom of the slopes, there are canyons and valleys.

The second part.

[3]The **floors** are the deepest parts of the ocean. They are so far down that man knows very little about them. They are a world of complete darkness. Do you think plants grow there?

The third part.

[4]For a long time man thought that no animals lived in this world of darkness. How could they live without plants, without light, and under such great pressure? Today, we know from research-vessel dives, from echo-soundings, and from specimens that have been pulled out of the depths that there are animals living there.

To what does "this world of darkness" refer? Answering that question tells you which part of the ocean bottom this paragraph is about.

[5]The depth of the ocean is measured in **fathoms.** A fathom is 6 feet. One of the deepest parts of the ocean is a long trench near the Philippine Islands about 5,700 fathoms deep. The highest mountain on land is about 29,000 feet.

A new main idea.

—from *Science for Tomorrow's World* 5

Building Skills

To Write

What are the two main ideas of this selection? In which paragraphs do you find details to support them?

To Discuss

1. How is Paragraph 5 related to the topic of the selection?
2. Why is *fathoms* written in boldface type? What arithmetic would you have to do to compare the depth of the ocean with the height of mountains?
3. Remembering that there are three parts of the ocean bottom should help you to recall what those parts are. Without looking back at the selection, can you name all three? If you have forgotten one or more, scan to find them.

Organization of Ideas in a Social Studies Lesson

Each paragraph you read has a purpose. The author is trying to give you a certain message. It is your job to read carefully enough to understand the purpose.

Keeping the streets clean. Keeping the streets clean was another problem of the growing towns. If a farmer decided to throw his garbage out his front door, he was the only one who would be affected. But in a town, throwing out garbage in this way made the streets filthy and caused disease and odors. It also made the streets unsafe for people who had to avoid the piles of rotting garbage.

The topic of the section.

The main idea of this paragraph.

The rest of the paragraph contains details which support the main idea.

New York was one of the first to pass a law about this problem, and soon the other towns followed. The New York law said that anyone who threw "any rubbish, filth, oyster shells, dead animals, or anything like it into the streets" would be fined. Every person was required to keep the street clean in front of his own house. One New Yorker discovered a very simple way to do this, but the town officials did not think much of his system, and he was fined. It seems he was keeping his own front clean by throwing his garbage in front of his neighbor's house.

What new idea is presented in this paragraph?

In most towns in America, street cleaning was done not by people but by hogs. They roamed the streets, eating the garbage. But roaming hogs were dangerous, especially to children.

What does this paragraph tell about solving the problem?

—from *Man and Society*

Building Skills

To Write

Write the three main ideas in the selection. Under each main idea put the related details.

To Discuss

1. Read aloud the main ideas in this selection. Discuss the importance of details in helping you to understand, to remember, and to enjoy the main ideas.
2. How does the first sentence in boldface help you read the selection? What sentence might you add to the beginning of the second paragraph?

Organization of Ideas in a Science Chapter

You have many skills to use to help you learn the material in your textbooks. One of the most important ones is *previewing*. Learn to look at the titles in each reading assignment *before* you begin to read. Doing this shows you the topics to be covered. When you begin to read, you read with more understanding because you know what to expect.

This selection comes from a chapter about foods. Read the two headings and one subheading to get an idea of what topics the selection will cover. Keep those topics in mind as you read each paragraph. When you come to a note in the margin, stop and read it. Those notes indicate the kind of thinking you should be doing as you read.

The Science of Nutrition

What is **nutrition?** The answer to this question is the main idea in the first paragraph.

The study of how your body makes use of food is called the *science of nutrition.* Nutrition is a process. It is the process your body uses to change foods into living tissues.

Foods contain nutrients. *Nutrients* are substances that promote growth and energy. Every living thing must have nutrients. Without nutrients, a plant or animal would soon die.

Every sentence in this paragraph contains an important idea. Read it again.

Your body uses nutrients to replace dead cells and to repair damaged tissues. It calls upon nutrients to regulate body processes. Nutrients also supply energy. They keep the body going from day to day.

These sentences give examples telling how nutrients are valuable to the body.

Perhaps many nutrients are familiar to you. At least you may have heard of them. Proteins, for example, are nutrients. Sugar is a nutrient. Various kinds of vitamins are nutrients.

Here are three examples of nutrients.

At one time or another in your life you probably have taken vitamins in the form of pills or as a liquid. Perhaps you still take vitamin pills. You also get vitamins from the foods you eat.

The foods you eat are important to your body because of the nutrients they contain. The foods provide a way of getting the nutrients into your body.

This paragraph summarizes the two most important ideas so far.

Nutrients

This heading tells you that you will learn more about nutrients.

By eating the proper foods from day to day, we can be sure our bodies are getting the nutrients they need.

There are six kinds of nutrients. These six kinds are (1) proteins, (2) carbohydrates, (3) fats, (4) minerals, (5) vitamins, and (6) water.

Let's examine these six groups of nutrients. First, we shall see what they do for our bodies. Then we shall go on to the foods that contain these nutrients.

What kind of paragraph is this? What will follow it?

Proteins

You know that proteins are one of the six kinds of nutrients. This subheading alerts you to look for the important ideas about proteins.

Proteins (prō′tēnz) help the body to grow and to mend itself when injured. The body burns some proteins for energy, but its chief use of proteins is for growth and repair. Without proteins the body could never grow and replace its many cells. –from *Today's Basic Science* 5

Building Skills

To Write

All of the paragraphs under the first heading, "The Science of Nutrition," help to explain a new word, *nutrients.* In two or three sentences, write a definition of nutrients in your own words.

To Discuss

If you were to outline the information given under the heading "Nutrients," your outline would begin like this:

Six Kinds of Nutrients

I. Proteins
  A. Used chiefly for growth and repair
  B. Contained in ______

Can you tell what the next topics in your outline would be? For example, what would be the topic for II? What would be the subtopics for A and B under II? What would be in the rest of the outline? How do you know?

Organization in a Math Lesson

Read the following lesson from a math book. Instead of answering the questions in the math lesson, think about its organization. This time there are no sidenotes to help you. Ask yourself: What ideas are presented? How are they related to each other? How are they explained? When you have finished reading, go on to "Building Skills."

NUMBER SENTENCES

A. How can you tell whether a number sentence is an **equation** or an **inequality**?

- Which equations at the right are true? Which are false?
- Which inequalities are true? Which are false?
- Which number sentences are neither true nor false? Why?

EQUATIONS	INEQUALITIES
a. $3 + 5 = 8$	**g.** $8 + 2 \neq 9$
b. $12 = 4 \times 3$	**h.** $7 - 3 \neq 4$
c. $9 - 6 = 4$	**i.** $3 \times 5 > 15$
d. $5 = 15 \div 3$	**j.** $21 \div 7 < 3$
e. $s \times 6 = 15$	**k.** $a + 4 > 10$
f. $14 - y = 9$	**l.** $18 - b > 12$

B. Number sentences that are neither true nor false are called **open sentences.**
You can make an open sentence true or false by thinking of a number in place of the variable.

- For each of these sentences, name a number that would make it true. Name a number that would make it false.

$a + 6 = 15$
$5 - x \neq 3$
$4 \times n > 16$
$y \div 3 < 10$

C. For each number sentence below, tell what members from the set of whole numbers would make it true.

$3 \times 5 = n$ $\quad$ $4 \times m < 36$ $\quad$ $6 - x > 12$ $\quad$ $20 < 5 \times y$

- A set from which you choose replacements for the variable is called the **replacement set.** What set did you use as the replacement set for the sentences above?
- The set of numbers that make a number sentence true is called the **solution set.** What did you find to be the solution set for each sentence above?
- Which solution sets were finite sets? Which were infinite sets?
- Which sentence had the empty set as its solution set?

EXERCISES

Write *Equation* or *Inequality* to identify each.

*1. $14 - 5 = 9$	*2. $7 + 5 > 10$	3. $8 + 3 \neq 14$
4. $12 - 6 < 9$	5. $12 + n = 15$	6. $7 + 4 < \square$
7. $5 \times 4 > \triangle$	8. $\square + \square = 8$	9. $7 \div \square = 7$

* 1. Equation. 2. Inequality.

Building Skills

To Write

1. What is the topic of this lesson?
2. What are the three subtopics? (Two of the subtopics have two parts.)

To Discuss

1. In the A section, the writer gives examples of the main idea. What are the examples? Where else are they given?
2. When you read the examples of equations, you read first "3 + 5 = 8" then "12 = 4 × 3," and so on. Why did you read *down,* instead of across?
3. What is the purpose of the little square that comes before some sentences?
4. Under "Exercises" should you read the items down the list or across the line? How do you know?
5. What does * mean? Why do you think the book gives answers to the first two exercises?

Summary

It is important to see how a writer puts paragraphs together to make his ideas clear:

—Using headings to understand how ideas are organized.
—Recognizing main ideas and noting supporting details.
—Watching for signals that help you find the main ideas.
—Recognizing paragraphs that make transitions.
—Watching for paragraphs that summarize.
—Noting paragraphs that give examples.

Books About Putting Ideas to Work

What's the Biggest? by Barbara R. Fogel.

Things that are considered biggest are delightfully described and illustrated in this book.

What Makes TV Work? by Scott Corbett.

This book gives a simple explanation of the sending and receiving of television pictures. There are labeled diagrams.

The Magic of Paper by Walter Buehr.

Papermaking has gone on for thousands of years. This book tells how the process started and how it has changed over the centuries.

Arithmetic for Billy Goats by Donald Barr.

We use a base of ten to count. Computers use a base of two. With pictures of goats and ears of corn, this amusing book shows you how to add, subtract, multiply, and divide in a two-digit numeration system.

Bridges and How They Work by Daniel Goldwater.

Man has built bridges for thousands of years. What holds a bridge up? It depends upon the kind of bridge it is. This book includes descriptions and diagrams of bridges.

Getting to Know UNESCO by Ella Griffin.

Why would happy parents in Haiti name their first baby girl Unesca? The UNESCO workers help the village people in Haiti and in other countries to build roads, to build schools, and to grow crops.

Benjamin Banneker, the Man Who Saved Washington by Claude Lewis.

Because Benjamin Banneker's father and grandfather used the good farming practices they had learned in Africa, their farm was a model for the neighborhood. But Benjamin was more interested in making clocks and studying the stars.

Unit 6

Communicating Through Art

Children drawing a chalk carpet in a city park.

SKILLS LESSON

SEEING TIME CLUES

In many kinds of reading, it is important to understand how events relate to one another in time. You have to understand what happened first, what happened next, and so on. Seeing time relationships is an important skill when you read the newspaper, a history book, the story of a person's life, and when you read to follow directions.

Following **time order** is easy in some reading. A writer may use time words like *first, second, third* to help you follow his organization. His words tell you the time order. You have learned to watch for many other kinds of words and phrases that tell time relationships:

now	within a few months	as soon as
before long	ten years ago	centuries earlier
finally	after a short delay	all at once

As your reading vocabulary grows, you will learn new words that indicate time relationships. Here are several. Can you use each one in a sentence? The Glossary will help you.

decade	subsequent	initially
fortnight	simultaneous	ultimately

Sometimes writers use time words that do not have an exact meaning. For example, in one context *soon after* might mean

"a few minutes later." In another context, the same phrase might mean "several years later."

Of course, dates are good time clues. When you see the name of a day or month, or numerals representing hours, days, or years, you have information about time.

Verbs are an important kind of time word. Two verbs in one sentence may tell you when one event happened in relation to another event.

All the time words and phrases help you to understand how events in time relate to one another. A good reader uses all of the time clues the writer provides.

TRY THIS

Find five time clues in the following paragraph. Write them on your paper. (There are more than five.)

Henry Tanner was born in Pittsburgh in 1859. Even as a young boy, he was fascinated by painting and was determined to study hard to become a good painter. He studied art in Philadelphia and had an exhibition of his paintings in Cincinnati. Interested friends helped Henry Tanner raise money to go to Paris for work and study. While he was there, he completed one of his best-known canvases, *Daniel in the Lion's Den*. . . . During his lifetime, Henry Ossawa Tanner received many medals and prizes for his outstanding work. Today his paintings are still treasured.

SKILLS LESSON

FOLLOWING TIME ORDER IN BIOGRAPHY

Biography is the story of a person's life. In a biography you must notice the order of events. You must also be alert for clues that tell in what period the person lived and what other events were happening then. Read the following beginning paragraph from a biographical sketch of the famous artist Rembrandt.

About three hundred years ago a child called Rembrandt van Rijn was born in Leyden, Holland. Van Rijn means *of the Rhine.* So the child was called Rembrandt Van Rijn to show where his home was. In Holland one can often tell from his name where a person lives.

About when did Rembrandt live? Is this an exact time phrase? The second and fourth sentences in the paragraph are true today. How do you know?

TRY THIS

Read these paragraphs from the story of Rembrandt's life.

[1] After a typical childhood spent with four brothers and sisters, Rembrandt was sent to school. He was well liked by his friends and teachers. Rembrandt grew to be a tall, strong youth.

[2] His parents asked him what trade he would like to follow. Rembrandt did not know which one to choose. He was sure, however, that he did not wish to be a miller, like his father. His parents hoped he would be a priest or a lawyer.

[3] Rembrandt was sent to the University of Leyden. It was surrounded by a park, and Rembrandt spent much of his time there. He was greatly interested in the odd plants that grew in the park. Rembrandt also sat for hours watching the procession of ships on the beautiful Rhine River.

[4] Rembrandt did not stay long at the university. He decided he did not wish to become a priest. He returned home and spent many hours studying the engravings and oil paintings that hung on the walls of the city hall.

[5] "What trade shall our son learn?" asked Rembrandt's father of his wife one day. "He will not be a miller and does not care to be a priest."

[6] "He is very fond of pictures," said the mother. "Shall we not send him to an artist to study?"

[7] Soon after, Rembrandt was sent to an artist in Leyden. The young artist worked hard to learn all he could from his master. His teacher was kind to him, and Rembrandt learned rapidly. At the end of three years, his teacher could help him no more. Then Rembrandt returned home and started a succession of paintings that were to make him the most famous of all Dutch artists.

Look back at the paragraphs to find answers to questions below. Since most of the time clues in this biography are not exact, your answers will not be exact either. Write the best

answer you can and then discuss them with your classmates.

1. Most boys and girls go to school *during* childhood. What age limits do you think the writer means for "childhood"?
2. About how old do you think Rembrandt was when his parents questioned him about a trade? What word in the first paragraph gives you a clue?
3. In the fourth paragraph, how great a period of time do you think "long" means? What makes you think so?
4. Note the phrase "soon after" in the seventh paragraph. Does it mean about ten years? three hours later? within a few weeks or months?
5. For how long did Rembrandt study with the artist?
6. About how old do you think Rembrandt was when he finished his study with the artist—about twenty years old? over thirty?

SKILLS LESSON

TIME RELATIONSHIPS

Often it is important to know *how much* time passes between events. Notice the sequence of the following events:

Man's discovery of fire
Man's use of fire to produce steam power
Man's use of atomic energy for power

These events are listed in correct order. But this order doesn't tell how much time passed between the events. Man's discovery of fire occurred many thousands of years before man used fire to produce steam power. Only two hundred years separated the steam-power engine and man's development of atomic power.

To show how much time passed between these events, an author might present the information this way:

Early man discovered that fire could help him keep warm and protect him from wild animals. **Many, many thousands of years later** he discovered how fire could produce steam and steam could, in turn, be used for power. Just **two centuries after this,** men learned to use atomic energy for power.

In order to understand time relationships, it is important to pay attention to phrases like "many, many thousands of years later" and "two centuries after this."

TRY THIS

Read the following paragraph, paying particular attention to the time relationships expressed in it. Then answer the questions.

The ancient Greeks used to paint most of their statues with bright colors in order to give an added feeling to them. Over the hundreds of years since these statues were made, they have lost their colors, and we are left with the white marble or brown wood from which the statues were carved. They still look beautiful, but they must have lost a great deal of their original appeal. Many primitive tribes of the past and the present use color on their carvings and masks in an attempt to give a stronger feeling than the uncolored surface would. But in most countries nowadays, sculptors tend to leave their carvings and statues uncolored. They believe that the surface of marble, stone, wood, or metal is interesting enough in itself.

1. What three groups of artists are referred to? What words give clues to the three time periods?
2. Write a sentence expressing the main idea of the paragraph. Underline the time words that you use.

SKILLS LESSON

OUT OF TIME ORDER

When writers describe events, they do not always begin at the beginning. Instead they may start with the most exciting or most important part of the story. This catches the reader's interest—but it may mix him up in following the time order. To understand the selection, the reader must rearrange the events in the order in which they happened. This isn't hard to do if you read carefully, paying attention to the words that tell *when* and thinking about time relationships.

TRY THIS

The following paragraph begins with today, but it tells about things that happened over a long period of history. Read it and then follow the directions on page 262.

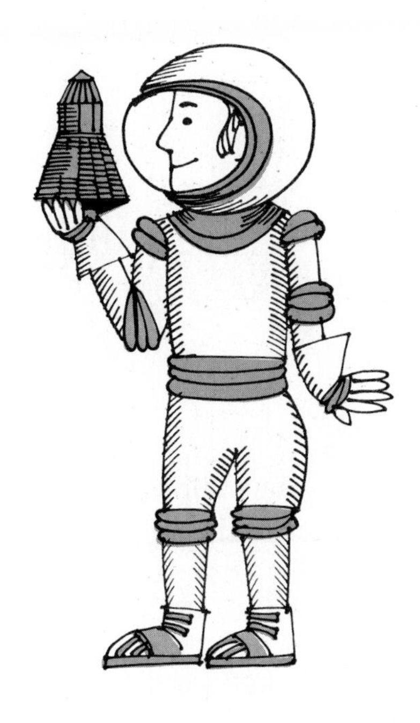

Today's space ventures depend on the careful preparation of many unusual materials. One of these is ceramics—material made from the shaping and heating of claylike substances. Ceramic materials are used in space rockets and jet engines where strength and ability to withstand heat are essential. During World War II, ceramic materials were also used to fulfill many other industrial uses. Actually, the use of ceramic materials is very old. Egyptian ceramic articles go back as far as 5000 B.C., and one piece of pottery is thought to be ten thousand years old. Later, when the explorers came to America, they found evidence of beautiful ceramic objects made by Indians in both North and South America. So when modern designers and builders use ceramic materials, they are simply continuing in a very old tradition.

Below are the facts in the order in which they appear in the selection. On separate paper write the letter of the event that happened first, then the letter of the event that happened next, and so on.

A. Ceramic materials are used in space rockets and jet engines.
B. During World War II, ceramic materials were also used to fulfill many other industrial uses.
C. Egyptian ceramic articles date from as far back as 5000 B.C.
D. One piece of pottery has been found that is thought to be ten thousand years old.
E. Explorers found evidence of beautiful ceramics made by American Indians.

WHAT DID YOU LEARN?

1. What are time clues? In what kinds of writing are they particularly important?
2. How can a reader follow events told out of time order?
3. Why is it a good idea to think of events in the order in which they happened?

A little dog helped to discover a wonderful painted cave. The pictures on its walls bring us messages from men who lived before writing was invented.

Entering the Lascaux Cave, one sees prehistoric paintings everywhere.

Four Boys and the French Cave of Lascaux

by SAM *and* BERYL EPSTEIN

An important time word in this selection is **prehistoric.** Watch for other time clues—exact and approximate—to follow the events.

Four boys discovered the wonderful prehistoric cave paintings of Lascaux, in the Dordogne region of France. Their story began one

Shaggy wild horses with tousled manes decorate one wall.

morning in September 1940, during the Second World War, in the town of Montignac.

Montignac is on the Vézère River, less than twenty miles from Cro-Magnon. Limestone cliffs rise up all about it. Among the cliffs are several caves which, by 1940, prehistorians had already explored. Like almost everybody in the Dordogne region, the boys knew about those caves. They had visited the nearest ones with their teacher, and listened carefully when he told them how to recognize ancient bones and stone tools. They hoped to be lucky enough themselves to find some new clues to prehistoric cave men.

On the morning their story begins, however, the boys weren't thinking about prehistoric times. France had been conquered by Nazi Germany just three months before, and the usually cheerful town of Montignac had become a sad and dismal place. When the boys wanted to escape it for a few hours, they wandered among the forested cliffs along the river. That's why they set off for the cliffs on the morning of September 12, with a little dog named Robot who belonged to one of them.

Suddenly, while the boys were climbing the hill called Lascaux, one of them noticed that Robot was no longer at their heels. Marcel, the dog's owner, whistled for him and called out his name. But the frisky dog didn't come bounding back to his place. Marcel's friend, Jacques, and the other boys called Robot too. Still he didn't appear or answer them with his bark. Finally they decided he must have been hurt, and they turned back anxiously to look for him.

Every few seconds they stopped to whistle and shout, and to listen for some kind of response. At last they heard a frenzied barking. But it sounded so faint and so far away that they couldn't imagine where the dog was.

They called again. Again the bark replied. This time they realized that the sound came from under their feet, from somewhere underground. A moment later they found a small hole not much larger than a rabbit burrow. They realized that Robot had somehow fallen down it and couldn't get out.

Swiftly the boys fell to work to enlarge the opening. They cut away the roots of shrubs with their knives and pried out small stones, calling to Robot all the while to assure him that he would soon be free. But the little dog didn't appear even when the hole had been doubled in size. His barking didn't seem to come any closer.

"I'll have to go down and get him," Marcel said.

So the boys made the hole bigger still, until Marcel could squeeze himself into it.

"Don't worry, Robot," he called. "I'm coming."

Marcel pushed himself into the opening head first and worked his way for several yards along a steeply slanting tunnel. When he thought he had reached the bottom and tried to get to his feet, he lost his balance and found himself rolling helplessly downward. His journey came to an end with a thud that jarred his bones.

The other boys heard the rattle of stones and the crash of their friend's landing. "Are you all right?" Jacques shouted.

Marcel shook himself. He felt bruised, but otherwise he was uninjured. And Robot was leaping about him, licking happily at his hands and face.

"I'm all right, and so is Robot," he called upward. "But it will be a hard climb to get out again."

"What's down there?" the other boys wanted to know.

Marcel flicked the switch on the small flashlight that had been in his pocket. "A cave, I think," he said. And then he added excitedly as he swung the beam around, "Yes—a cave! Come on down! But be careful or you'll fall the last part of the way."

One after another the other boys slithered down, clutching at roots and rocks in an effort to slow their swift progress. Finally they all stood together on the bottom, brushing themselves free of dirt while Robot barked his welcome.

"Look!" Marcel told them, pointing his flashlight. "Over there!"

Only a few feet away an enormous animal loomed out of the surrounding darkness, bright red against a paler background. Then they saw another animal, and still another.

After a startled moment, the new arrivals realized that the beasts were figures painted on the wall of the cave in striking black and vivid yellow and red.

"They're like the pictures at the Font-de-Gaume cave!" one boy whispered in awe. "Only there are so many more of them!"

"Let's explore!"

With Marcel in the lead, they moved forward slowly into the center of a great, hall-like cavern almost a hundred feet long. The pictures were all around them, on both long walls and even stretching up onto the arched ceiling.

There were prancing wild horses with tousled manes. There were prehistoric bulls—four of them, three times larger than life, sprawled across the ceiling. There were bison and long-antlered deer. One row of deer heads looked exactly like a group of animals swimming across a stream—across the Vézère River itself, perhaps—with only their heads showing above the water.

It was late when the boys reluctantly scrambled back up the steep slope, taking Robot along with them. By then they knew that they had made a discovery so important that they would have to show it to other people, their teacher first of all. But they had already promised each other that they would keep their exciting find a secret until they had a chance to explore it completely themselves. Cautiously they made their plans.

The next morning the boys left Montignac one by one so that no one would become curious as to the group's purpose. Each boy carried a flashlight in his pocket. They met at the entrance to the cave, and again Marcel led the way down the sloping tunnel to the cavern thirty feet below the surface.

That day they explored not only the big hall at the foot of the slope, but the two passages leading out

The cave artist painted an enormous bull against a pale background. ►

These animals are painted in red, yellow, and black hues.

of it at its far end. One passage ran straight forward. The other ran to the right and divided into two smaller branches after a short distance.

The walls of both the passages were painted too. Altogether there were so many pictures, some painted on top of others, that the boys couldn't begin to count them all. There were pictures of single animals, some bigger than life, like the bulls on the ceiling of the hall, others scarcely larger than a man's hand. There were groups of animals shown together. There were animals that seemed to be standing still, and others that seemed to be leaping or falling or racing. Here and there were criss-crossed lines that looked as if they might be pictures of animal traps, and long straight lines that looked like spears.

The strangest picture of all was right at the bottom of a deep pit at the end of one of the passages. It was strange because there was a man in it, drawn in single lines like a stick figure drawn by a small child. He seemed to be hurt, for he was toppling backward. On one side of him was a wounded bison with wildly staring eyes, looking right at the boys as they crouched at the bottom of the pit. Perched on a stick on the other side of the man was a bird, crudely drawn, but looking very much alive, as if he were watching over the death of the beast and the man.

The next day and the day after

that, the boys returned to their cave. At each visit they found something they hadn't noticed before, and grew more excited than ever about their own secret prehistoric art museum. But they knew they couldn't keep their secret forever. On the fifth day they told their teacher what they had found. At first the man thought they must be joking. Even when he was convinced that the boys had actually discovered a prehistoric painted cave, he couldn't believe that it was as remarkable as they insisted it was. But finally he agreed to go and look at it himself.

The teacher didn't speak at all when he first stared around the big painted hall. He just gasped in amazement. Then he said, "We must waste no time. We must send at once for Abbé Henri Breuil."

The boys knew that name. They knew that the French priest Abbé Breuil had been chosen to copy the famous paintings at Altamira. They had heard the story of how the young man had lain on his back for weeks, under the low Altamira ceiling, in order to set down every line and every shade of those paintings. The copies he had made of them, published in a book, had introduced the whole world to the glories of that Spanish cave.

Since that time Abbé Breuil had become France's—perhaps the world's—greatest expert on prehistoric art. If Abbé Breuil decided that the paintings the boys had discovered were worth copying, too, then the cave on the Lascaux hill would also become famous throughout the world.

Abbé Breuil came at once. Not even the difficulties of transportation in wartime France could delay him. And after his first words the boys knew that the town of Montignac would never seem such a sad and dismal place again. They knew that from then on there would always be something exciting happening on the Lascaux hill.

For Abbé Breuil and the other experts who soon joined him in Montignac agreed that the cave was one of the greatest art treasures in France. They said it must be opened to the public so that all the world could marvel at the paintings. But the experts also agreed that the priceless paintings might be ruined if the cave were opened to the public without careful preparation.

Those men knew that the paintings had survived for thousands of years only because the air in the sealed-up cave had remained at the same degree of temperature and moisture all that time. If the cave were opened and outside air poured through it, those conditions would change and the pictures might soon begin to fade and peel off the walls.

So they sent for engineers to plan a special air-conditioning system to protect the prehistoric art. Other engineers made plans to enlarge the cave's entrance and provide it with massive airtight doors. Still other technical experts designed a lighting system that would show the paintings to their best advantage. Until 1945, when the war ended and France became free once again, very little actual work could be done. Even after the war it took a long time to build the special air-conditioning and ventilating machinery that was needed.

Finally, in 1948, everything was finished. The famous Lascaux cave was opened to public view, and people began to arrive at Montignac from all over the world. Two young guides were waiting to show them through the Hall of the Bulls, as the big cavern had been named.

The guides had been carefully trained for their job, and could tell the visitors many things about the Lascaux paintings. They could point out, first of all, how cleverly the artists had used the roughness of the rock. By drawing the outline of a bull around a bulge in the wall—instead of drawing it on a smooth flat place—a prehistoric artist had made a picture that seemed to have thickness as well as height and width. The bulging rock made the animal look real and alive.

The guides could also explain that the cave men probably made their paints by mixing certain substances with animal fat. Charcoal from a fire, the guides said, gave the artists their black paint, and powdered minerals gave them their red and yellow colors.

The guides could explain the painting methods the artists used, too. The earliest cave men simply dipped their fingers in paint and used their finger tips for drawing lines on the stone. Later artists probably used brushes made out of feathers. Some of the prehistoric painters also used a method something like our modern spray painting. They spread fat on the wall, and then blew powdered color at it through a hollow reed. The color stuck to the greasy surface and formed a layer of paint that had a light misty look.

The guides told the visitors that no one knew for certain why prehistoric men—who apparently never decorated the shallow

Deer are swimming across a stream with only their heads showing.

shelters and cave fronts where they lived—had made hundreds of pictures deep inside Lascaux and certain other caves. But most experts agreed, the guides said, that the pictures were made because the cave men believed in magic. When a cave man went into a dark corner of a cave and drew a bison with a black line like a spear piercing its body, he was—the experts believed—trying to work a magic spell that would make him a successful hunter.

The guides could tell the visitors all those things because they had learned them from scholars like Abbé Breuil. But when the young men described the discovery of Lascaux, they were telling a story they knew better than any of the experts did.

The two guides who were on hand in 1948 to show the wonders of the Lascaux cave were Marcel Ravidat and Jacques Marsal. Eight years before, on an autumn day in 1940, they had been two of the four teen-aged boys who had followed little Robot down a hole and found, deep in the earth, the greatest collection of prehistoric cave paintings yet known to the world.

At first, man plucked music from strings—even from the bow that launched his arrows. It was a long way from that time to the perfecting of the violin.

From Bowstring to Violin

by FANNIE R. BUCHANAN *and* CHARLES L. LUCKENBILL

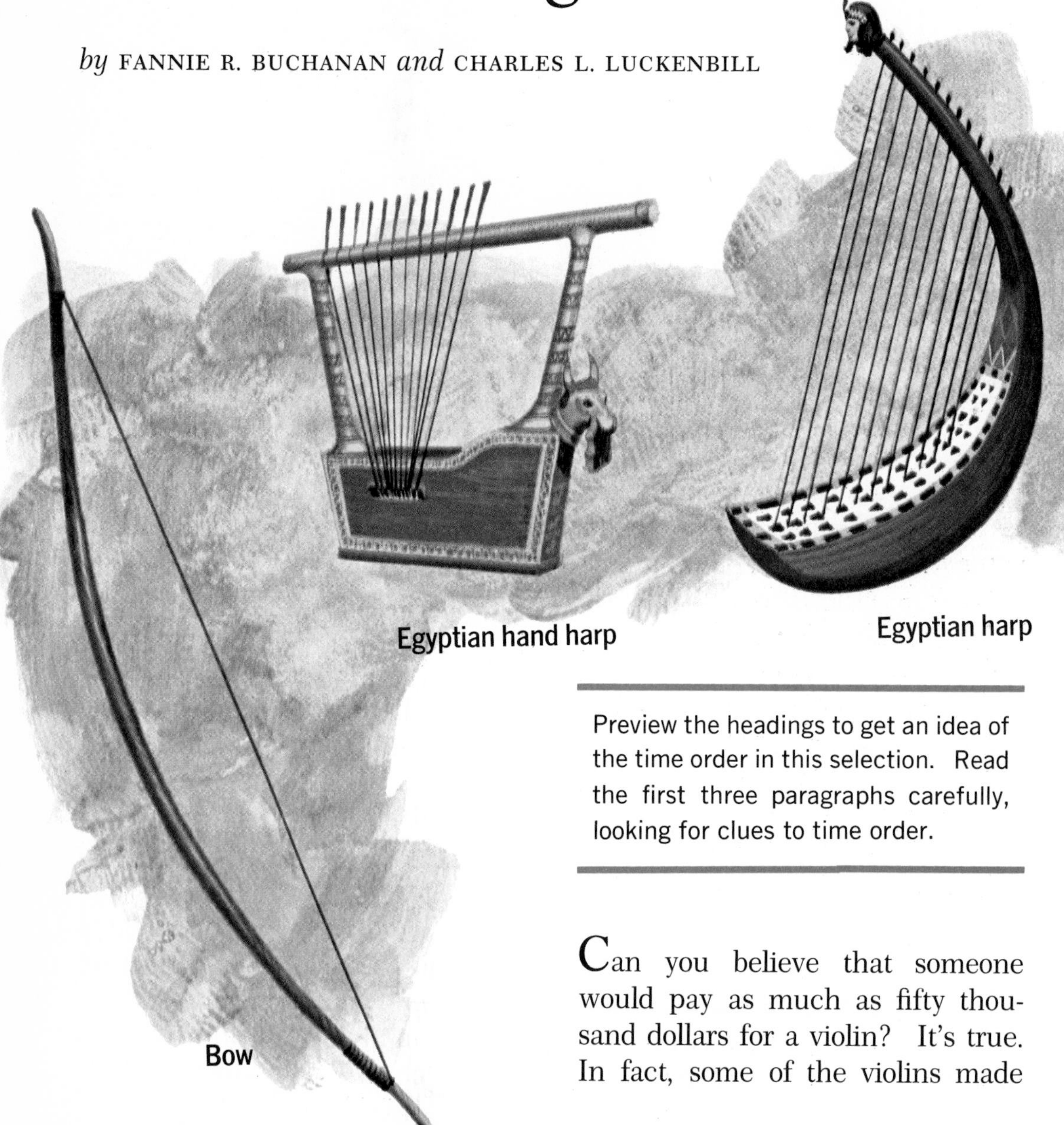

Preview the headings to get an idea of the time order in this selection. Read the first three paragraphs carefully, looking for clues to time order.

Can you believe that someone would pay as much as fifty thousand dollars for a violin? It's true. In fact, some of the violins made by Antonius Stradivarius are worth even more today. Stradivarius was an Italian violinmaker who lived from 1644 to 1737. His violins are considered the finest ever made. There are many stories about the famous Stradivarius violins and the great musicians who played them. But even an ordinary violin has a long and interesting story behind it.

The story begins in the days when the hunter's bow was a part of every man's equipment. He depended upon it for his food, his clothing, and his protection from lurking foe or stalking beast.

The hunter of those times had to be sure of his bowstring. A good string on a well-bent bow always hummed as it sent the arrow flying. The hunter learned to listen for this humming sound. He noticed that long bowstrings twanged with a deeper tone than the shorter strings. He liked the sound of the short and long strings together.

MUSIC FROM THE BOW

Perhaps at night about the campfire these old-time hunters twanged the bowstrings with their fingers, just for the sake of hearing them hum. Perhaps as they sat there they made a little song to go with the humming sound. In some way the bowstrings must have been used for pleasure as well as for protection, because somewhere in those forgotten times man began to make music from stretched strings. He had learned to make drums to help with his dances. He had learned to make pipes that would sing to him when he was lonely. Now he was to learn to sing with the strings, and afterward to find new ways to make them sing for him.

There was a long, long time, thousands of years, from the first singing strings to the music of the violin. Before such an instrument could be made, man had to learn many secrets about singing strings. How could one string produce tones of different pitch? How could several strings be tuned to sound in harmony? How could the tones be made stronger? How could strings be made to play the melodies of his songs?

These were puzzles which man was to work out. While doing so, he discovered that strings could sound in many different ways. He made many kinds of stringed instruments. Some were *pickers*, and some were *scrapers*. The pickers must have been made before the scrapers because they were more simply constructed.

The harp was the first picker. It probably began when one of

those early hunters, in the arch of his bow, put a short string back of his long string. He had made the first harp.

Ruins of ancient cities tell of early harps. In Babylonia a few years ago explorers discovered a buried city. Among the ruins was a slab of stone ornamented with carvings representing musicians, one of whom is seated and playing a harp with eleven strings. When this stone picture was made more than four thousand years ago, man had already learned to tune strings. He had a way of stretching them with varying tightness, for in this way strings produce tones of different pitch. All this can be seen from the picture, although it can never be known what melodies the strings sounded.

The tombs and ruins of ancient Egypt are picture galleries of the past which tell fascinating stories about music. More than four thousand years ago the Egyptians decorated the walls and columns of their great buildings with pictures and sculptures and sacred writing. Because of the dry atmosphere of Egypt, these are still preserved. Even the paintings have not lost their colors.

Processions of singers and dancers and harpists are there on the monuments. Along with these are sign stories which tell of choruses of twelve hundred singers and orchestras of six hundred players. Things were done on a large scale in ancient Egypt!

These pictures show harps more than six feet high. The base, which rests on the floor, is richly decorated. Some are carved with the head of the king, and others with the great lotus flower which was such a favorite among Egyptians. The base extends upward in a bent bow shape which curves forward at the top. Such harps were used in the temples. They show as many as twenty-three strings.

There are also pictures of smaller harps. Some have strings and are being played as they are carried, resting upon the shoulder in an almost horizontal position. All the Egyptian harps were without the front pillar which is so important in harps of the present time. But their form plainly suggests the curve of the old hunting bow.

In all ancient harps, this bow has been very greatly broadened, which proves that four thousand years ago man had already worked out another of the puzzles. He had found how to make the tones stronger by using a board which vibrated with the strings. Such a device is called a soundboard.

While experimenting with the harp, man made other stringed instruments with different kinds of soundboards. The guitar with its hollow body to increase the sound was used in Egypt before the Children of Israel made their famous passage through the Red Sea.

There were lutes, too, with graceful pear-shaped bodies which were hung from the shoulder with ornamental cords or sashes. The long finger boards of lutes and guitars show that man had worked out another of his problems. He had found that, in effect, a string may be instantly shortened by pressing it against the finger board.

ANCESTORS OF THE VIOLIN

For hundreds and hundreds of years the harp was the most important stringed instrument. Other pickers came and went, but the harp remained. The scrapers seem to have been little used.

About the time Columbus discovered America many changes were taking place in the world. Books were printed, colleges were founded, schools were opened. Music, too, was changing. More attention was paid to instrumental music. New kinds of songs were being made. The singer no longer furnished the only musical entertainment. Princes in their castles had orchestras and bands. The church had instruments to help the singers. Neighbors and friends met to sing, much as people today meet to play bridge. The practice of singing soprano, alto, tenor, and bass parts together was the newest pastime. Everybody was doing it. If an alto or bass was missing, that part was taken by an instrument. An instrument also helped choir singers learn their different parts.

Here the scrapers began to be important. A bowed or rubbed string produced a more singing and prolonged tone than could be made by picking. The stringed instrument of those days which was best suited to this use was called a rebec. It was something like the mandolin of today, but was played with a bow. The English called it a "fiddle." The Germans called it a word which meant "jig." Its tones were loud and harsh. An old Spanish poem speaks of the "squalling rebec." Such an instrument was good enough for use in street bands, and for fairs and village dances. But something better had to be made for these new ways of using music in the church and in the home.

BIRTHPLACE OF THE VIOLIN

For many years before Columbus was born, the best stringed instruments of the world had been made in a small district of northern Italy. It was a land of new ideas, for in those years it was a meeting point of East and West. Travelers from distant places halted there. Merchants and sailors passed that way. Pilgrims and soldiers made it a stopping place. Minstrels sang brave tales. There Italian painters mixed rich colors for their pictures, and there Italian sculptors gave to their marble the grace which was all about them.

It is not strange that the men of that region took the greatest of pride in their workmanship. The cabinetmakers were expert craftsmen. The instrument makers were artists. They dreamed of bringing wonderful new music from the strings. Yet they were doers as well as dreamers. They listened to the music brought by travelers from East and West. Ideas which

Violin

Viola

Violoncello

might help were borrowed and passed from workman to workman for testing. Each was striving in friendly competition to make the instrument which would produce finer music than had ever yet been heard.

These workmen believed that the strings with a hollow box for a soundboard held the secret of this unheard music. The best that had yet been made was the clumsy heavy-toned viol. But no workman was satisfied with it. They made viols of different sizes. They changed the shape of the body. They altered each different part.

As they worked, the voice of the viol took on a brighter sound. But yet it did not satisfy the workmen. Still they tried to make it better. They changed the curve of the sides. They altered the shape of the top. They arched the front or the back. They used different kinds of wood and thinner pieces. They raised the bridge on which the strings rested.

Year after year they never tired of experimenting. The town of Cremona became famous because of its skillful workers. Patiently and happily they tested and tried each pattern.

At last a small, fine, clear-sounding viol was made. The master of the shop and his workmen gave the new viol an endearing name such as they would give to a beautiful child. They called it the violin (little viol).

STRADIVARIUS, MASTER VIOLINMAKER

But there was one among the craftsmen, young Antonius Stradivarius, who still was unsatisfied. When he drew the bow across the strings of the violin, he bent his ear above the delicate shell of the body, seeming to catch an echo of tones that had not yet been sounded.

Year after year the boy worked on in the Cremona shop. He helped to make instruments of the violin family to replace the family of viols. His fingers grew more skillful as he helped to make the tenor violin, which is the *viola* of today. His ears grew keener in the years he helped to perfect the *violoncello,* known today as the cello.

The years as they passed seemed to weave a spell for his working. He had a magic sense of touch. His fingers on wood told him just how it should be shaped. Each smallest one of the more than fifty pieces of the violin was shaped according to its own character. His charmed fingers curved and molded soft wood for the front. They rounded and shaped the strong wood for the back. They joined front and back together with sides that fitted as exactly as the halves of a shell that have grown together. Every hidden slip of wood, every least peg, was perfectly made. The varnish, under his brush, did its part in creating a violin which at last gave to Stradivarius the magic music of his dreams.

The secret of the perfect Stradivarius violin was known only to its maker. The thin, shell-like little body, less than fourteen inches long and weighing less than nine ounces, is so perfectly balanced that it supports the pull of its four strings when they are stretched to a tension of sixty-eight pounds. No one has been able to rediscover the secret of Stradivarius's design. The varnish, which gave the violins their special singing quality, is also a lost secret. Never since has such a varnish been mixed.

Violins made by other Cremona craftsmen bring fabulous prices, but a violin bearing the signature "Antonius Stradivarius" is an almost priceless treasure of the music world.

A young man with a sketchbook and a taste for adventure painted some of the best pictures we have of the West when it was really wild.

Thomas Gilcrease Institute, Tulsa, Oklahoma

Remington called this painting "Stampeded by Lightning."

Frederic Remington, Painter of the Last Frontier

edited by CARL CARMER

Some of the time clues are hidden. You must read carefully to follow the events. For each scene, ask yourself: "When was this happening?"

The Apache Indian sat on his horse, silhouetted against the sun. A wild figure in a wild landscape, he looked as if at any moment he might shout a war cry, then lift his rifle and send a bullet right between your eyes.

"I am most certainly glad," said the art critic, "that it's only a painting."

He stepped back to get a better look at the framed canvas hung on the gallery wall. "Between you and me," he went on, "if this were the *real* thing, I'd be under the bed, hiding. I understand the Apaches are on the warpath again. How *does* this fellow Remington do it? The details are superb, but how does he get close enough to study a warrior like that?"

"Bosh," another New York critic said. "If you want my opinion, Remington's not a bad painter, but he's a faker."

"Oh, come now," the first art critic protested. "He's constantly making trips West, to Arizona and the Indian Territory. Why, look at the details in this picture; you can't fake a thing like that."

"I'll lay you a wager," the other critic scoffed, "Remington hired that Indian to pose for him in a nice peaceful attic. Here – I'll prove it. Look at those moccasins. Just look at them! This Indian – *no* Indian – ever wore such fancy moccasins. You'll find such things only in a theater!"

In a way, the skeptical critic was right. That particular Indian wasn't wearing those fancy moccasins when Frederic Remington first saw him. And, even if he had been wearing a pair *like* them, the Apache was too far away for even Remington's sharp eyes to take in such a detail. Off at a distance, the Apache, followed by several of his tribesmen, was racing his horse around a water hole, yipping a war cry and taking a few pot-shots. And in the dried-up water hole, three men crouched, listening to the whine of the bullets overhead.

Two of the men in that water hole were white. The third was a friendly Indian guide, who lay on his back, his feet almost in Frederic Remington's face. But Remington didn't seem to mind. In fact, he was studying the moccasins the Indian wore.

"Never seen that type of beadwork before," Remington said. "How about it, One Horse? Will you sell them to me?"

A bullet whined overhead.

"What for?" the Indian guide asked calmly.

"Do you see that Apache on his horse, up there? See, he's stopped to reload his rifle. See how he's silhouetted against the sun? I've made a sketch of him. Look." Remington displayed his pad.

"Good," One Horse grunted admiringly.

Thomas Gilcrease Institute, Tulsa, Oklahoma

"The Coming and Going of the Pony Express" catches the spirit of the Old West.

"Well," Remington explained, "when I get back East, I'd like to do a painting of him. And I'd like the model to be wearing your moccasins."

One Horse grunted. "One dollar."

"Remington!" the other white man shouted. "Are you crazy? Two dozen Apaches shootin' at us, and all you can do— Don't you realize we may be *dead* any minute?"

But as Remington told his wife later in New York, "None of us got hurt. When the United States Cavalry came riding up, those Apaches scooted for the hills. One dollar," he said, holding up the moccasins. "Aren't they beautiful?"

Eva sighed. "Yes, dear, they're lovely. But must you take such risks?"

"Well, it wasn't my idea to get caught in the water hole," Frederic protested. "And I can't say it was much fun. But—risks? Well, I'm afraid I do have to take them once in a while, Eva. It can't be helped. That is, if I'm to accomplish what I'm after."

What *was* he after?

At Yale University, where Remington had played football, he had taken a fine-arts course. Having graduated, he had become an illustrator for magazines. He found the work dull. "I'm sick of 'em!" he said to his wife one day. "Men with whiskers in frock coats kissing women in bustles. I'm sick of drawing them. I'd like to paint—paint anything that comes into my head."

"Why don't you, dear?" Eva said. "We can get along for a while on what we've saved. You could start tomorrow—go into the woods, paint some mountain laurel, perhaps, or—or ferns. Or you could paint . . ."

But mountain laurel or ferns, houses or church steeples—these subjects were too tame for Remington in 1884. Alone, he took a train West for Arizona and the Indian country. Here the skies were a pure cobalt, contrasting with the powder blue of the immense hills. At first, Remington didn't like the great emptiness, the silence. One day, that silence ended abruptly. An Indian put a bullet hole through the crown of his hat.

This was a dangerous region for a man armed only with a sketch pad and a pencil. Remington took to carrying a gun. And he took to something else, as well—the country.

Still, the West *was* changing; even he could see that. The old wild days were going. The herds of buffalo were thinning out. Civilization was reaching more deeply into these parts. The Indians still caused trouble. Comanches, Sioux, Apaches—one never knew when they might ride out of their reservations and wage war. But soon this excitement, too, would be gone. In future generations, school children would marvel over these things, but only from reading about them in their history books.

When Remington came East again, loaded down with drawings and sketches, he said, "We were born too late, Eva. We're only just in time to see the end of three American centuries of smoke, dust, and sweat. In a little while, it'll be gone. Gone without a sign, without a trace. Out there, I talked to some of the old-timers. 'Paint what you see here,' they told me. 'Paint this dying West, and you'll be doing a darn sight more than all the history books ever printed. You'll be preserving the memory of this country, saving it

Frederic Remington at his easel.

for future generations to *see.*' "

"Well," Eva said resignedly, "when do you leave again?"

"What?" Remington said. "And leave you alone again? I love you, Eva. I can't—"

But Eva knew what he wanted, what he now hoped to accomplish. And she would not stand in his way.

"I'll only stay three months this time," he promised.

He kept that promise. Later, however, he made other trips. He lived with cowhands, with cavalry troops, with half a dozen Indian tribes. Everywhere he went, he carried his sketch pad. And when he came home, he would say, "Got some great ones this time. Comanches and Kiowas. And horses, all kinds of horses. Pintos, mustangs—and here—a herd of wild ones, stampeding over a cliff. See those Indian scouts chasing them? Those horses would rather die than be caught."

Today, in the great museums of our country, you will find them: the sketches, the paintings, the statues in bronze. These are Frederic Remington's gift to us, a record of that vanished time and place—the Old West.

Feliciano in concert.

A guitar, a song—
and an adventure in courage.

Feliciano!

by RICHARD B. LYTTLE

The events in this selection are told in the order of their happening. Watch for time clues that you can relate to what you already know.

The scene was Tiger Stadium in Detroit; the occasion, the 1968 World Series. But this time it was not the game that made history. It was the way the game was introduced.

With guitar and high tenor voice, Jose Feliciano sang "The Star-Spangled Banner" with feeling and spirit, the way he thought it should be done.

When it was over, some in the crowd were too stunned to applaud. Some even thought it unpatriotic. Some thought it was great and rushed to buy a quickly issued recording of the rendition. Others condemmed it. Everyone wanted to know who Feliciano was.

They soon learned he was something special in the world of modern music. In six years as a professional, the young Puerto Rican had climbed from ghetto poverty to success. But his was more than just a rags-to-riches story. It was a story of stubborn determination and courage. For Jose Feliciano was born blind.

He was the second of eight sons born to the family in a poor farming district of Puerto Rico. When Jose was five, his father quit trying to wrest a living from the soil, and like thousands of other Puerto Ricans, he moved to New York City.

They settled in the ghetto area known as Spanish Harlem. The Felicianos remained poor, but the children were full of spirit and good fun. Jose, blind and over-protected by his parents, was cut off from much of the fun, the ball games and the other play. He had to learn to amuse himself. Very early in life, the radio and its music became important to him. And at six, he learned how to play the concertina.

Popular singers were his heroes, and he saw the life of a singer as one way to become independent in spite of his blindness. By the age of nine, he had learned to play the guitar.

Jose's parents were proud of their son's talent, but they continued to feel that the blind boy would always be dependent on them. Jose felt differently.

The flame of self-reliance burned strong in Jose. It was an almost unbearable shame when he got lost in the streets of New York and was forced to call home, asking someone to come get him.

Fear also drove him to music. He did not want to spend his life making chairs or mops, trades often taken up by the blind. That might be all right for some, but Jose dreaded the idea.

Of course, he was not the first blind youth to try for a career in music. Many others had led the way.

One of these, Ray Charles, was already tops among Jose's list of heroes, and when Jose learned that Charles was blind, too, he determined to make music his career. He could do it. He had to do it.

Being blind, he could not read music. He had to learn by ear, but he had a natural talent. The talent and hard work began to bring him recognition. His first public appearance was in El Teatro Puerto Rico in New York. He was not yet ten years old.

Later, at Charles Evans Hughes High School, Jose was in demand for school assemblies. He was an expert mimic, and his songs, imitating the styles and voices of famous singers, delighted his fellow students—although the mimicry was later to become a problem for him.

School assemblies gave Jose a chance to test audience reactions, but these performances did not satisfy his ambition. If he was to become independent, he would have to start singing for pay.

With his guitar in a large paper sack, Jose began making the rounds of the coffee houses in New York's Greenwich Village.

After entering a coffee house, he would ask the manager if he could play a few songs. Usually, the managers expected little from a blind boy. Most said they had no time to listen to Jose.

Jose would shrug and ask if he could at least tune his guitar before leaving. Even the busiest manager could not turn down that request.

Of course, the guitar would already be in fine tune. As soon as Jose pulled it from the paper sack, he would play with such zest that both manager and customers were at once delighted.

The customers wanted more of Jose's music and they would pay to get it.

While playing in coffee houses, Jose met Janna Perez, a college student. She like Jose's style, and Jose like the way Janna talked. She said Jose was absolutely right in seeking independence, and there was no reason he should not have as full a life as anyone else.

Jose was seventeen when he quit high school to take his first professional job in a Detroit night club. When he returned to New York, he played Gerde's Folk City. Critic Robert Shelton in the *New York Times* recommended Feliciano to those who wanted to see the birth of a star.

The review brought the singer more public attention. Jose signed a recording contract. Night club bookings started stacking up, and by the fall of 1963, Jose was playing in a night club in Miami, Florida.

In Miami, Jose and Janna decided to get married. Because Jose's parents would not consent to the marriage, the couple eloped to Brandy County, Georgia, and were married October 19, 1963.

Though Jose always worked hard at his music, his marriage made him even more aware of his responsibility to his career. He worked harder than ever. Jose appeared on national television for the first time in July, 1964, as a guest on the "Al Hirt Show." At about the same time, RCA released his first album, *The Voice and Guitar of Jose Feliciano.*

It seemed he was really on his way.

Most reviews of the album were good, but one critic said Jose's original guitar style overshadowed his singing. His voice sounded too much like other singers. Jose realized that his high school performances as a mimic had slowed the development of a style that was all his own.

The criticism was sound, and Jose knew it; furthermore, he did not yet feel right about recording. Jose was more at ease with a live audience than in making records. With an audience, he could judge the response as he went along, and Jose had developed a knack for getting on friendly terms with audiences.

Early in his career, he determined never to try to win an audience through sympathy. He had to score by talent—talent and good showmanship. If he spoke of his blindness, it was to joke about. At times he would jolt the crowd by saying he had driven himself to the concert. Then he would get a laugh by explaining that he did not drive very well. Such humor would turn sympathy into admiration.

Jose enjoys hearing a joke as much as he enjoys telling one.

A second album, *Bag Full of Soul,* came out in January, 1966. Then he and Janna left New York for California. In a way, the move was tied up with Jose's search for himself, his search for his own singing style. In California, he and Janna picked out a home, a large and comfortable ranch-style house in

Orange County, about an hour's drive from Los Angeles, and a long, long way from New York's Spanish Harlem.

Soon after the move, Jose went on tour in Latin America. There he sang his songs in Spanish. He was a great success. Better still, the songs in his native tongue proved to be just what he needed to build a special style. He played for Spanish-speaking audiences in the United States.

RCA International recorded three Spanish albums from Jose's tours. They sold well in both North and South America. Two songs, "La Copa Rota" and "Amor Gitana," were hit records in Latin America. The next step was a television show for Spanish-language stations in the United States.

By the spring of 1968, he was ready to try another English-language album. This was called *Feliciano!* It was his best, and one song in the album carried Jose to national fame.

The song was Jose's special treatment of "Light My Fire." Jose changed it to a slow soul song. He gave his own special stamp to the song. That was all he was trying to do when he recorded it. He never expected it to become a big hit. But a hit it was! "Light My Fire" throbbed from radios and jukeboxes across the land.

Pictures and stories about Feliciano appeared in magazines. Jose wore success well and lost nothing of his touch in working with an audience. One time when the lights went out, interrupting the music from the band, Jose suggested to the sell-out crowd in the Greek Theater that all musicians should be blind. Then they, too, could play in the dark.

In addition to his talent, style, and humor, Jose makes a fine stage appearance. He has a broad, handsome face and a good build.

It was no surprise when he was invited to sing the national anthem to open the fifth game of the 1968 World Series. The surprise came when he raised his head and sang.

In addition to the fifty-three thousand fans in Tiger Stadium, millions of television viewers heard Jose's soul version of "The Star Spangled Banner." He distorted the melody, changed the meter, and filled the old song with new passion.

Jose's treatment of the song produced a great deal of disagreement, some of it bitter. But he has no regrets. By singing the anthem his way, he remained true to himself.

The incident certainly did not seem to slow his career. At twenty-four years of age, Jose was a success

Feliciano finds time to relax, too.

by every measure. And there are few men today whose careers offer as much promise for the future.

Skillful at reading and writing braille, Jose has turned to composing music. He has learned to play the banjo, bass, piano, organ, harpsichord, mandolin, harmonica, and trumpet.

Jose also finds time for fun. Few enjoy their success as thoroughly as he. The Felicianos own six dogs, scores of tropical fish, chinchillas, and birds.

Jose likes to swim, and he can ride a bicyle, and swing a bat when a friend pitches. Jose brags about his ability to clout the ball out of his yard. He has a natural feel for sailing and needs only an occasional word from a friend in guiding the boat.

Of course, Jose puts great stock in music as the ideal career for the blind.

"If you are blind," he says, "and have talent as a musician, you probably can make it if you really give it everything you've got and make sure that it is the only thing on your mind."

Anyone who has heard Jose Feliciano knows he gives his music everything he's got.

Following Time Relationships

You have seen how important it is to understand time relationships in many kinds of reading. In your textbooks, too, following time clues is often necessary. These lessons will give you practice in using your skill in understanding such relationships.

Time Clues That Are Not Exact

Sometimes exact dates show the time order of the events that are being described. But there are many time clues which are not exact. These also help you to keep events in order. Look for such clues in the following selection.

What Are the Chief Sources of Energy?

[1] In the beginning, people depended on their own muscles and, later, on those of animals to supply themselves with food, clothing, and shelter. To warm themselves, to cook their food, or to scare away wild animals, they used the heat and light energy of burning wood. For thousands of years, they used only human and animal muscle and burning wood to produce the energy they needed.

This phrase is not exact, but it tells you that the author is writing about earliest man.

[2] After a long time, some people discovered how to use the energy of wind and moving water. One of the first uses of wind power was propelling boats by sails. The ancient Romans used water wheels to run sawmills and flour mills.

Why do you think this clue is not more exact?

[3] Until about two hundred years ago,

This clue is more exact than the others. About what years does it mean?

these were the only sources of energy known. But there were not nearly so many people in the world in those days. So there was plenty of energy for all their needs. There were always wind and running water, and wood was plentiful.

When does this mean?

[4]But then the steam engine was invented. And suddenly people began to devise a great many other kinds of machines. They needed much more energy than before, to run these machines. They began to use more coal as well as wood to do this. They also used more coal to heat their houses. When electricity came into use, coal or water power was used to produce it.

—from *Science Is Discovering*

Building Skills

To Write

1. Each of the four paragraphs begins with a time clue to help you keep the events in order. Write the four clues.
2. Find three or more time clues besides those marked and write them on your paper. Be prepared to explain what each one means.

To Discuss

1. Find examples of time clues in this selection that must be related to other information before you can understand them completely.
2. What do you need to know in order to find out approximately when coal and water power began to be used to produce electricity? How could you find out?

Time Order in Reading Biography

Most biographies, whether long or short, are organized in time order. Usually they begin with a person's birth, tell of his childhood and youth, and then tell of the things he did in adult life. Often dates help you keep the events in order. Look for such clues as you read the following biography.

Martin Luther King, Jr.
Preacher of Nonviolence

Martin Luther King, Jr., was born in Georgia in 1929. When he was still a boy Martin learned that his people, the black Americans, were often treated differently from most of their fellow Americans. Many could not attend good schools, get good jobs, or live in nice houses because of the color of their skin. Martin knew that in a free country this was wrong. He wanted to help his black brothers, so he decided to go to school and become a minister. He became a pastor in Montgomery, Alabama. This is where Martin Luther King's "peaceful fight" first began.

Dr. King worked for equality in other cities. He knew that the only way people could win their rights was to remain peaceful, even in the face of danger. Dr. King won the Nobel Peace Prize in 1964 for his courage and achievements.

The whole nation mourned the terrible event that happened on April 4, 1968, in Memphis, Tennessee. Martin Luther King, Jr., was shot. The man who had preached nonviolence died violently.

But Dr. King's dream can never die. Many Americans are still struggling to make that dream come true.

—from *When Greatness Called; Stories of Courage in America.*

Building Skills

To Write

1. Write these events of Martin Luther King's life in time order:
   a. Received the Nobel Peace Prize.
   b. Became a pastor in Alabama.
   c. Was shot in Memphis, Tennessee.
   d. First learned that blacks were often treated differently.
   e. Born in Georgia.
2. Some time words, such as dates, are exact. Find the three events in Martin Luther King's life that are indicated by dates.

To Discuss

1. Besides dates, what words in this selection give you time clues? Look in the first and last paragraphs.
2. What time relationships can you see between the dates that you know? For example:
   a. How old would Dr. King be if he were living today?
   b. Do you know someone that age?
   c. How old was Dr. King when he was killed?

Time Relationships in Science, Geography, History, Health

Read the paragraphs below. They come from several textbooks. Show that you understand the time relationships by answering the questions about each passage.

Note Selection A. Part of the skill in completing a science activity is to follow the directions as they are outlined.

A

ACTIVITY Take a slat from an orange crate (or any very thin piece of wood about 3 feet long and 2 inches wide). Place the slat on a table, allowing about 4 inches to extend over the edge of the table. Then place two double sheets of newspaper

Note the sequence of steps in this set of directions.

over the part of the slat that is on the table. Smooth the papers, leaving no space between the paper and the table. Now strike the end of the slat with a baseball bat. What happens? Why?

—from *Science: A Modern Approach* 5

Building Skills

To Write

List the steps in this activity.

B

The first large ironmaking factory in America was built near Philadelphia more than 250 years ago. Another early iron works gave America one of the famous names of history—"Valley Forge." George Washington and his army once spent a winter near Valley Forge.

About what year was this? Was this before or after the Revolutionary War?

Bethlehem, Pennsylvania, north of Philadelphia, is an important steel city. Recently, the largest steel mill ever built at one time was constructed on the Delaware River just north of Philadelphia.

To what time does this refer?

—from *The American Continents*

To Discuss

1. What time is described in the second paragraph of B—the past or the present? How do you know?
2. You know that George Washington spent a winter at Valley Forge during the Revolutionary War. Was the first large ironmaking factory in this country built before or after that time? How do you know?

C

Fluoride is a chemical compound of the element *fluorine* (flü′ə rēn). Long ago, an Englishman named Sir James Crichton-Browne thought that there might be some relationship between fluoride and tooth decay. No studies were made at that time to see if this were true.

This word can also be pronounced as floo′rēn.

Later, in 1908, a Colorado dentist named Dr. Frederick McKay began a study of the enamel of teeth. He noticed that the drinking water of certain communities was different from that of other communities. He noted that the teeth of people in some of these communities had fewer cavities than the teeth of the population as a whole. In 1931, Dr. McKay concluded that certain amounts of fluoride in drinking water help prevent cavities by making the enamel harder and more resistant to the action of the acid-forming germs in the mouth. Since that time, other studies have supported his findings.

–from *Health* (Second Edition) 5

To Discuss

1. Does the first paragraph contain any clues as to when Sir James Crichton-Browne was thinking about the relationship between fluoride and tooth decay?
2. What clue in the second paragraph tells you that Sir Crichton-Browne was doing his thinking before 1908?
3. How many years did Dr. McKay devote to his study before he drew any conclusions?
4. When have other studies supporting his findings been made?

Using a Time Line to Understand Time Order

Textbooks frequently use time lines to make time relationships clear. A time line is a kind of graph. The line itself stands for a long period of time. Most time lines are divided into equal parts that stand for certain amounts of time. In the first time line below, each part stands for one hundred years. The lines dividing the time line and the years those lines stand for are marked above the line. Certain events are named below the line, and arrows point to parts of the line that stand for the year when they occurred. This time line is a kind of picture that helps you see how these three journeys of exploration are related in time.

The second time line does not have any dates marked on it. This time line shows approximate time relationships. The years it stands for are described under the line. Certain events are marked above it. A dotted line leads from each event to the part of the line that stands for what happened. The time line is broken in the middle because there is not enough space to accurately show "many, many thousands of years."

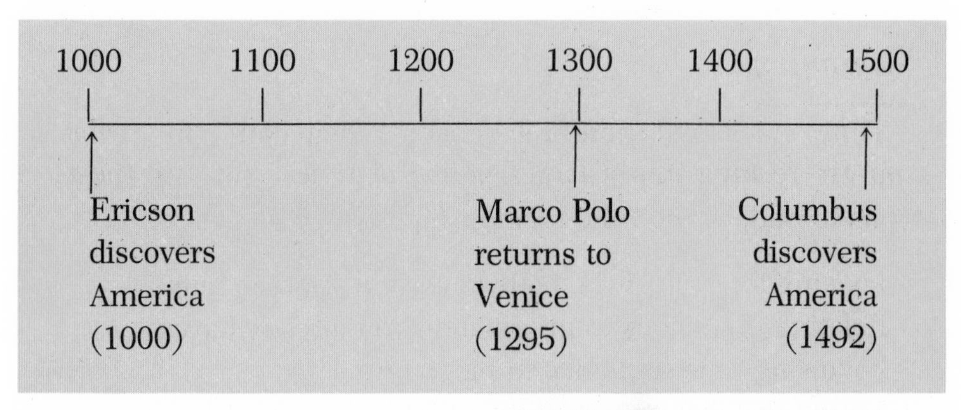

–from *The Story of American Freedom*

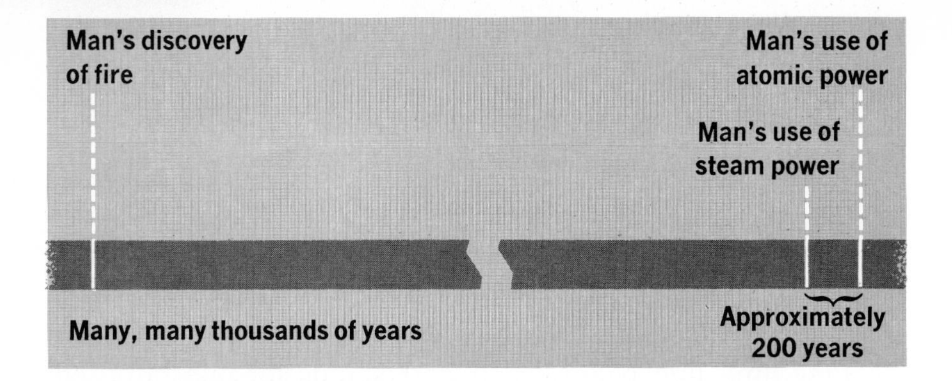

Building Skills

To Discuss

1. What period of time does the first time line cover? How many centuries?
2. Approximately how much time passed between Ericson's discovery of America and Columbus's discovery of America? Did more time pass between Marco Polo and Columbus than between Ericson and Marco Polo?
3. The second time line shows some important events in man's use of power. What comparison does it help you make? You know in which century man started to use atomic power. Can you figure out in which century man started to use steam power? Why does the time line not show in which century fire was discovered?

Summary

Time clues and time relationships help you "fit" what you are reading into a larger period of time. You use these skills to understand time relationships:

– Looking for time clues, both exact and approximate.
– Relating time clues to information you already have.
– Following time sequence in biography.
– Noting the sequence of steps in following directions.
– Reading a time line that shows a series of events.

Books About Art

Jazz by R. P. Jones.

A small, attractive book with a lot of information about swing, bop, rock 'n' roll, and other styles of music. Many pictures show performers with the instruments that made them famous.

Edvard Grieg, Boy of the Northland by Sybil Deucher.

The life of the great Norwegian composer makes a story full of interest. Many of Grieg's compositions for the piano are included.

Famous Modern Artists: From Cezanne to Pop Art by Charlotte Willard.

Great painters are also inventors and discoverers. They find new ways to use materials and they think up new ways to describe the world. Fifty paintings are shown in color.

Paint, Brush, and Palette by Harvey Weiss.

This guide for the young painter tells what materials are needed for oils and water colors and how to use them. Helpful illustrations are included.

What Makes an Orchestra by Jan Balet.

One page explains and illustrates each instrument in the orchestra, and a diagram shows how the players are arranged for a performance. The role of the conductor is also described.

Drawings to Live With by Bryan Holme.

Drawings of all kinds, ancient and modern, make this a beautiful picture book. The brief text suggests ways of looking at drawings.

Young Dancer's Career Book by Regina J. Woody.

A well-informed writer tells what training is needed for ballet and modern dancing. Photographs of both young and adult dancers illustrate each chapter.

Unit 7

Learning About the Earth

A guide pointing out the ichthyosaur fossil to tourists visiting the Ichthyosaur State Monument in Nevada.

SKILLS LESSON

USING A TABLE OF CONTENTS

If you wanted to know where chocolate comes from, where would you look for information? Knowing how to find information is important. It is a skill you will use all through your school years and in later life.

Suppose you do want to know where chocolate comes from. In the library you find a book about spices and flavorings. Will it help you? One way to find out is to turn to the table of contents. Here it is:

CONTENTS

CLOVES

CINNAMON

CHILI

The numerals at the left stand for chapters in the book. Those at the right stand for pages. The information you want is probably in Chapter 2, which begins on page 14.

Most books that contain information have a table of contents. It is always in the front of the book. The table of contents tells what is in the book and the page on which each part begins. It tells something else, too: how the writer has organized the major ideas.

Most textbooks have detailed tables of contents which give a great deal of information about what is in each part of the book. Look at the table of contents of this textbook. What does it tell you about the organization of the book? Where would you look to learn something about communication? Do you see how helpful a table of contents can be in finding information?

TRY THIS

Write answers to the following questions by referring to the table of contents on page 302.

1. To what chapter would you turn in order to find out where the Spice Islands are?
2. You might find a recipe for gingerbread in either of two chapters in this book. Which chapters?
3. In what chapter would you look for information about honey?

SKILLS LESSON

USING AN INDEX

An index is an alphabetical list of the names and topics that appear in a book. It is much more detailed than a table of contents. An index gives a page number for each topic. Sometimes there are subtopics under each topic; these are listed in alphabetical order, too, with page numbers for each entry. Let's use part of the index from the book about spices and flavoring to find out how an index works.

Look at the entry for **Chocolate** in the first column. On the first line, after that word, are listed all of the pages on which chocolate is mentioned in a general way. You might find the answer to your question about where chocolate comes from on one of those pages. But perhaps you can find an answer more quickly by looking at the listing of subtopics. Read down that list until you come to the line that says "source of, 19." That entry shows where to find the answer to your question.

Notice how the items in the index are listed. When you read each subtopic, remember that it is related to the main topic. For example, the first subtopic under **Chocolate** means the

origin for the name for *chocolate* will be found on page 14. Notice that the listings under **Chocolate** are continued into the second column.

Index

Here is another part of the same index. Again, note how carefully the subtopics are listed under the topics.

A *cross reference* is an entry that tells you to look at another entry. Look at **Spice Islands.** You see that Spice Islands are mentioned on pages 46, 47, 48. The next words, "*See also* Indonesia," tell you to look at the entry for Indonesia. That entry will direct you to more information about the Spice Islands. What other cross reference do you find?

TRY THIS

Read the questions below, and find the answers in the two parts of the index on pages 305–06. Write your answers.

1. On what page would you find something about King Solomon?
2. On what page or pages would you look to find out what saffron is?
3. What kinds of sugar are discussed in this book?
4. On what pages might you find several uses for cinnamon?

SKILLS LESSON

FINDING INFORMATION IN AN ENCYCLOPEDIA

An encyclopedia is a book or set of books that contains information about many subjects. An encyclopedia has hundreds of articles about science, history, famous people, art, sports, and other subjects. The articles in an encyclopedia are usually arranged in alphabetical order.

You can tell what part of the alphabet is in each volume by looking at the spine of the book—the part that you see when the book is standing on the shelf. If the letters on the spine are **P–Q** you know that all topics beginning with those letters are in that volume. If the spine says "Renner to Sibelius," for example, you know that any topic that comes between those two words in alphabetical order will be in that volume.

Most encyclopedias have an index to help you locate topics. The index may be a volume by itself, telling where to find the information in all of the other volumes. Or there may be an index at the end of each volume, telling where to find the information in that volume only.

Often you can find the information you want in an encyclopedia without using the index. Suppose you want to read an article about earthworms. You could go directly to the **E** volume. At the top of each page you would find guide words. On the left-hand page, the guide will name the first entry on

that page; on the facing or right-hand page, the guide will name the last entry. If you found pages with the guides "earthquake" (on the left) and "Edinburgh" (on the right), you would know that the entry "earthworm" would be on one of those two pages.

TRY THIS

In the list under A below are five topics that you might look up in an encyclopedia. Under B there are guide words and page numbers for pairs of facing pages from an encyclopedia. On your paper, write the numerals 1 to 5. Write the numbers of the pages where you would find each topic.

A.

1. Opal
2. Salvador
3. Orlando, Florida
4. North Atlantic Treaty Organization
5. Rural Free Delivery

B.

366	North America	North Cape	367
274	Running	Rush, Benjamin	275
594	Ontario, Lake	Open Shop	595
648	Orion	Orlon	649
384	Salt River	Salvation Army	385

Key Words

When you look for information in an encyclopedia you have to think of the right entry word. Suppose you want the answer to this question: What effect would physical activity, like skipping rope, have on your pulse?

To find the answer to that question in an encyclopedia, what entry would you look for? You might find "activity" as an entry, but that is a very general subject and would certainly include much information that had nothing to do with the pulse. You would not expect to find "skipping rope," but you might try "pulse."

To answer the next question, what entry would you look for? Why? What are the chief occupations of the people in the Northwest Territories of Canada?

Often a cross reference will help you find the entry you need. Information about dolphins, for example, may not be given under **Dolphins.** If you looked under **Dolphins** you might find a cross reference saying "See Whales and Dolphins." If you looked in one encyclopedia for the topic **Reaper** (a machine for cutting and gathering grain), you would not find it; but under the topic **Reaping and Threshing,** you could find the information you needed.

TRY THIS

Suppose that you are asked to use an encyclopedia to find answers to the questions below. For each question, write the key word or words that you would look for.

1. When was Nebraska admitted to the Union?
2. Why is Oklahoma called the Sooner State?
3. What is the work of a public health nurse?
4. Where is Rocky Mountain National Park?
5. How long did Dr. Jonas Salk work to find an effective vaccine against polio?
6. How is glass manufactured?
7. What are the natural resources of Arkansas?

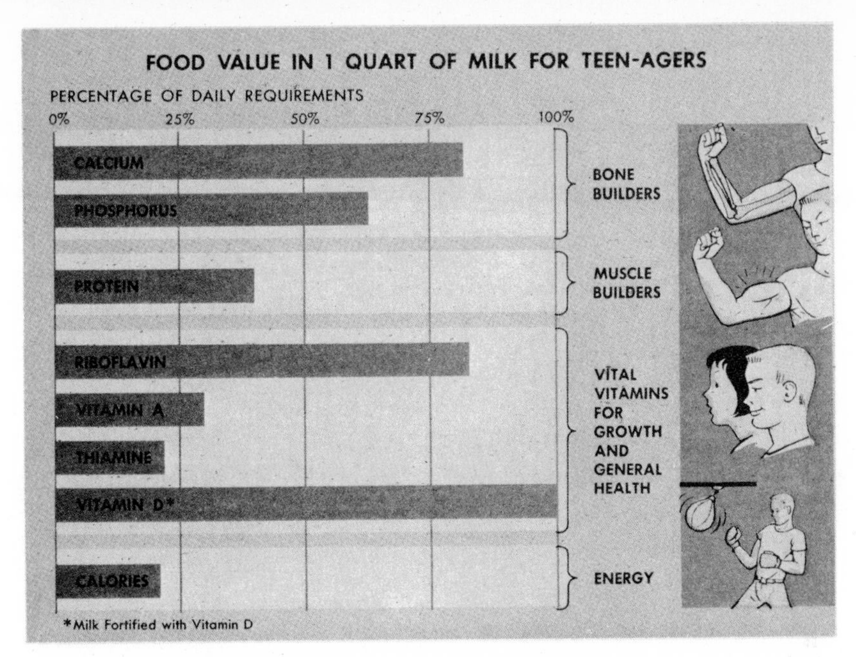

–from *Compton's Encyclopedia*

SKILLS LESSON

LEARNING FROM GRAPHS AND PICTURES

Usually the words and the pictures in a graph work together to give information. Let's study the graph at the top of this page.

The title tells you what information to expect. The next line shows what the percentages mean. For example, the line labeled "50%" means "50% (or half) of the amount of something that teen-agers need each day." To find out what "something" is, look at the horizontal bars. Each of these eight bars has a label printed on it. You can see that one quart of milk provides more than 50% of a teen-ager's daily needs in four of the elements: calcium, phosphorus, riboflavin, and vitamin D. When you read the line for vitamin D, the asterisk (*) tells you to refer to the footnote. What does the footnote tell you?

Read *all* the words on a graph, and read the pictures, too. The words and pictures at the right of this graph tell you that calcium and phosphorous are bone builders. What do calories do?

The TOOLS of the BARN BUILDERS

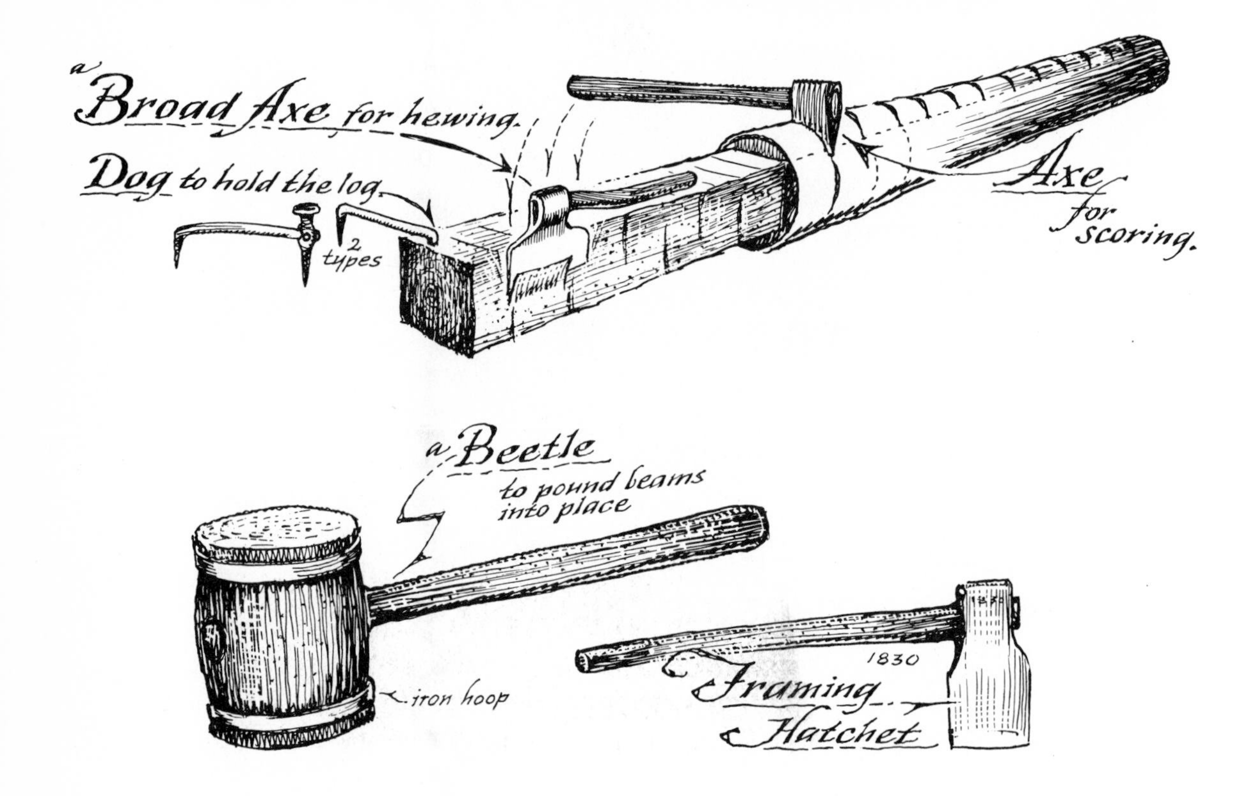

The illustration on these two pages shows some of the tools that early American settlers used to build barns. The artist has drawn each tool to show more than one side, if possible, and to show the grain of the wood. Here again you must read the words as you look at the drawings. Some words that may be unfamiliar are explained by the drawings. For instance, the position of the axes in the log at the top of the picture make clear what **hewing** and **scoring** mean. The names for the tools that are illustrated are underlined, and the arrows point to the pictures of the tools.

TRY THIS

Study the picture of the tools and write answers to the following questions about them.

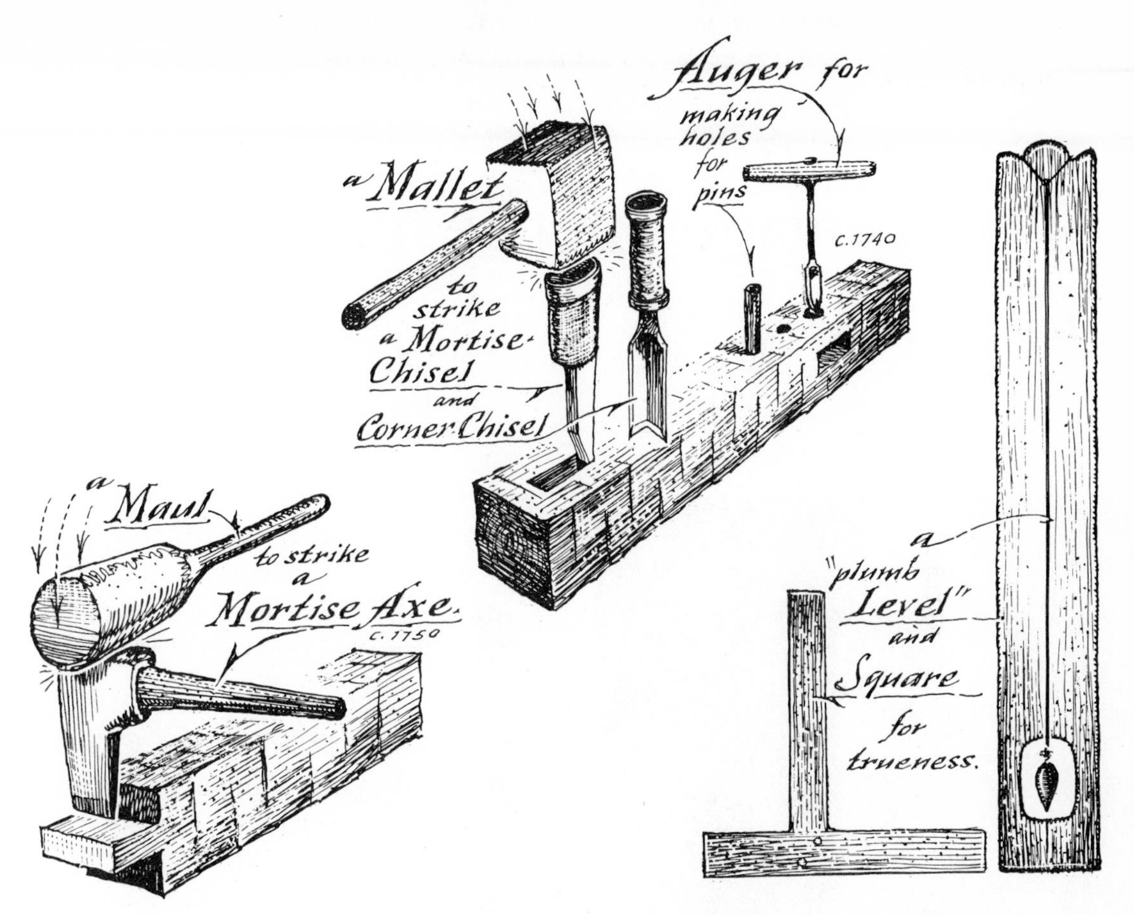

1. What two familiar words did you learn new meanings for?
2. An auger was used to make holes. What were the holes for?
3. What do the dotted-line arrows show?
4. Are there any words that the drawing does *not* make clear? How could you learn about them?

WHAT DID YOU LEARN?

1. Describe some situations in which you would consult a table of contents. When is an index more helpful?
2. When do you use an index?
3. What steps would you take to find the answer to a question in an encyclopedia?
4. How can illustrations give information?

Much of what we know today about the earth and its creatures can be traced to a young Englishman and—

The Voyage of the *Beagle*

by MILLICENT E. SELSAM

As you read, study the pictures and their captions. Think about how they add to the information in the text.

Marco Polo, Christopher Columbus, Ferdinand Magellan, Vasco da Gama, and Captain James Cook are famous explorers who discovered new lands, new peoples, new plants, and new animals. But there was one sea voyage taken by a small British warship, the H.M.S. *Beagle,* that made scientific history as no other voyage had before.

On board was a young Englishman just out of college, Charles Darwin. Captain Fitzroy, the commander of the *Beagle,* had invited him to come along on the voyage as the ship's naturalist, which meant that he was to observe and collect everything that could be of

◄ **Prickly pear cactus in the Galapagos Islands.**

interest to the scientists of the day. This included plants, animals, rocks, minerals, and fossils. Charles Darwin was not very well trained for the job. But he was a good observer and he was curious about everything. He had a great opportunity, too, for the *Beagle* was going out to map the coasts of South America and possibly to sail around the world.

The *Beagle* left Plymouth Harbor, England, on December 27, 1831. It took two months to reach South America, and Darwin was seasick much of the time.

For two years the *Beagle* sailed up and down the coast of South America. Darwin went on shore whenever he could and walked or rode on horseback up and down the countryside, stopping now and then to crack rocks with his hammer and to collect all the mammals, reptiles, and birds he found interesting. He also made detailed notes describing the things he observed.

Darwin found animals in South America that were unknown to most of the people in Europe. On the pampas of Argentina, Darwin saw *guanacos,* which looked somewhat like small camels; *agoutis,* which resembled rabbits; and *armadillos,* little animals with shells of bony plates.

On the coast of Argentina, Darwin found fossil bones of gigantic animals – huge ground sloths, giant armadillos, and other great beasts. There were no such animals alive then, and Darwin realized that these giant animals had died out. Yet these animals apparently were similar in some ways to the living animals Darwin saw around him. The evidence was clear. Animal life had been different in the past; yet it was linked to present-day life.

The *Beagle* sailed through the Straits of Magellan to the Pacific. On the coast of Chile, Darwin got clear evidence of how the Earth's surface was constantly changing when he experienced an earthquake. He felt the ground move beneath him, and later saw for himself that it had raised the land two to three feet above sea level. From Valparaiso, Chile, Darwin traveled across the Andes Mountains.

High in the mountains he found trees that had been preserved as fossils. Darwin figured that the trees had grown ages ago in volcanic soil at the edge of the Atlantic Ocean, and this land had sunk into the ocean. Buried under mud, sand, and lava from an underwater volcano, the trees did not decay, but some of the chemicals in them were exchanged for minerals that hardened the trees and preserved their shapes. Later the bed of the ocean rose to form a chain of mountains more than 7,000 feet above the level of the sea. Then mountain streams and the wind cut valleys through the lava and the mud and sand that had been changed into rock, leaving the fossil trees uncovered.

Still higher up, Darwin found fossil shells of animals that had once lived on the bottom of the sea. They, too, had been buried under thousands of feet of rock that was later thrust up from the ocean, forming high mountains. They, too, had been uncovered by the winds and waters that had worn away the rock over the ages. Slowly but surely young Darwin grasped the sense of geologic time—the ages upon ages during which the Earth's surface has been gradually changing.

In August 1835, the *Beagle* sailed to the Galapagos, a group of volcanic islands about 600 miles off the coast of South America. The animals of these islands—such as giant tortoises and lizards—were even more surprising.

Toward the end of his visit, Darwin discovered that the animals and many of the plants were different on each island of the Galapagos. The settlers could tell which island a particular tortoise or bird came from. This was a strange thing, and Darwin puzzled over it. How could plants and animals a few miles apart in the same climate differ so much? If he could answer this question, he realized he would be getting an answer to the bigger question: "How had so many different animals and plants come to be on the Earth?"

Five years after the *Beagle* had left England, the ship returned home with Darwin still aboard. For twenty years after the voyage, he worked on his tremendous collections of plants, rocks, fossils, and skinned and preserved animals. He got other scientists to help him identify the specimens.

Naturalists of Darwin's time knew from their studies of rocks and fossils that there were different kinds of fossils in buried layers of rock. Most of these scientists tended to believe that these different forms of life were all separate creations. They believed each layer held different kinds of animals and plants because floods and earthquakes had destroyed life again and again and new plants and animals were created.

However, there were some who thought otherwise. One scientist had proposed that the Earth had

The marine lizard, or iguana, in the Galapagos Islands is the only lizard in the world that finds its food at sea.

been shaped by the same forces that cause changes you can see taking place every day—wind and water wearing down rocks and carrying soil from place to place, volcanoes spouting molten lava, and earthquakes splitting and heaving the Earth's surface.

Darwin had seen these same forces at work and came to agree that the Earth was millions of years old. But Darwin added something new. He suggested that living things could have been changed over long periods of time by processes as natural as those that have changed the Earth's surface. The fossil animals he found in South America had convinced him that the animals he found still living there were descended from ancient creatures.

The Galapagos Islands had taught him that animals and plants isolated on islands could develop into different types, so that, in time, each separate island in the Galapagos group would have its own kinds of living things.

Darwin organized his facts and slowly developed a theory that explained how living things had changed, or *evolved,* in the course of time.

For example, take the horse. The earliest horse we know about lived over 55 million years ago in the forests of North America. Fossils show that it was like a present-day horse in many ways, but it was only about the size of a fox terrier. How did this creature develop into the long-legged horse of today?

Scientists suggest that the first prehistoric horses to go out of the woods onto the plains were chased by flesh-eating animals. Horses with the shortest legs would be more likely to be caught than would horses with slightly longer legs that enabled them to run faster. If more short-legged horses than longer-legged ones were killed, the next generation of horses would include more with longer legs, like their parents. And if this process of natural selection continued for several generations, the shorter-legged horses might disappear entirely, leaving the field to those with longer legs.

But the legs of all these horses would not be the same length, either. Those with shorter legs would still be slower runners—and therefore easier for other animals to catch—than the longer-legged horses of their generation. Down through the ages, the horses that could run fastest were better able to survive than those with shorter legs. Slowly, generation after generation, the dog-sized horses of prehistoric times developed into the long-legged animal we know today.

In 1859 Darwin published his book called *The Origin of Species.* Plants and animals, he said, have gradually changed from earlier forms of life by a process of *natural selection.* Animals and plants vary. Some are better suited to their environments than others. Those that are best equipped for getting food and defending themselves from enemies survive. Their heredity is passed on to their offspring. Others less suited to their environment die out. During the course of time, this "struggle for existence" has led to a natural selection of those animals and plants found alive in the world today.

What was the secret that American whalers knew and English sea captains would not learn?

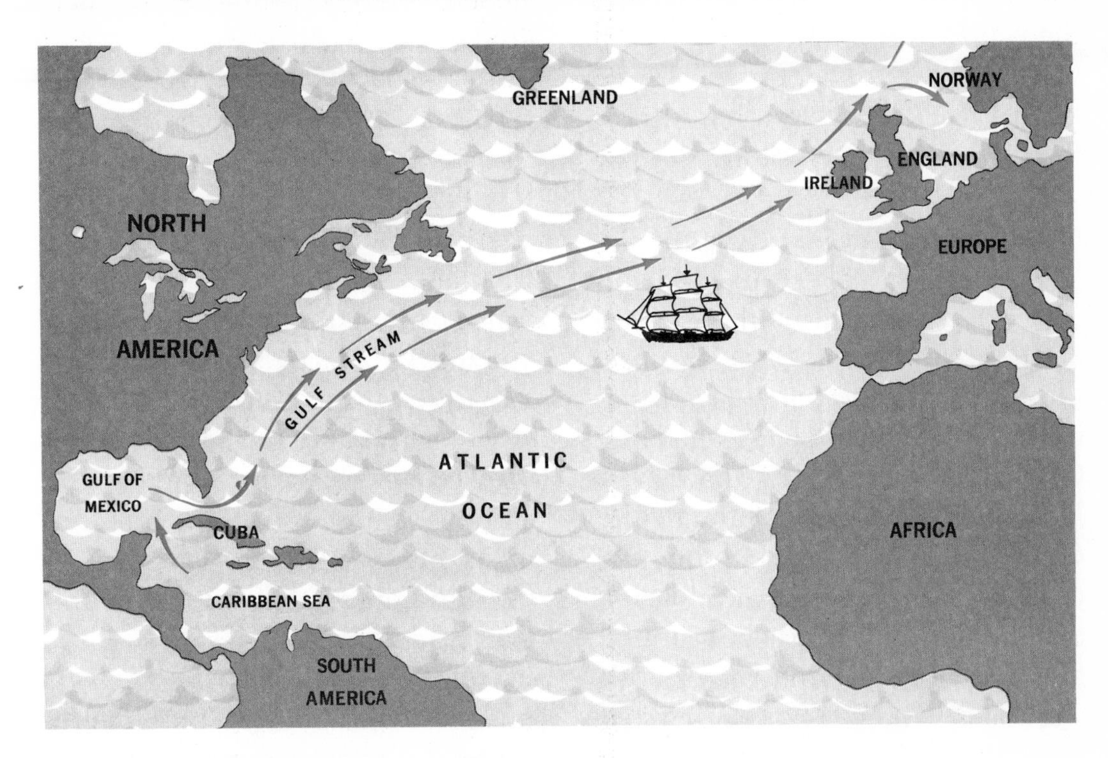

A River in the Ocean

by RUTH BRINDZE

Look at the headings before you begin to read. They tell you the time and the topic of this selection.

This is the story of a really extraordinary river. There is no other quite like it in the world.

This river of which we are speaking is mightier than the Mississippi, and it is longer than the Amazon. But its immense size is not the reason it is interesting. The fascinating part is that this great current, which is called the Gulf Stream, is a river that flows through the ocean.

A true river cuts through the land and has solid banks of sand, or of mud, or of stones. But the banks of the Gulf Stream are simply the ocean waves. There is nothing to wall it in; yet, so far as anyone knows, the Gulf Stream has always flowed along the same course.

PATH OF THE GULF STREAM

This ocean river, like inland rivers, has many tributaries. One of these tributaries flows through the Gulf of Mexico, and because of it the entire current is called the Gulf Stream. Another, and even larger, tributary flows through the Caribbean Sea and around the west coast of Cuba. It joins the waters of the Gulf current, rushes around the tip of Florida, and then northward along the coast of the United States. After a while the Stream slows down, turns east, and drifts across the Atlantic Ocean, carrying the warm water from the tropics to the shores of Ireland and England and Norway, and even on to Russia.

If it were not for the warmth carried across the sea by this ocean river, northern Europe might be as bitterly cold as Greenland. England might be covered with snow and ice most of the year, and part of Norway which is within the Arctic Circle might be hemmed in by icebergs. The wind that blows across the Stream toward Europe is warmed by the water, and this helps to temper the climate of western Europe.

Scientists who study the ocean have traced the course of the Gulf Stream and have recorded the speed at which it flows. We know that if a corked bottle were tossed into the Gulf Stream near the coast of Florida it might be picked up by a person walking along a beach of a country thousands of miles away, for such experiments actually have been made. In some parts of its voyage this bottle might be carried as much as one hundred miles in a single day, so rapid is the flow of the blue water of the Gulf Stream.

Long before scientists experimented with bottles, the mighty Gulf Stream carried strange plants and seeds to the shores of Europe. They made men wonder what lay beyond the horizon. They may even have changed the world's history. They helped convince important people in Spain that it was worthwhile to send Columbus on his expedition of discovery.

A Spanish explorer, Ponce de León, discovered the Gulf Stream in 1513 as he sailed along the coast of Florida. During the centuries that followed, seafarers learned much about the Gulf Stream and its powerful current. But nobody made a real study of it until after

1750. The first person to make actual scientific observations of the Gulf Stream was Benjamin Franklin.

BEN FRANKLIN ORDERS A MAP

"Perhaps, Mr. Franklin, you can explain this riddle."

Benjamin Franklin shrugged his shoulders. "Perhaps," he replied. Since his arrival in London everyone seemed to want an answer to some problem relating to colonial affairs.

"This question has nothing to do with taxes," the Lord of the Treasury hurried to say. "We have had a complaint from the Board of Customs that there is undue delay in the arrival of the packets sailing between Falmouth and New York. They say it takes the mail ships a fortnight longer to make the crossing than is required by the merchant ships, which sail the farther distances between London and Rhode Island. Why, Mr. Franklin, should that be?"

"I do not know," said the American, who was famous for his scientific discoveries in the Old World as well as in the New. "But there is a sea captain in London who may be able to supply the answer."

A few days before, Ben Franklin had chanced to meet an old friend,

Captain Folger of Nantucket Island, one of the famous whalers of the time.

"The very man to ask," thought Franklin. And he lost little time in inviting him to call.

"No riddle at all!" roared Captain Folger in a voice that could have been heard over a gale of wind. "The answer is simply this: The captains of the merchant ships are

Rhode Islanders and they know how to avoid the Gulf Stream. The English captains of the packets sail right into the Stream and lose time because they stay in it."

Franklin had crossed the Atlantic many times, but he knew nothing of the Gulf Stream. So he began to prod the captain with questions.

"Every whaler knows the Gulf Stream," Captain Folger said, "for the whales are found there. Often when I have crossed from one side to the other, I have seen the English packets bucking the current and making little or no headway. I have observed this many times.

"I have advised the captains that they were stemming a fast current, but they were too wise to heed a simple American fisherman."

Franklin disregarded his friend's scornful remark. "If there were a chart showing the course of the Gulf Stream," he said, "every captain would know how to make use of the current to forward his progress when sailing to Europe, and how to steer clear of it when sailing west to the colonies."

After some further conversation, Captain Folger agreed to mark out the course of the Gulf Stream. He did this on an old chart of the Atlantic Ocean. Although his drawing is not quite the same as those made by modern scientists, it is remarkably accurate. Franklin spread the map on the table and watched closely while the whaler pointed out the course of the Stream.

"A fine piece of work, sir," said Ben Franklin. "Many a seaman will thank you for this map."

To have pleased Franklin was thanks enough for the old seaman. As for the gratitude of captains, well, he was not sure of getting it.

"They won't listen," he objected. "Why should they follow what I have drawn?"

Ben Franklin thought they would. And he took the map to an engraver, who made copies of it. But Captain Folger was right. The English captains paid no attention to the map. They thought they knew as much as any colonial.

A few years later the thirteen colonies declared their independence, and the Revolutionary War began. Then Ben Franklin was glad that so little attention had been paid to Captain Folger's directions. For the chart, which showed the fastest way to cross the Atlantic Ocean, became a military secret.

FRANKLIN STUDIES THE GULF STREAM

After the war, when Ben Franklin was again sailing the ocean on business for the new United

States, he began a scientific study of the Gulf Stream. It was the first one ever made. Franklin noticed that the air was always warmer when the ship was sailing through the current than when it was in other parts of the ocean.

"Is the air warmer because the water is warmer?" he wondered. He decided to test the temperature of the water with a thermometer.

He made these tests many times, and he found the water in the Gulf Stream warmer than the water in the surrounding ocean. "A thermometer may be a useful instrument to a navigator," Franklin noted in his record.

He reasoned in this way. The master of a ship could determine whether or not he was in the current by testing the warmth of the water. Then if he were sailing to the westward, he could lay a course to take him out of the Stream as soon as possible, since the current would be flowing against him. But if he were sailing east, then the current would be with him and he could keep with the Stream, gaining speed from it.

These first tests made Franklin eager to try others. "How deep a layer of warm water is there?" he wondered.

To solve this problem, Franklin "fished" for water. He lowered a glass bottle at the end of a rope to bring up water from far below the surface. But this experiment did not give exact results. Franklin needed a better instrument—one that would trap water deep beneath the surface, then automatically seal it in. He made a small keg with special valves to trap the water. Unfortunately, the valves did not work exactly right, and the experiment was not a success. Franklin did not try another.

But he kept a record of the temperature of the air when the ship on which he was traveling was passing through the Gulf Stream. He wrote down the strength of the wind and the direction from which it blew. And he persuaded friends who were crossing the ocean to keep similar records. It was an interesting and a really useful job.

Few people know of Benjamin Franklin's scientific study of the Gulf Stream. They know of his work with electricity, of the discoveries he made by flying a kite during an electric storm. But little notice was taken of his study of the Gulf Stream. In fact, not until nearly seventy years after he had noted his observation on this great current did the government start a thorough study of the Gulf Stream.

A part of our earth that we know little about is the ocean floor. Explorers of this mysterious region have lived underwater for weeks, in a specially designed steel vessel. From their underwater home, they study the life around them.

SEALAB II at the right with her surface support ship, the *Berkone*.

Men in the Sea

by PETER R. LIMBURG

Pay attention to the time order in the part of the selection headed "Importance of the Experiment." Study the illustrations, too.

One August day in 1965, Astronaut Scott Carpenter put on his tight-fitting foam-rubber suit and strapped an 84-pound breathing tank to his back. He was preparing to make a dive into the Pacific Ocean. Carpenter had been one of the first men in the world to make the dangerous flight into outer space. Now with a "buddy" diver he was going to follow a thin, yellow guideline and swim 205 feet down to the floor of the ocean. It would take only two minutes, but he would spend the next thirty days there as leader of a team of divers and scientists who had been chosen to carry out a daring experiment for the U.S. Navy.

Besides Carpenter, the group was made up of twenty-eight men. Some were Navy men; some were civilian scientists. The men were divided into three teams. Each team was to spend fifteen days under water, carrying out scientific tests and learning how men reacted to the dark and coldness of the depths. Carpenter would stay down with both the first and second teams; a medical officer named Dr. Sonnenburg would go down twice with the first and third teams. While under water, they

Divers work on deck as SEALAB II is towed to its diving site.

would spend most of their time in a specially designated habitat, or living chamber, called SEALAB II. (SEALAB is short for Sea Laboratory). There they could move about freely without their diving equipment. They could relax, eat, sleep, and write reports on their work. If successful, this experiment would prove that men with the proper equipment could live and work under water for days and weeks at a time.

IMPORTANCE OF THE EXPERIMENT

Why was this experiment important? After all, men in diving suits and helmets had been making dives as deep—and occasionally even deeper—for more than half a century. Scuba divers had been exploring the ocean floor for more than twenty years.

But neither an ordinary diver in a suit and helmet, nor a scuba diver with a tank on his back, can stay under water very long. The deeper a diver goes in water, the greater the pressure becomes. At 200 feet below the surface, a force of 100 pounds is pressing against every square inch of his body! To keep this force from crushing his chest and lungs, the diver must be supplied with air at an equal pressure. The trouble is that, under this high pressure, nitrogen (a gas that makes up four fifths of the air) dissolves in his bloodstream. If the diver comes up to the surface too quickly, the nitrogen comes bubbling out of his bloodstream like the fizzy gas in soda pop. This causes the diver severe pain. It can cripple or even kill him. To prevent this from happening, the diver must come up very slowly to give the nitrogen a chance to pass gently and harmlessly out of his system. Every few yards he must stop and rest. A diver who has spent an hour in 200 feet of water must spend more than three hours coming up. This process of changing gradually from a high pressure to a lower one is called "decompression." The slowness of the decompression process as well as other reasons, chiefly the bone-chilling cold of the water, limit a deep diver's actual working time under water to an hour or less. And a diver cannot do much work in an hour.

But with a living chamber such as the SEALAB, the diver wouldn't have to return to the surface. Since the air in the living chamber would be at the same pressure as the surrounding water, he would not have to spend any time in the long, slow decompression process. Although he still might not be able to work longer than an hour at a time, he could rest between dives and make several working trips a day. In this way, he would be able to spend much more time working under water.

Scientists had for some time been interested in the idea of underwater stations where divers could live. There were many reasons for their interest. One was the opportunity to study the sea and its animals and plants at close range. Another was the opportunity to raise the wrecks of ancient ships. These ships and their cargoes give valuable clues to our past history. Ships that have been wrecked or sunk more recently often contain valuable cargoes that are worth salvaging. Divers working from the surface could study wrecks and undersea life, but stay-down divers could work better and faster. Another reason for underwater stations was to study the mineral wealth of the sea. The floor of the sea contains rich deposits of metals and oil that cannot be reached from the surface. But teams of men trained to work under water could locate and mine these valuable resources.

Project SEALAB II was not the first attempt at underwater living. In 1962 Captain Jacques-Yves Cousteau, the French naval officer who was the father of scuba diving, set up the first undersea living quarters. The place he chose was the Mediterranean Sea off the south coast of France. Two of Cousteau's men spent a week in this underwater shelter, which Cousteau called "Conshelf I." (Conshelf is short for *continental shelf*, the underwater region around the edges of each continent where the ocean bottom slopes gently down before it makes a steep plunge into the ocean depths.) Encouraged by the success of Conshelf I, Cousteau set up a larger station in the Red Sea. There five men spent a month under thirty-five feet of water, studying marine life and carrying out experiments.

In 1964 the U.S. Navy undertook Project SEALAB I in the Atlantic Ocean near Bermuda. This project was more challenging than Cousteau's, since the divers had to work in considerably deeper water—192 feet. At this depth the pressure is nearly seven times as great as at the surface. Nevertheless, the four men who took part were able to work six hours a day. In the ten days they stayed down, they accomplished almost as much as they could have done in a year, working from

Scott Carpenter gives the signal for the dive.

the surface. Now SEALAB II was carrying on where the earlier projects had left off.

In charge of the project was the man who had planned and directed the first SEALAB, Captain George Bond, a Navy doctor and an expert diver himself.

The site chosen for Project SEALAB II was half a mile off the Southern California coast, near the town of La Jolla. The SEALAB itself rested near the brink of Scripps Canyon, a gigantic gash in the ocean floor. From a scientific viewpoint, this is one of the most

Two aquanauts adjust the supply line.

interesting areas of the ocean that can be reached by a diver.

AT HOME UNDER THE SEA

The vessel the aquanauts called home was a giant steel cylinder 57 feet long and 12 feet in diameter. The walls were made of inch-thick steel. For safety's sake, they were designed to stand a pressure one and a half times greater than they would actually encounter. As an extra safety measure, there was a hatch in a little tower on top of the hull.

Inside, the living compartment was divided into a laboratory, a kitchen, and sleeping quarters. Electric heaters in the floor kept the living compartment comfortably warm. There was always hot water for showers when the men came in cold and tired from a dive. Electricity and fresh water for drinking and showers were supplied through lines from the shore.

The men entered and left the vessel through a four-foot-wide hatch on the underside of the cylinder. A sturdy wire cage around the hatch protected them from sharks. The hatch was always kept open, since the pressure of the air inside SEALAB kept the water from coming in.

Perhaps "air" is not exactly the word to use for the atmosphere of SEALAB. Because of the depth at which they were living and working, the aquanauts had to breathe a special mixture of gases. The SEALAB had been filled with this special breathing mixture before being sent down. The mixture was passed through chemical filters to purify it, so the aquanauts could breathe it over and over again. As the mixture was gradually used up, it was replaced from storage tanks attached to the hull. The air cylinders of the men's diving tanks were filled with the same mixture from the storage tanks.

This special atmosphere, which was mostly helium, played some funny tricks on the men. For one thing, it affected their vocal cords so that they couldn't speak normally. Their voices came out in funny, high-pitched, rapid squeaks like Donald Duck or the chattering of chipmunks. Carpenter later wrote that at first the aquanauts couldn't keep from laughing when they heard each other talk. It took them a while to learn to understand each other's funny Donald Duck talk.

THE "TILTIN' HILTON"

The ocean floor on which SEALAB II rested was not quite even, so that the whole vessel slanted upward slightly at one end. This did not cause any serious inconvenience, although the aquanauts did have to tie their cooking pots to the stove to keep them from sliding off. They ate their meals standing up or sitting on the floor. The men quickly named their undersea home "The Tiltin' Hilton," after the famous chain of Hilton hotels.

Meals aboard the "Tiltin' Hilton" were surprisingly good. There was no regular cook, so the men took turns preparing the food. Some of them had quite a knack for cooking. For the most part, the men ate canned foods and prepared mixes, but now and then ready-cooked roasts and steaks were sent down from the surface in a waterproof container. A birthday cake baked by an aquanaut's friend came down the same way. Unfortunately it was squashed. Sometimes the men caught fish in the open hatch of the vessel and ate them raw, Japanese style.

There was not much spare time in the busy schedules of the aquanauts, but now and then they relaxed with a singing session. Some of the men had brought guitars, harmonicas, and other musical instruments, and these furnished the accompaniment. Another favorite activity, of which they never tired, was watching the ever-changing parade of the fish past SEALAB's eleven portholes.

Although the men had seen almost no fish around the site when SEALAB was first lowered, within a few hours hundreds of fish had gathered around the capsule. Apparently the light streaming out of the portholes attracted them. The fish seemed just as curious about the men as the men were about them. They stared by the hour through the portholes at the men inside the hull. When the men went out on dives, clouds of fish followed them. Some fish even learned to come into the hatchway to beg for food. At times the fish were so many that they completely hid SEALAB from a diver's view.

All these fish attracted sea lions, which came down to feed on them. The men could feel thumps as the big animals rested briefly on top of the hull. One friendly sea lion, nicknamed Samantha, became a sort of pet. She playfully followed the men around in the water and even learned to come in answer to a buzzer. A chunk of fish was her reward for answering promptly.

Unfortunately, many of the fish that clustered around SEALAB were annoying sculpins, or scorpion fish. These ugly fish, which grow to be about two feet long, have sharp spines in their fins. The spines contain a poison that usually causes a slight sting. The anti-shark cage around SEALAB's entrance hatch was a favorite resting place for the scorpion fish. Several of the divers were stung by them. Scott Carpenter was severely stung. His arm was swollen for more than a day.

Although the aquanauts were separated from the "topside" world by 205 feet of water, they were not completely cut off. They were in constant touch with their surface support ship, the *Berkone,* by means of a two-way speaker system and closed-circuit television. There was also a special telephone line, which the aquanauts used to make calls to their families and friends all over the country. These calls had to go through a special "speech unscrambler" that turned the aquanauts' high-speed Donald Duck gabble into normal speech. Perhaps the most exciting call of all was made at the end of the first day in SEALAB II, when Carpenter spoke to two of his fellow astronauts, Gordon Cooper and Charles Conrad, in orbit in Gemini 5. Another exciting call came from a group of French aquanauts working at the bottom of the Mediterranean Sea, half way around the world.

AQUANAUTS AT WORK

The aquanauts had many different kinds of tasks to carry out. Each team had a different project. The first team's main job was to get SEALAB set up and operating properly, to map the ocean floor

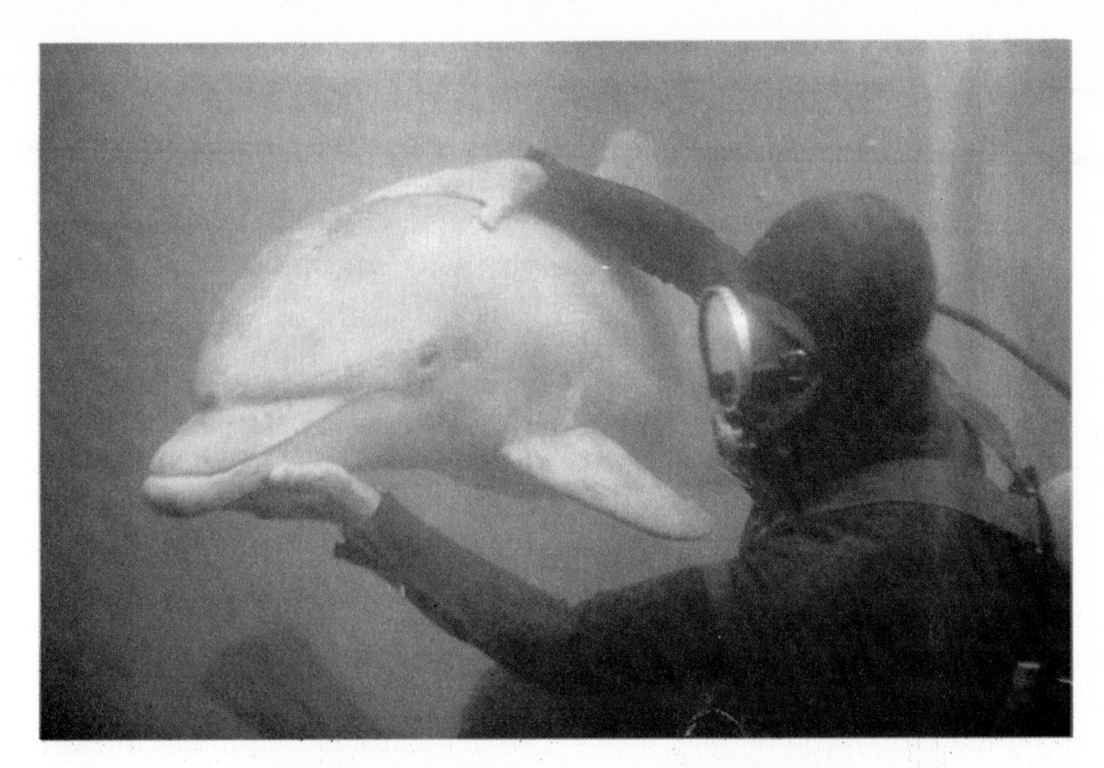

Tuffy's trainer prepares him for work with the aquanauts.

nearby, and to set up an underwater weather station. By measuring such things as the speed and direction of undersea currents and the temperature of the water, scientists hoped to learn whether changes in the undersea climate had any effect on the weather at the surface. Another part of the mission was to set out marker stakes to guide men on dives.

The second team was mainly concerned with biological experiments. They counted the numbers and kinds of fish and other sea life. They tagged fish, crabs, and starfish to learn how far they traveled. They performed experiments on fish. They even tried to raise plants to learn whether future aquanauts could grow some of their own food supplies.

One of the most enjoyable experiments involved a porpoise named Tuffy. The Navy has long been interested in training porpoises and other sea animals to help men. With Tuffy, they had a chance to find out how well their theories worked. Tuffy carried mail pouches and small tools from the surface to the divers. In one test, a diver who pretended to be lost signaled Tuffy with a buzzer.

Tuffy swiftly swam to his rescue, carrying a guide line to lead him back to the safety of SEALAB. These tests showed that porpoises can be valuable helpers to men working under the sea.

The third team's main task was testing new methods for salvaging sunken wrecks. They pumped the body of a Navy airplane (sunk there for that purpose) full of plastic foam to raise it to the surface. They used special explosive tools to attach a metal patch over a hole in a steel plate curved to resemble the hull of a submarine. They fastened lifting attachments to the plate. The "hull" was then raised with the help of a giant air-filled rubber bag that acted like an underwater balloon. The third team also tried out new power tools and tested methods of underwater mining. But probably their biggest job was simply getting things ready to wind up the experiment. Unhooking the scientific equipment and taking it apart to be sent back to the surface and just plain tidying up the area took a great deal of time.

Both the second and the third teams made short dives into Scripps Canyon. Carpenter and a companion made the first dive, to the 266-foot level. Later, other men dove to the same depth in turn. The third team descended to 300 feet. The purpose of these dives was not to break records—deeper dives had been made before—but to explore the unknown world of the underwater canyon and to learn more about men's ability to work at such depths.

Because of the danger involved, special permission from the Navy was needed to make the dives. The Navy took no chances with the aquanauts' lives. In fact, safety was one of the keynotes of the whole project. Divers never went out alone. They always had at least one "buddy" to look after them and help them in case of trouble. Inside SEALAB itself, the closed-circuit television allowed the men topside to keep a constant watch on the aquanauts, so that help could be sent instantly in case anything went wrong.

Project SEALAB II was very successful, and many important things were learned. One of the most important was finding out how well men can stand up to the hard conditions of underwater life. Every one of the aquanauts received a thorough physical checkup daily. His heart, breathing, blood pressure, temperature, and other physical reactions were tested. While outside in the water, the men went through a series of tests that measured their vision, co-ordination, and mental alertness. One such test involved fastening metal rods together to form a triangle—a kind of giant puzzle. In the cold and dark 200 feet below the surface of the ocean, this was not as simple as it sounds.

One of the aquanauts' worst problems was the cold. Even with their foam-rubber suits, the divers found that the chilly water drained heat from their bodies at an alarming rate. However, they got used to the cold little by little. Each day they found that they didn't get cold quite as fast. By the end of their two-week stints, the men found they could stay out for as long as an hour. By using electrically heated suits, they could stay out even longer. The Navy is now working on different types of heated suits for future projects.

Poor visibility was another problem. The depth and the muddy water cut off the sun's light, so that the men could see only a few feet. Perhaps lightweight underwater searchlights will help.

Coming up to the surface was the only dull part of the project. Because the aquanauts had spent so much time under pressure, their bodies were saturated with gases. That is, they had soaked up as much gas as they could possibly hold. This meant that the decompression period had to be very long.

The men rode up to the surface in a pressurized capsule, then went through an airtight entrance into a decompression chamber. There the pressure on them was gradually reduced to the normal pressure of the atmosphere at the surface. This took from thirty-one to thirty-five hours. During this time the men could not leave the decompression chamber.

SEALAB II proved that men could indeed live and work deep beneath the sea. The experiment also showed that the men in those forty-five days had accomplished work that would have required nearly four years to do if they had been unable to live in the ocean. In the years to come, similar projects will push the deep frontier even deeper.

Learning to Use Sources of Information

A textbook includes special aids to learning: a table of contents, headings, pictures, and an index. Some textbooks contain special kinds of illustrations that give information: diagrams, charts, graphs, and maps. All such aids are of great help if you know how to use them.

This section will give you practice in the efficient use of textbooks. You can increase your skill not only by studying these lessons but also by learning to use all of the aids in your own textbooks when you study.

A Table of Contents in A Language Book

What can you learn about a book from reading the table of contents? Find out by answering the questions that follow.

Contents

[Part of the table of contents has been omitted here.]

Section 4

—from *The Roberts English Series: Fifth Book, Second Edition.*

Building Skills

To Write

1. What kind of literature does the author use to introduce each section?
2. What page would you turn to if you:
   a. want to learn how dictionaries show pronunciation?
   b. want to learn how to write a caption?
   c. want to take the tests on a part of the book?
   d. want to read the poem "Pop Goes the Weasel"?

To Discuss

1. This table of contents has two listings on each line. What is the difference between the listings on the left side of the page and those on the right?
2. Read all the listings that are labeled **Phonology.** Do they help you know what *phonology* means? Where else might you look to find the meaning of the term?
3. Can you figure out what *syntax* means?

A Table of Contents in Science

Printed below is the last part of a table of contents from a science book. What can you learn about the book from reading the table of contents? Find out by answering the questions.

—Concepts in Science 5

Building Skills

To Write

1. What two aids to study are included at the end of the book?
2. What can you learn about light by reading the Table of Contents?

To Discuss

1. Both this book and the language book are organized in units or sections. How are the units different?
2. Notice that there is a section called "The Main Concept" at the end of each unit in the science book. What do you think of the purpose of this section?

Geography and Science Indexes

The index in each of your textbooks is one of the most useful parts of the book. You can use it to find information quickly. Using the indexes below, do the exercises on pages 341–42 to increase your skill in using indexes efficiently.

A

With the aid of the pronunciation key, you can use this index as you would a dictionary. The index will also help you find pictures and maps in the book as well as topics. The abbreviation *ill.* after an entry means there is an illustration on the page given; *m.* stands for a map.

–from *Our Country*

B

A sign like this * next to a page number means that the name is on a map on that page.

–from *In the Americas*

C

(Page numbers in **boldface** refer to illustrations.)

–From *Science 5*, Silver Burdett

Building Skills

To Write

1. In Index A what symbol indicates a map?
2. In Index B what symbol indicates a map?
3. Which indexes provide help in pronouncing some of the entry words?
4. In Index C how are pages with illustrations marked?
5. Using Index A, on what page or pages would you look to find–
   a. the location of the capital of Alabama?
   b. when Alaska was first settled?
   c. who the Allies were in World War II?
6. Using Index C, where would you look to find–
   a. information about chlorophyll and carbon dixoide in plants?
   b. an illustration to help you understand the carbon dioxide-oxygen cycle?
   c. information about cacti making chlorophyll?

7. Using Index B, where would you look to find—
   a. a map of Africa?
   b. something about agriculture in different parts of the Americas?
   c. where Aconcagua is?

To Discuss

1. In what ways are these three indexes alike? In what ways are they different?
2. What is the first thing you should do when using a new index?

Illustrations in a Health Book

Some information can be shown in a picture more clearly than it can be given in words. This is why textbooks often include many kinds of illustrations: charts, diagrams, graphs, and drawings, as well as photographs. You get information by "reading" the illustrations as well as by reading the words that go with them. What can you learn by studying the words and illustrations that follow?

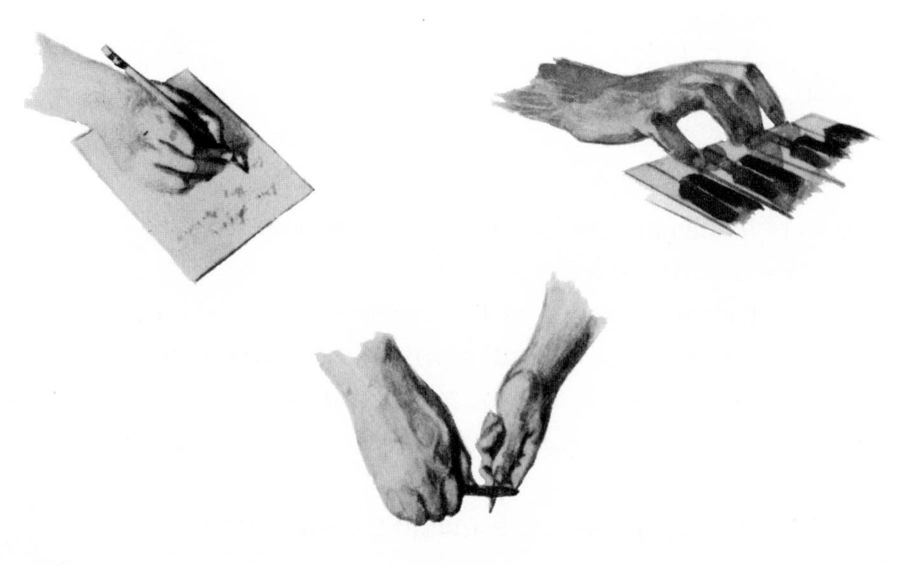

The Bones of the Hand

Just think of the many short, fast movements you so often make with your hands. To help you make such movements, you have many short bones in your wrist, palm, and fingers.

The bones of the hand

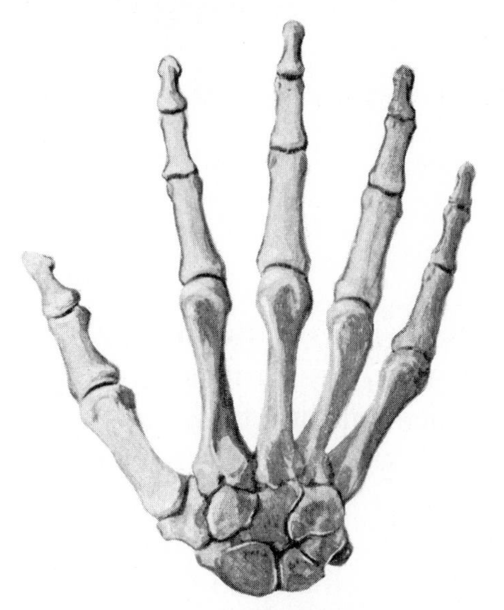

–from *Health for All, Book 5*

Building Skills

To Discuss

1. In the diagram, on which side of the hand is the thumb? How can you tell?
2. Compare the diagram of the bones of the hand with your own hand. Where in your hand do the finger bones begin? How many bones are there in each finger?
3. Where in your hand are the small round bones shown at the bottom of the diagram?
4. What idea do the small drawings on the left illustrate?

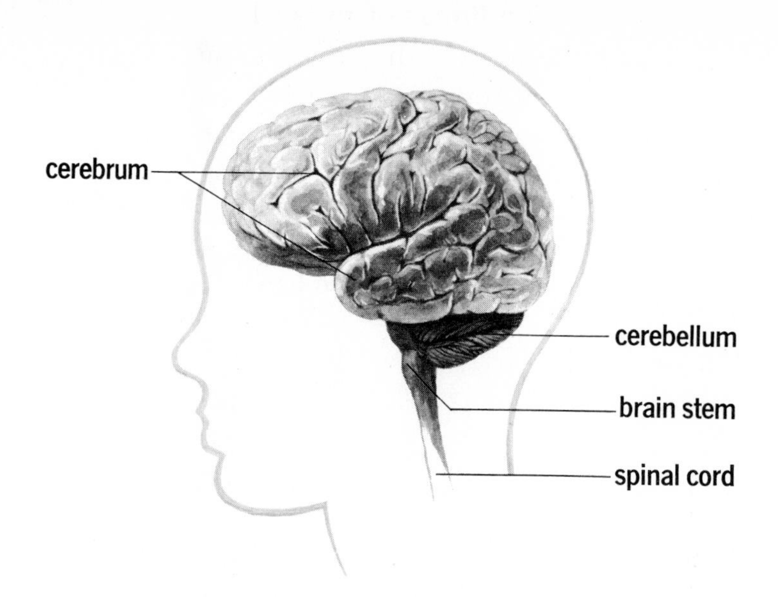

The Brain

You may be curious to learn more about your amazing brain.

Your brain, as you know, is in your head and is well protected by the bones of the head. It is protected, too, by a liquid that is all around it.

Your brain has three main parts: the *cerebrum,* the *cerebellum,* and the *brain stem.* The lowest part of the brain stem is the *medulla,* which leads into the spinal cord.

—from *Health for All, Book* 5

Building Skills

To Write

1. What are three things you learn about the brain from the picture that are not mentioned in this text?
2. What are two things you learn about the brain from the text that are not shown in the picture?

A Chart in a Social Studies Book

In this section, the drawing below is used to help you understand the paragraph about moisture from Pacific winds.

See if you can discover why little moisture from the Pacific Ocean reaches the western part of this great region.

This refers to the North Central states.

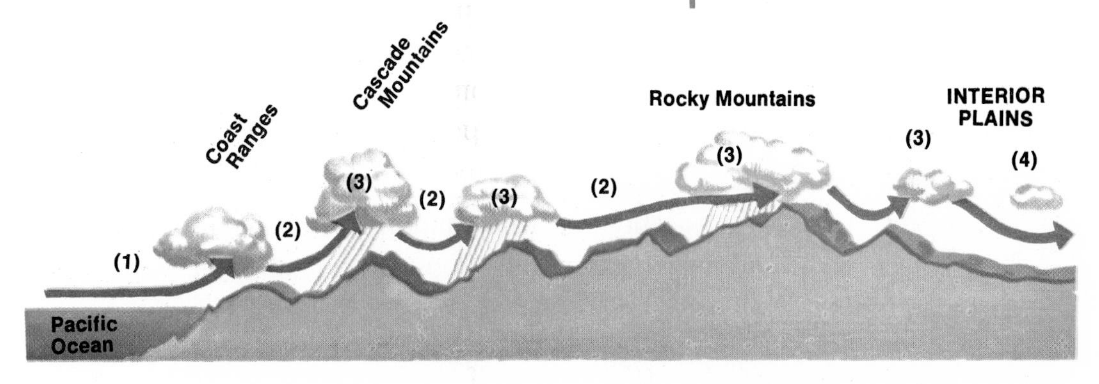

Follow these steps on the diagram: (1) Warm westerly winds cross the Pacific Ocean. They pick up much moisture. (2) As the winds move eastward, they must rise in order to cross the high mountains. (3) As the air rises, it cools. Because cool air cannot hold as much moisture as warm air, most of the moisture in the air falls as rain or snow. (4) By the time the westerly winds reach the Interior Plains, they contain little moisture. So this western part of the region is dry. Farmers have discovered that wheat is a profitable crop in these dry western plains.

A diagram is a simple drawing used to explain an idea.

Look at each number on the diagram as you read about it.

The diagram explains the reason for this important fact.

—from *Exploring Regions of the Western Hemisphere.*

Building Skills

To Discuss

Read the first sentence again and recall your purpose for reading. Could you get that information from the diagram above? from the text alone?

Summary

A good student uses all the aids available to find information in a book. You have been:

– Reviewing a table of contents to see the organization of the book.
– Finding different kinds of information – pronunciation of entry words, illustrations, maps, topics, and subtopics – in an index.
– Studying pictures, diagrams, and charts that accompany the text.

Books About the Earth

The Earth Is Your Spaceship by Julius Schwartz.

On this trip you will learn about the moon, gravity, and how the earth moves and spins.

Our Wonderful Wayside by John Hawkinson.

Are there things to learn as you walk along country roads? There are if you know what to look for. This book gives recipes for making jelly from berries, directions for making a pen from a reed, and many drawings to help you identify plants, birds, and butterflies.

Deserts: Silent Lands of the World by Alonzo Pond.

What plants and animals live in deserts? Of what use are deserts to man? Where are the deserts of the world? A map, photographs, and lively text answer these questions.

Natural Wonders of the World by Robert Stock.

Can you name thirteen natural wonders in the world? This book describes the Sahara Desert, the Greenland Icecap, the Giant's Causeway, and ten others.

Deep-sea World: The Story of Oceanography by Charles I. Coombs.

Modern explorers are discovering the life of the little-known ocean depths. Many photographs help the reader share their adventures.

The Story of the Earth by William Henry Matthews.

Rocks, minerals, volcanoes, earthquakes, mountains, soil, fossils—each is explained in words, drawings, diagrams, and photographs.

The Amazing Seeds by Ross E. Hutchins.

Many photographs show seeds that float or fly, seeds that have the strength to break glass, seeds that grow after being stored for years.

Unit 8

Action!

Basketball players in action.

SKILLS LESSON

MAKING INFERENCES

Often you read sentences that have a meaning the writer wanted you to understand but didn't actually say. For example, what does this sentence mean?

When the captain heard the news, he threw his sword to the floor and pounded the table violently.

Without actually saying so, the writer has told you that the captain was angry. Two clues help you to know this: he threw his sword to the floor and he pounded the table violently. You know that people who behave in that way are usually angry, so you *infer* that the captain was angry. To **infer** an idea means to arrive at it by reasoning. We call this process *making an inference.*

Writers depend on the reader to make inferences. They expect a reader to use his knowledge and his powers of reason-

ing or thinking to infer important ideas. Here are two sentences in which the writers did not state the full meaning directly:

Henrietta studied many hours for the test and made careful notes.

What inferences do you make? Did Henrietta want to do well on the test?

The day they arrived at the lodge, the boys were hoping for a snowstorm.

Why do you think the boys hoped for a snowstorm? The word **lodge** gives you a clue. A hotel for skiers is often called a lodge.

It is easy to make a wrong inference. In fact, sometimes writers want you to infer ideas that may not be there. For example, an advertisement might say:

The three highest-rated TV stars drive Power Jets. Success goes hand in hand with Power Jet styling.

Which of the following inferences would you make?

– If you want to be successful, drive a Power Jet.
– The styling of a car causes good things to happen to its owner.
– The writer of the advertisement wants the reader to *think* there is a connection between Power Jets and success.

What is wrong with the first two inferences?

TRY THIS

Read the statements below. Look for meanings that are not directly stated. What meaning do you infer from each? Write that inference on your paper, and be ready to discuss it.

1. Early settlers used whatever material was available for building. In the northeast, they built with wood. On the prairies, they made sod houses.
2. When the principal described the new school calendar, the students cheered enthusiastically.
3. This year's basketball team won the league championship. All the players wear Sportsman gym shoes.
4. Gale warnings are up along the coast, and the small boats are making for shore.
5. Jean's lip trembled and her cheeks were wet. She couldn't seem to find her voice.

SKILLS LESSON

DRAWING CONCLUSIONS

A skill closely related to making inferences is that of drawing conclusions. You have been drawing conclusions most of your life. For instance, when you have to cross a busy street where there is no traffic light, you look both ways, wait until all vehicles are far enough away for you to cross safely, and then cross. You collect the necessary facts, think about them, and then reach a conclusion.

In reading, you sometimes find a writer drawing conclusions based on the evidence he has presented. Notice how this is done in the following paragraph:

> In France and Spain within the last hundred years, a great many caves have been discovered where there are paintings that have been preserved for more than ten thousand years. One strange thing about the caves is that they are very hard to get into. Most of the paintings are in the darkest, most difficult part of the cave to reach. From these facts, we can be quite sure that they were not "art galleries;" in other words, the paintings were not put there just to be looked at. We think that the paintings were a part of religious and magical practices.

From the facts he has given, the writer draws two conclusions. These are stated in the last two sentences. Both conclusions have qualifying words ("we can be quite sure," "we think") that show the writer is not presenting these ideas as known facts. Notice the evidence that is given to support each conclusion. Do you think the conclusions are justified?

A conclusion is usually an important idea. (It is often the *main idea.*) When you read, you should examine the writer's conclusions carefully. Ask yourself whether the conclusions are based on facts or on opinions that are supported.

The next paragraph is about the different skills people need in doing work. An important idea is presented, but it is left to the reader to draw a conclusion from it.

Sometimes we talk about people who work with their hands and people who work with their minds. Some people are more proud of the great skill of their hands, others of the skill of their minds. But those who think they are working with their minds have to use their hands to do it; and those who think they are working with their hands wouldn't have their skill if the mind were not cooperating with the hands.

The conclusion we draw from this paragraph is also the main idea. We might state it this way: *No one works with his hands alone or with his mind alone.*

TRY THIS

Here are two paragraphs about the election of the Indian leader Nehru. The writer presents both facts and opinions, which will lead you to make inferences and draw conclusions. Read the paragraphs and answer the questions.

[1] The new nation was to have its first general election in 1952. [2] Nehru and the other leaders traveled widely, talking to the people. [3] They went by train to the big cities. [4] They reached even the smallest villages, sometimes traveling by cart on mules or on foot. [5] For the first time in India's history, every citizen could have a say in the election. [6] For those who could not read, ballot boxes were marked with signs to identify the political parties.

[7] It was the largest free election ever held. [8] When Nehru and his followers were elected, there was widespread rejoicing. [9] Since Nehru had been in school in England, he understood Western ideas. [10] He also knew India thoroughly. [11] No one was better prepared to lead the new country into the world community.

1. Which of the following inferences can you make from Sentences 2, 3, and 4?
   a. Nehru was willing to work hard to reach as many people as possible, in all parts of India.
   b. The other leaders forced Nehru to travel constantly.
2. What sentences give evidence supporting this inference: The election was run in a democratic way?
3. Is Sentence 11 a fact or an opinion? What supports it?
4. Which of the following conclusions can you draw from these paragraphs?
   a. Nehru was an important leader in the first days of India's independence.
   b. Nehru was the most famous Indian hero of all time.

SKILLS LESSON

RECOGNIZING FACT AND FICTION

When you read about events that happened in the past, or about people who lived in earlier times, do you ever wonder where the author got his information? As you read the following paragraphs from a book about George Washington, think about which details may be historically accurate. Which details do you think the author may have imagined?

A house, high above the Rappahannock, had a comfortable look against a line of tall trees. Nearby, a barn, the kitchen, poultry house, storeroom, smithy, and quarters for the slaves made a little settlement such as was usually found on prosperous Virginia farms in that year of 1739.

This first paragraph is mainly a description of the farm buildings. We know what farms in that time and place looked like, because people who lived at the time wrote about them and made drawings and paintings of them. Based on such information, the description here is probably quite accurate. The selection continues:

At the horse lot a boy tugged at the heavy gate bar, while his pony, Whitefoot, pawed impatiently, eager to be gone.

"Want help?" Tim, the stableman, called.

"No, I can do it myself," George Washington said quickly. As he tugged again, he noticed that Whitefoot was suddenly still, ears cocked as though he heard a new sound.

"Someone coming, Whitefoot?" George asked, listening. The rhythmic sound of hoofbeats came from far down the lane leading to the main road to Fredericksburg.

Are the names of the pony and the stableman real names? It is possible that there is a written record of those names, but it is more likely that the author made them up.

What about the conversation? Although the words of famous people were often written down, no one would write down such an unimportant conversation between a boy and a stableman. The author must have imagined these remarks, as well as the details about the hoofbeats and George climbing the fence in the next paragraph.

George climbed onto the fence for a look. He was sturdy and tall for a boy in his eighth year. Freckles sprinkled his straight nose, and his hands were tanned from long hours out-of-doors. Now he brushed a lock of sand-colored hair from his forehead and squinted his gray blue eyes down the land.

Look at the sentences describing young George's appearance. These are probably factual details. We know from

pictures of Washington that his hair was light in color, his eyes gray blue, and that he was tall and sturdy. So the description is believable, based on facts we know.

In order to have books about the past seem real and interesting, writers often imagine conversations and actions that may not have happened. They do this after learning everything they can about the person or the time they are writing about.

Of course, a reader cannot always know which details are based on facts and which are imagined. But it is a good idea to think about that question as you read about earlier times or about people who are no longer living. You will learn more from your reading if you ask yourself, "Is this a record of something that really happened? Or is it imaginary?"

TRY THIS

Read each of the paragraphs below carefully. Do you think the information is factual or imagined? Or is it mixed—part factual and part imagined? Be prepared to tell why you think that this is so.

A. In 1908 Robert Peary made his last attempt to reach the North Pole. He was fifty-two years old that year, but he looked older. His many years of exploring in the Arctic had been hard

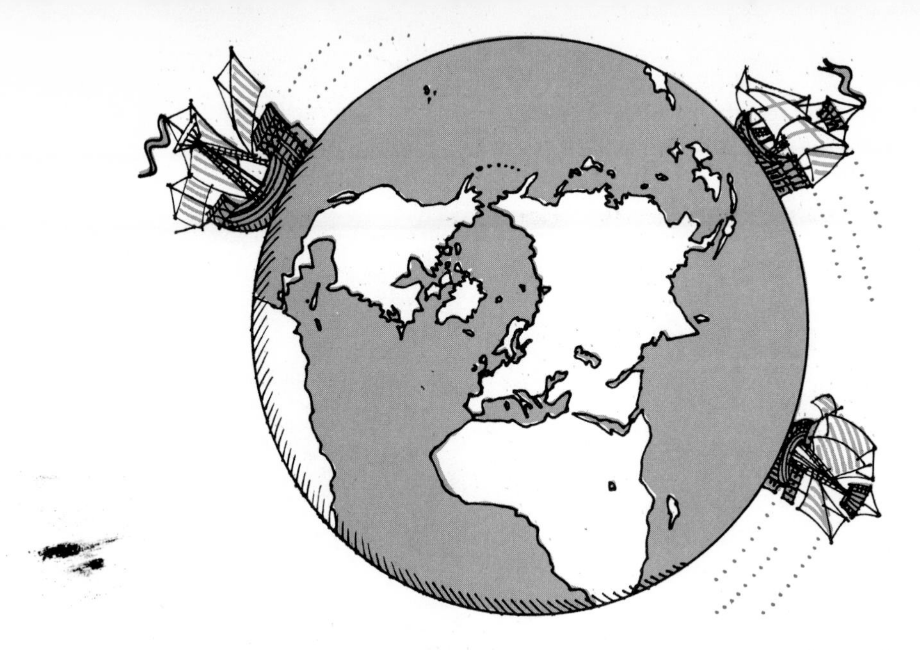

on him. Peary had decided that he must reach the Pole on this trip or die in the attempt.

B. In the 1930's Franklin Delano Roosevelt became the first President to speak regularly over radio to his fellow citizens. He had a strong, clear voice that was easy to recognize. Many people today still remember his broadcasts.

C. Columbus's voyage of discovery to the New World took more than two months. Many of the sailors became afraid or discouraged and wanted to turn back. But Columbus insisted that they continue. "We must sail on!" he cried.

WHAT DID YOU LEARN?

1. How can a reader get a meaning that is not expressed directly by the printed words?
2. When a writer draws a conclusion, what should the reader notice?
3. How do writers get information about people and events from the past?

■ The crowds of football fans cheered this star running-back—

Floyd Little

by BILL LIBBEY

As you read, think what you can infer about Floyd as a person. Look for details that support the conclusions you draw.

It was midseason, and Floyd Little had finally become a top pro football runner. After two ordinary seasons with the Denver Broncos, the former Syracuse University All-American now led the American Football League in rushing. Despite missing one full game with an injury, he had rushed for more than five hundred yards, averaging more than five yards a carry. The tough, tricky, little runner had gained a place at the top.

"BADGES OF BATTLE"

It was the night before a game with San Diego. Joyce Little, his wife, beat Floyd seven games to five on the pool table in the basement of their Denver home. They were wisecracking but serious. Floyd laughed, "She gets me in the mood for winning football by beating me at pool."

He watched TV for a while, fell asleep about eleven, then slept until eleven the next morning. He skipped breakfast, as he always did on the day of a game, because food did not feel good in his stomach when he was nervous. He grew more nervous as his wife drove him to Mile High Stadium and the game drew near.

The Mile High Stadium—home to Floyd Little and the Denver Broncos.

It had snowed on Saturday, and more snow swirled down now as he entered the dressing room. He had his legs rubbed down and his ankles taped while the other players drifted in, clowning to cut the tension. They pulled on their bulky gear and their red and white uniforms and then sat quietly as their coach, Lou Saban, talked to them about how to beat the Chargers.

Finally, it was time. Floyd pulled on his blue helmet and ran out onto the field with the rest of the Broncos. It had stopped snowing, but the sidelines were white and the field was brown.

At five-foot-ten and 195 pounds, Little *seemed* little among the giants who were warming up for combat. At first he was used sparingly. The Denver quarterback would fake to Floyd, then give to another back. When Little did get the ball, he moved it, darting quickly through openings in the line, shifting speeds smoothly, faking out defenders with jitterbug steps, breaking tackles with surprising strength, and pushing forward for extra yardage.

"Fluid" was the word that kept coming to mind when you watched him. He ran hard, but with fluid motion, breaking a hard tackle to get twenty-one yards on one run. He reached out to catch a long pass on his fingertips and pivoted away from two defenders to get seventeen yards on another play.

There was no scoring and the Broncos took command in the second half. Passes produced one touchdown. Another score was set up when Little shook loose on a screen pass for twenty-one yards. Then Floyd himself rammed the ball home from two yards out. He and his mates on the offensive team trooped happily to the bench.

Late in the third quarter, Little took another screen pass for a fifteen-yard gain, but he was tackled viciously. Floyd writhed in pain on the frozen ground and was finally carried to the bench. As a doctor worked on his right leg, someone helped him off with his helmet, revealing his face, numb from cold and caked with mud.

He did not get back into the game, which ended as a two-touchdown triumph for Denver. The weary Broncos trotted jubilantly into their dressing room under the outfield bleachers as the chilled fans stood and cheered them. Little limped in last.

He stripped and hobbled into the trainer's room, where he sat on a table with his legs spread and his back pressed against the wall. Despite his injury, he was smiling. All around him the players whooped and hollered in the steamy warmth.

Little's shins were scabbed from old sores and scraped bloody with new ones. "Badges of battle," he said, grinning. He pressed an ice pack against a large bruise on his right thigh, but it was his knee that worried him. It had been twisted severely, and he was told he would have to have it examined the following day.

"The tackler was so close to me I didn't think he could hit me heavy," Floyd explained. "If I had lowered my head and just rammed into him, I'd never have been hurt. But I knew another touchdown would put us out of reach. I could see that if I could get by this one tackler, I'd go, so I began to put down some stuff. He wasn't fooled and hit me hard while I had both feet off the ground."

Little probed his sore knee gently with his scuffed-up fingers and shrugged his shoulders. "You can't tip-toe through games. If you're cautious, you're through. You go all out and hope for the best."

Earlier in his career he had been handicapped by a cracked collarbone, a wrenched back, a sprained ankle, and a severely torn finger. He also had been slowed down by a bad case of flu.

He got up from the table and limped into the shower room. Although he was not a big man, he was thickly muscled. He also had severely bowed legs. "They help

Floyd addresses his fans as his wife, with baby, looks on.

me not be grounded. They're so bowed tacklers can't get their arms all the way around them. If they were straight, I'd be three inches taller and a great pass receiver."

He returned drying himself off. Most of the other players had departed by then. Painfully, Floyd dressed, pulling on slacks, a white turtleneck sweater, and a heavy coat. He went out into the darkness, for it was night now, and even colder than it had been during the game. A group of youngsters stood outside by the dressing room door, waiting for him to sign autographs. He stopped and gave them out patiently.

Someone called, "Hey, Floyd, your wife says to hurry before she freezes to death." Floyd grinned and limped to the sidelines where she waited. She was dancing from foot to foot and clapping her hands in an effort to keep warm. "Oh, baby, beautiful," she said, hugging and kissing him. Then her victory smile faded, her face grew concerned, and she asked him, "Are you hurt bad?" He said he thought he was all right. She was relieved.

Unfortunately, the injury turned out to be more serious than expected. It did not require an operation, like so many knee injuries in pro football, but Floyd's leg was in a cast for a long time. In the meantime, Little got around on crutches and missed four games. "Those were the worst four weeks of my life," he said later. "I lost eight or nine pounds worrying."

After Little was hurt, Denver failed to win in its next five games and won again only in the last game of the season. Little said, "It's a deep disappointment, but you have to learn to handle disappointment in sports. You have to keep trying your best and hope things will get better."

READING, WRITING, AND FOOTBALL

Floyd Douglas Little was born on the Fourth of July, 1942, in Waterbury, Connecticut. His father died of cancer when Floyd was six, leaving Floyd's mother to raise six children on welfare payments. They lived in a poor, black section of town and had few luxuries.

Floyd was a homely, nervous child, who for a long time would go out into the world only when he could hang onto an older sister's skirt. When he mispronounced a word in the third grade and others laughed at him, he refused to read aloud in school for many years afterward.

His mother moved her family to New Haven when Floyd was thirteen. There they settled in another ghetto. In one house in which they lived, there were twenty-six children on three floors. There was little hope for the future for any of them. Floyd, however, found hope in sports.

He was a fast, agile youngster, who played all games brilliantly. Unfortunately he was too busy making a badly-needed five dollars a day as a shoeshine boy to practice with his teams. He got to Hillhouse High School late, learned little there, and became too old to play high school football before he finished school. But by then he was already recognized as a great football player.

Many colleges offered Little football scholarships. He could not imagine himself in college, so he looked for work. He applied for a job as a janitor but was rejected when he was unable to fill out the application properly. The company considered him illiterate.

Bordentown Military Academy, a college preparatory school, was seeking a black athlete to integrate the school. They offered Floyd a scholarship and he accepted. He played brilliant football for them and they worked hard on giving him an education. "There was nothing wrong with my mind, but no one had reached out to help me before," he explained. "With help, I began to do well in my studies. Finally,

Floyd divided his time between the classroom and the football field.

I felt I could make it in college."

Many colleges sought him, including Syracuse, which sent its All-American runner, Ernie Davis, to recruit him.

At Syracuse, Little was given the number 44, the same number worn by the famous Syracuse players Jim Brown and Davis. Floyd surpassed their accomplishments there. A spectacular breakaway runner, Floyd became one of the few players to attain All-American honors for three straight seasons. And he helped his team to great success. He blossomed as a leader who often tongue-lashed lagging teammates on behalf of his coach.

Floyd also blossomed in the classroom, studying history and religion and reading and writing poetry, which he came to love. He also came to love Joyce Green, the lovely daughter of a New York schoolteacher. Joyce stepped up her program in order to graduate with Floyd and to finish in just three years, with honors. After graduation, they were married.

Little called college the saving

experience of his life. He said, "It used to bug me to sweat for hours over books for C's, while others fooled around and got A's; but I had a lot of catching up to do. I may have gotten more from my studies than those to whom everything came easy. While others could take jobs for extra money, I had to attend summer school. I was an old senior, twenty-five. But while a lot of athletes never graduate, I did, and in four years."

The year he graduated, Denver drafted Floyd and signed him to a four-year contract worth about $130,000.

ONE OF THE GREAT ONES

A twenty-six-year-old rookie has his troubles. Little made many mistakes and fumbled frequently. His true ability emerged only in solo performances. The team won only three games, and Little was considered a disappointment.

Floyd autographing footballs for his fans.

Perhaps he proved himself as a pro against Buffalo. He caught a pass for a sixty-six-yard score to help the Broncos to a 31–29 lead with a minute to play. Then he fumbled deep in his territory. Frustrated and furious, Little pleaded for the opportunity to atone.

After the kickoff the Broncos had the ball deep in their own territory. Floyd's number was called on a pass play. He faked free, caught the ball, and gained sixty-six yards before being downed. Bobby Howfield rushed on to kick a field goal, giving Denver a dramatic 34–32 triumph. Floyd wept with joy.

Little was approaching his first thousand-yard season when he broke a bone in his back in the twelfth game. Though not too serious, the injury was painful, and it handicapped him in the last two contests. He fell short of the thousand-yard mark, but he still won the American Football Conference rushing crown.

He received more votes than any player on the conference All-Star Team and was named All-Pro for the entire NFL. "Individual recognition is just great," he admitted, "but it doesn't mean as much when your team hasn't done well. I'll just have to keep trying to do more and hope it helps the team do better."

He said he would like to go into youth counseling in the future. "I am not a militant and I do not believe in violence. I do not believe a person should waste his time in college creating turmoil," he said. "I am black and proud of it. I'd like to work with black boys, with minority groups, with all boys who have a hard time getting started. If I had been counseled, I wouldn't have left high school too dumb to fill out an application for a job as a janitor. I'm one who knows now how much good college can do for a person. I'd also like to coach, because I love football.

"Basically, I'm an old-fashioned sort. I believe in doing right. I believe in making the most of your God-given abilities. I'm a natural-born runner. It's something I do well and I've worked to become better at it. I believe in becoming the best you can at the things you do best, whether it's playing a game, singing, selling something, or working on cars. I feel fortunate that what I do well is glamorous and exciting and pays well. I've had to endure a lot of injuries, but that's part of it."

In the age of the passer there is still room for the runner, the most exciting performer on the football field. Floyd Little is one of the great ones.

A motor plus two wheels adds up to an exciting sport.

Whirling Wheels

by EDWARD RADLAUER

As you read, decide which details about the past are factual and which are imagined.

As the morning sun brings its first light to the hilly country, there are sounds of roosters, dogs, and cows from the farms nearby. Suddenly, a different sound fills the air. It grows from a distant rumble to the roar of powerful engines. As the thunder grows, a huge cloud of dust swirls up from the ground. Out of the cloud of dust comes a group of motorcycles. The riders wear helmets, leather suits, and boots. As they make sharp turns, their heavy-soled boots cut grooves in the dirt. The powerful machines whine and growl as they go up and down the steepest hills.

What is going on? Who are these strangely dressed people riding two-wheeled mountain goats?

These are the members of a motorcycle club. They are testing each other and their machines on the steepest hills they can find. This race really started long ago.

BIKES WITH MOTORS

Let us go back to a small German village in the year 1885. Since there are no automobiles, airplanes, or trucks, it is very quiet. Suddenly,

Gottlieb Daimler (1834-1900)
Daimler was a German engineer, inventor, and pioneer. He improved the internal-combustion engine and was one of the first to use it on a bicycle. But he didn't stop there. He adapted the engine for use with boats and cars. These successful experiments made important contributions to the growing motorcycle and automobile industries.

the air is filled with a loud, popping, snapping, and hissing sound. Down the road comes a machine that sends chickens running for cover, sets dogs to barking and the children to hiding behind their mothers' long skirts. But these aren't the ones who should be frightened! The one who should be fearful is Paul Daimler, riding the world's first motorcycle.

Daimler may not have been afraid, but he was certainly shaken up. Taking the first ride on the first motorcycle may have been an honor, but it was not a pleasure.

On that day Paul's father, Gottlieb Daimler, had just finished building this two-wheeled monster. Paul was taking his first ride and, although he didn't know it, he was making history.

The motorcycle Paul rode was invented by accident. Gottlieb Daimler had built one of the world's first small gasoline-burning engines. Most engines of his day were giant things, not intended to be moved at all. These heavy engines burned gas from pipes, the same pipes that supplied homes with fuel for cooking, heating, and lighting. There was no electricity in use yet. No one had found a way to mix liquid gasoline with air in order to make it burn in an engine. Until Gottlieb Daimler, no one had found a way to mix air and gasoline and force it into an engine. He had not only discovered how to make a lightweight engine, he had also discovered how to make a *carburetor*—the chamber in which air and gasoline could be mixed. Without a carburetor, we might still be riding horses. With his engine built and running, Daimler needed a place to try it out. He decided to build a two-wheeled vehicle like a bicycle. The result was the world's first motorcycle.

What a ride Paul Daimler must have had on his motorcycle back in 1885! The road was rough and bumpy and, even at slow speed, his motorcycle bucked and snorted like an angry horse. It must have been a sight! Certainly no one had ever heard such a thing. It would look strange to us today. The seat of the cycle resembled a horse's saddle. The frame, wheels, and spokes were made of wood. There were tires, though! Each wheel had a rim of steel, but the steel rim was not meant to cushion the ride. The rim of steel was designed to hold the wooden wheel together. Such a rim did not do much to soften a ride on a rough road.

The world's first gasoline engine did not run smoothly at all. The engine would speed up and slow down so suddenly that the rider jolted forward and backward in a way that made his head shake. In spite of the rough ride, Paul is said to have reached a speed of seven miles per hour. While seven miles per hour is not much speed nowadays, the Daimlers showed the world that a motorcycle could be built and ridden.

About 1900, a company started to build an engine for bicycles. It was called a *clip-on engine.* The engine clipped on under the handlebars, where it could turn the front wheel through a belt drive. But the engine, being in front, sprayed oil and fuel in the face of the rider, caused difficulty in steering, and made the whole bicycle top-heavy and out of balance.

Even so, most bicycle riders thought oil spray, poor balance, and hard steering were preferable to pedaling so hard.

Before long, people decided that mounting an engine under the handlebars was probably a poor way to provide a bicycle with gasoline-engine power. Then a few folks managed to find worse places for the engine. Some tried putting it above the rear wheel. A few bicycles appeared with engines mounted between two rear or two front wheels! One unfortunate rider tried a bicycle with the engine mounted under the seat. The first time it backfired, the driver

Motorcyclists lean forward, anticipating the start of the race.

decided he had better find a different place for the engine. Finally, people discovered that the best place for the engine was right by the bicycle pedals. This is just about where present-day motorcycle engines are located.

MOTORCYCLE RACES

No one knows exactly where the very first motorcycle race took place. It probably happened when two riders met on a road. No doubt, there were, and still are, many such races. They usually bring about long arguments about who won. These are races without rules.

We do know that some of the first organized motorcycle races *with rules* took place on the Isle of Man, off the coast of England. The race was to be for *touring cycles.* That meant motorcycles which people used on the public roads for everyday riding. But people could not agree on what was really meant by a touring cycle. Even back in 1907, it was hard to make up rules that pleased everyone.

Finally, someone made a suggestion to have two races, a race for cycles with one cylinder and a race for cycles with more than one cylinder. That saved the event!

So, on a gray, cold day in May, 1907, two important events of motorcycle history took place. The competition on the Isle of Man will be remembered as the first organized motorcycle race and also the first motorcycle event in which machines were placed in classes. Today, in almost every kind of racing, machines are still placed in classes according to speed, engine size, or driver experience.

A whole story of motorcycle competition has come out of that beginning of racing at the Isle of Man. The story seems to say, "Give two people two motorcycles and you have a race."

Let us look at some of the many kinds of races that have been tried, as well as those that are still popular.

Flat Track Racing

One of the simplest and most common races is on an oval dirt-track. Before the race, the track is often soaked to pack the dirt. One rule common to all flat-track racing is that bikes must have no brakes! Some flat-track cycles are specially built without brakes. Riders who enter with a street-style machine disconnect their brakes before entering the flat-track race. The reason for the no-brakes rule is that on a small oval, a quick stop can mean a *spin out*. A spin out means a rider gets dumped and may cause others to spin out. Instead of brakes, the rider uses his boots for stopping, and he may wear a steel sole on his left boot because the race is run in a left-hand direction. The steel shoe helps while stopping or sliding through left-hand turns. Obviously, flat-track racers need sturdy left legs.

Hill Climbing

If the flat-track riders need strong left legs, those who enter hill-climb events need strong legs on both sides. Hill climbing takes plenty of muscle. It is more a test of skill than a race. The course up a steep hill is timed. The rider who makes the climb in the shortest time wins. It isn't easy to climb through the dirt on a steep track. Too much power or acceleration causes spinning wheels to dig into the dirt. Too little speed means a driver loses balance and ends up by trying to carry his bike to the top! Hill climbing is *not* an event for beginners.

Drag Racing

In recent years, more and more cyclists have entered drag racing. Professional drag races are run on a straight, flat, hard-surfaced track. The course is a timed run from a standing start. Specially built drag bikes have reached speeds of over one hundred sixty miles per hour at the end of the quarter mile. This kind of machine usually has a giant engine and burns fuel other than gasoline. Many drag cycles have

Enthusiastic crowds add to the excitement of a scrambled race.

no seats. The driver just stretches out on top of the bike. Since he may cover the distance in ten seconds, there is really no need to sit down. Besides that, with the driver stretched out on top, the bike makes a more streamlined mass to cut through the air.

Scramble

Scramble racing is popular with motorcycle people. A scramble track is a rough piece of countryside. The run goes up and down hills, over small jumps, around sharp turns, and maybe even through water! The riders, in classes, gather in a pack for the start. The race is run in *laps*. A lap is once around the required course. A scramble-race lap is anywhere from three to five miles. The first rider across the finish line after running the required number of laps is the winner. But there have been scramble races where *no one* finished.

Enduro

For those who like even longer races, there is the enduro. The name comes from the word *endure*. That is what one must do in this race. The rider and his bike have to endure long enough to run one hundred fifty to five hundred miles. Some enduro events last two days. The course is one that includes public roads, desert or mountain trails, and perhaps just for fun, a shallow water crossing or two. This competition is between each cyclist and a time schedule. Enduro rules require riders to stop at checkpoints along the way. If a rider arrives at a checkpoint on time, he gets a number of points. But if he arrives too early or too late, he gets a lower number of points. Therefore, enduro rules suggest that riders carry a good watch.

Enduro rules also require machines to be equipped with a license, a muffler, and a speedometer. Enduro cycles are built to be dependable; they are not built for speed. But an enduro rider must be on the lookout for course markers; and if he misses a marker or takes a wrong turn, he is out on a pleasure trip, not in an enduro race.

Road Racing

Road races are run on paved courses, sometimes on parts of public highways that have been closed to regular traffic.

Road-race machines have light frames and engines tuned for speed and endurance. Many road-race machines have *fairings*. These are shields to protect the rider from wind and dirt.

By using extra-large fuel tanks, riders can run longer between fuel stops. Road-race machines have extra-large brakes because of the need to slow down quickly and often.

Riders race in classes, and either the first to finish or the one with the shortest running time is declared a winner. Factory-sponsored teams participate in some of the big road-race events. Each of these teams consists of drivers and mechanics paid by a company to test its equipment under racing conditions. In this way, a manufacturer proves the value of his product for himself. At the same time, he demonstrates what his cycle, oil, tires, or other products can do. These are popular world-wide events. In fact, road races are popular wherever there are roads and motorcycles.

Road Run or Rally

The road run or rally is not actually a race. It is an event for fun. Participants in the rally travel, either singly or in groups, over a course laid out by club officials or an association. The course is almost always on public roads. The club usually emphasizes safety, careful riding, courtesy, and attention to traffic laws. Participants must stop at "checkpoints" marked on their maps. Prizes at the end of

A cyclist wearing the proper gear practices signaling.

the run might be for the best-looking cycle, the youngest participant, the best watermelon eater, or for other games and contests. Road rallies are a good family sport. They give motorcycle riders a chance to show the public that riding is both safe and fun.

MOTORCYCLE SAFETY

More and more people are turning to motorcycles for transportation and sports. With so many cycles in use, there is a great need to teach the owners to ride correctly and safely. Some people say there should be driver education for cyclists as well as for automobile drivers.

There are various ways to learn to ride. One can learn from a friend who is a good rider, from books which give lessons on safety and correct driving rules, or from dealers who sell motorcycles. The important thing to remember is that a motorcycle is *only as safe as the person riding it.*

Safety starts even before a rider mounts his machine. This first safety rule is about clothes! People who know motorcycles, especially those with a great deal of riding and racing experience, wouldn't think of mounting without wearing heavy shoes, helmet, pants, and jacket. They want motorcycling to be fun without being dangerous. They get very angry with people who do reckless things that give motorcycling a bad name.

Another safety rule starts *before* the actual ride. This is the rule about checking the condition of the machine. We have talked about the flat-track racing where no brakes are allowed. This is the *only* place in motorcycle sports where brakes are not wanted. But driving on a busy street is not a flat-track race. At a race or cycle event, the official inspector is an experienced rider. If he believes a bike is unsafe and says no, the contestant just does not run. Cycle riders must learn to be their *own safety inspectors.* It is dangerous to have brakes that don't work or an accelerator cable that sticks in the wide-open position.

It is also very important for the rider to become familiar with the motorcycle he rides. Even an experienced cyclist should drive a new or a borrowed motorcycle slowly around the block or in a parking lot before he drives in traffic at normal speeds.

In traffic, the motorcyclist must remember that the other fellow may not be as careful a driver as he is. Even if an automobile driver remembers his safety rules, there are places around his car where he cannot see the motorcycle rider!

There are places in traffic where no motorcyclist should go. While it may look faster to sneak in between a moving row of cars and the curb, or between a row of cars and those parked along the curb, once in there, the rider is caught. If someone in a car changes lanes or if a car pulls out from the curb, the motorcyclist is in a tight spot.

The fun in motorcycle riding runs out when someone gets hurt. Safety experts, race riders, and the police are working to keep all the fun in motorcycle riding.

The enduro cycle is not built for speed but for dependability.

Learning how to take chances the safe way is part of a stunt girl's education.

Hollywood Stunt Girl

by WALTER PRICE BURRELL

Think about the details of Peaches' life. What conclusions about Peaches can you draw from these details?

The place is Durango, in Mexico. The day is hot and still. A girl, sweet-faced and freckled, walks through the desert town. Her clothes are those of the 1860's. Except for the girl, nothing moves in the quiet, sleepy town. Suddenly, a man rides out of the choking dust at breakneck speed. Hoofs strike the girl and knock her to the ground. Man and horse ride off, leaving the trampled girl in the dust. Horrible!—or so it seems.

One of Peaches' best stunts is jumping from one horse to another.

"Cut!" cries director Sidney Poitier. The girl, Peaches Jones, rises unhurt and smiling from the road. She brushes the dust from her clothes and pats her hair back into place.

Peaches Jones is a Hollywood stuntwoman. She has just doubled for actress Ruby Dee in a scene too dangerous for most actresses to play.

If the scene is too dangerous for other actresses, why isn't it too dangerous for Peaches? How does she manage to keep from being hurt? And how did a girl like Peaches get into such a risky profession?

Peaches doesn't get hurt because she carefully plans and practices every stunt. These stunts require perfect physical condition, split-second timing, and practice, practice, and more practice. After weeks of training, a stunt like falling off a horse is as easy as, well, falling off a horse.

Shortly after moving pictures were invented, stuntmen began replacing the actors in dangerous scenes. Over the years there have been only a few stuntwomen. Peaches Jones's father was a Hollywood stuntman. He and a few other men founded the Black Stuntmen's Association. Peaches loved to watch her father practice his movie stunts. Soon, she started trying a few of them herself. Today, she is one of the leading stuntwomen in Hollywood. Peaches does some stunts that no other stuntwoman in the movies is qualified to do. She is the only woman in films who can "fall" a horse. "Falling" a horse means getting the horse to fall on command as if it had been shot or wounded—without hurting either itself or its rider.

A stuntman or stuntwoman must be in perfect physical condition. At Pasadena's John Muir High School, Peaches was one of the top athletes in her class. She was on the gymnastics and basketball teams. She high-jumped and broad-jumped. She was a cheerleader, and she was voted Miss Physical Fitness. She took part in the city's Junior Olympics. Peaches's father felt that she was so good in gymnastics that she could have made the Olympic team. Peaches still keeps in good physical condition by playing tennis, scuba diving, and riding horses.

Peaches mastered horseback riding when she was still a child. Now she has two horses of her own that she keeps in a neat corral in her backyard. These horses play an important part in Peaches's work. Many of her stunts are done with horses. Besides "falling" horses, Peaches can ride two horses at once

Peaches practicing motorcycle stunts.

while standing up in both saddles. She can jump from one moving horse to another without losing stride. She can fall in front of racing horses and roll away unhurt.

Peaches is constantly practicing her old stunts and perfecting new ones. She is becoming an expert in motorcycle stunts. Peaches practices these tricks with her father. Soon, she hopes to be able to jump a motorcycle over a row of barrels. Cars also take some of Peaches's time. She is learning to handle cars for crash scenes in movies. Crashing a car is not difficult, but not getting hurt is.

Of course, there is danger in her work, and Mr. Jones admits that he worries about his daughter. "I tell her not to try anything she isn't sure she can handle. There is no need to take unnecessary chances. The chances she's faced with after she knows what she's doing are enough."

Some of Peaches's stunts look very dangerous and they are. Some look very dangerous and they aren't. In one movie, Peaches was dragged down the stairs by her hair. That stunt was "one of the easiest of my career," said Peaches. "I had lots of pads to cushion the bumps. But it looked terrible on camera."

But in another film made for TV, Peaches was almost hurt doing her stunt. She played a blind girl who steps off a curb and falls in front of a speeding car. The cameras would show most of the action, then turn to the driver's face. The audi-

Peaches Jones relaxing after a day of stunt work.

ence would not see the girl get hit. (Of course, stuntmen are not actually hit by cars, but clever photography makes it seem as if they are.) In this "take," the driver could not stop the car as soon as planned. The car stopped only inches from Peaches's head. That was a stunt that should have been easy, but wasn't.

Doing stunts is not the hardest part of Peaches's job. She has to do them better than the stunt*men*. Stuntmen aren't any easier on Peaches because she is a woman, and some of them resent it when Peaches does a better job than they do. "I have to keep up with them. That's all right with me. They don't really like the idea of my being as good as they are at stunt work."

Everyone, including the stuntmen respect Peaches's ability and hard work. Her willing-to-try-anything attitude has won her a great deal of praise. Sidney Poitier was so pleased with her work that he added stunts to one of his films for Peaches to do. He even put in a small acting role for her. Ruby Dee says that "Peaches makes everybody on the set feel good. Everybody likes her immediately. She's a very good stuntwoman. I was constantly amazed at what she could do."

The best part of Peaches's unusual job is that she likes it. Every day she works at it, she likes it even better. "Even after I get married, the more I do and learn, the more I am convinced that this is what I want as a life's work."

Thinking While Reading

In textbooks a writer often gives you information and then draws a conclusion from it. You have to ask: Is the conclusion supported by the information given? Sometimes a writer gives information and allows a reader to draw his own conclusion. Then you have to be careful to infer only the meaning that is justified. You have to think about the evidence and weigh the ideas carefully in your mind.

When you are reading about people and events from the past, you must be alert to the kind of evidence that is imaginary and the kind that is probably factual. In short, you should always be thinking while you are reading.

Inferences and Conclusions in Social Studies

Read the paragraphs about "Famous Routes Used in New Ways." Note how the information given helps you to make inferences and draw conclusions.

Famous Routes Used in New Ways

Very few people know that ocean-going ships can sail all the way to Chicago. Milwaukee, Detroit, and Cleveland, too, are ocean ports.

Ask yourself: What connects these cities to the ocean? Read to find the answer.

The St. Lawrence River, which flows from Lake Ontario to the Atlantic Ocean, is a fine waterway for much of its length. But in the upper part of the river, the water is shallow and there are many rapids. More than one hundred years ago, a canal was built along the St. Lawrence River from Montreal to Lake Ontario. Yet, this canal is shallow and its locks are small. Only very small ocean ships can use the canal.

From which details in these sentences can you infer that the St. Lawrence is not entirely satisfactory as a waterway?

A new way to the sea

In 1959 a new canal along the St. Lawrence River was completed and opened for traffic. This canal is called the St. Lawrence Seaway. It is wide and deep, and its locks are big enough for large ocean freighters.

What effect do you think the St. Lawrence Seaway has had on water traffic?

Now that the St. Lawrence Seaway is finished, it is possible to ship large loads of western wheat directly from Chicago to countries overseas. Iron ore from eastern Canada can be shipped through the Seaway to the Great Lakes.

What would be the advantages of these new shipping routes?

Chicago and other lake cities are working to build new harbors for larger ocean ships. The lake cities believe they may become great seaports like those along the Middle Atlantic seaboard.

Why does having an outlet to the sea help cities to grow?

Another waterway goes back to work

For many years after the coming of the railroads, the Mississippi and Ohio rivers carried less and less traffic. But times have changed. Diesel-powered towboats and barges have replaced the steamboats, and the rivers now carry more cargo than ever before. St. Louis, Louisville, and Cincinnati are again important river ports.

Why would the railroads have an effect on river traffic?

Powerful towboats like the one in the picture can push a string of as many as thirty barges. Steel, grain, chemicals, pipe, animal feed, and soybeans are shipped this way. But the most important cargoes are now petroleum and coal. The new barge traffic on the Ohio-Mississippi-Illinois waterway has brought new industries to the river banks. River towns that seemed forgotten for more than fifty years are building homes and shcools for the workers in the new factories. It seems likely that, as more and more people go to work in the factories of the Middle West, there will be more and more traffic on these famous waterways.

Why does good water transportation attract industries?

—from *The American Continents*

Building Skills

To Write

Which of the following inferences would you make from the facts about the St. Lawrence Seaway? Write the letter of each statement that you think is justified by the text.

a. The Seaway is the most important development in Canada in the last twenty years.
b. The Seaway has had an important effect on the transportation of goods in both Canada and the United States.
c. Many cities around the Great Lakes expect the Seaway to help them grow.

To Discuss

1. In the last sentence of the selection, the writer draws a conclusion about traffic on the Ohio and Mississippi rivers. Is his conclusion justified? How does he support it?
2. Based on the information about these waterways, what conclusion can you draw about the importance of good water transportation to modern cities and towns?

Conclusions About People in History

The paragraphs below tell about John Smith, the leader of the earliest American colony at Jamestown. The writer draws a conclusion about Smith in the first paragraph. As you read, ask yourself whether the details that follow support that conclusion.

It was due to John Smith that the Jamestown settlers were able to survive at all. More than any other person, he furnished the energy, ability, and common sense that saved the colony.

Most of the men who had sailed with Captain Newport had never worked with their hands. They were unprepared for the hard work of building houses and a stockade. They had come to Virginia expecting to find gold and riches. Instead they found nothing but hardship.

From the beginning, the Indians were unfriendly toward the settlers. Also, many other troubles lay ahead.

Summer arrived with its hot moist days and nights. With summer, the mosquitoes came, spreading malaria among the unhappy colonists.

Then the food spoiled, and the water turned bad. Many settlers died, and the others almost gave up hope.

Cooler weather in the fall brought some relief. But hunger, disease, and death haunted the settlers. By winter, only thirty-two of them were still alive.

It was John Smith who set the example for the colony. He worked hard at building a fort. He made sure everyone else had shelter before he thought about shelter for himself. When the men complained of the hard work, he issued orders that anyone who did not work would not eat.

Later, when the food supply was nearly gone, Smith went to the Indians. These were the same Indians who had been planning to destroy the tiny settlement. Yet, somehow, Smith managed to trade with them for food.

—from *This Is Our Land*

Building Skills

To Write

1. Did you make some inferences about the men described in the second paragraph? Write the words from the list below that you think might be used to describe those men. If you think of some words of your own that give a better description, write them, too.

unskilled	gentlemen	weaklings
selfish	lazy	greedy

2. Which words below could you use to describe John Smith? Write some words of your own if you prefer.

fair	strong	industrious
cruel	clever	hard-hearted

To Discuss

1. Reread the first paragraph. Are the writer's statements supported by the evidence he gives?
2. Give four facts that tell of the hardships the colonists had to suffer. Do they help to explain why the author wrote "Many settlers died, and the others almost gave up hope"?

Reported and Imagined Details in History

The selection below is about an early American patriot, Haym Salomon, who came to this country from Poland before the Revolutionary War. During that war, he was on the American side against the British. As you read, watch for details that show how Salomon felt about his adopted country.

Haym Salomon still fought for his new country. The British soldiers heard about him and arrested him for helping the American cause. This was September of the year 1776.

Although Haym Salomon was put in jail, he did not stay there long. The British had brought over some Hessian (hĕsh′ăn) soldiers to fight for them. These soldiers were not British. They came from a part of Prussia called Hesse (hĕs). England paid the Hessian government money for the services of these soldiers.

The Hessians spoke only German. This made it hard for the British to talk to them.

"We hear that you can speak the German language," the British said to Haym Salomon. "We will let you out of jail if you will help us talk to the Hessians."

Haym Salomon thought about this offer. Maybe this was his chance to do something for the cause of freedom.

"The British will not really set me free even if I do talk to the Hessians for them," Haym Salomon thought. "They will keep me under arrest and watch me. But I cannot help my country while I am in jail. If I agree to this British plan, maybe I can find out some of their plans and get the news to General Washington."

Haym Salomon agreed to speak German to the Hessians and to help the British understand what the soldiers said.

The British let Salomon out of jail, but they did not set him free. They put him to work for General Heister (hī′stûr), a Hessian general.

The British kept Haym Salomon under close watch. But he did manage to help America! He talked to the Hessians for the British, but he also talked to the Hessian soldiers about America and her fight for freedom. And he talked so well that many Hessian soldiers ran away to join the American army to fight against the British!

—from *Great Names in Our Country's Story*

Building Skills

To Write

1. Which of the following details do you think are factual and which are imaginary? Write FACTUAL or IMAGINARY after the letter of each.

   a. The length of time Haym Salomon spent in jail.
   b. The Hessian soldiers spoke only German.
   c. The words the British used in speaking to Salomon.

d. The words that express Haym Salomon's thoughts about the British offer.

2. What do you think Salomon said to the Hessian soldiers that made them join the American army? Imagine two or three sentences that he might say to them, and write them on your paper.

To Discuss

1. Why did the British keep a close watch on Salomon after he was out of jail?
2. How do you think some of the Hessians felt about fighting for the British? What clues help you to know?

Summary

In studying textbooks, thinking about what you are reading is especially important. You have learned to use these thinking skills:

– Making inferences based on given details.
– Drawing conclusions that are supported by facts.
– Determining whether the writer's conclusions are justified.
– Determining whether material is factual or imaginary.

Books About Action

Super Bowl! by John Devaney.
Exciting accounts of the teams that reached the world championships of football and of the games in which they won or lost the title. Read about Vince Lombardi, Joe Namath, Bart Starr, Johnny Unitas, and many others as they compete for victory in America's biggest sporting event – the Super Bowl!

Veteran and Vintage Cars by David B. Wise.
The steam carriages and the earliest internal combustion engines are shown along with the first sports cars. Most of the beautiful color pictures show the great variety of cars produced between 1905 and 1930.

Car of the Year, 1895-1970, a 75-Year Parade of American Automobiles That Made News by Henry B. Lent.
Each car was selected by the author as the "car of the year" because he felt it was newsworthy for one reason or another. The book begins with the Duryea, the Ford Quadricycle, and the Stanley Steamer, and ends with the 1970 Maverick.

Mighty Hard Road, the Story Of Cesar Chavez by James Terzian and Kathryn Cramer.
At the age of ten, Cesar Chavez learned how it felt to be poor. His family lost their farm and became migrant workers. Later, he became a leader of the migrant workers.

Action! Camera! Super 8 Cassette Film Making for Beginners by Rick Carrier and David Carroll.
This is an easy and exciting book for those of you who want to make your own movies. The authors explain how to plan, time, and "shoot" many different kinds of pictures using your own family and friends. "Stills," or photographs taken from movies and used to illustrate the text, also help in understanding the techniques.

Glossary

This glossary is a little dictionary. It contains the difficult words found in this book. The pronunciation, which tells you how to say the word, is given in the parentheses following the word. The meaning of the word is given next. Sometimes, a different form of the word follows the definition. It appears in boldface type.

The special symbols used to show the pronunciation are explained in the key that follows.

PRONUNCIATION KEY

a	add, map	m	move, seem	u	up, done
ā	ace, rate	n	nice, tin	û(r)	urn, term
â(r)	care, air	ng	ring, song	yo͞o	use, few
ä	palm, father	o	odd, hot	v	vain, eve
b	bat, rub	ō	open, so	w	win, away
ch	check, catch	ô	order, jaw	y	yet, yearn
d	dog, rod	oi	oil, boy	z	zest, muse
e	end, pet	ou	out, now	zh	vision, pleasure
ē	even, tree	o͞o	pool, food	ə	the schwa,
f	fit, half	o͝o	took, full		an unstressed
g	go, log	p	pit, stop		vowel representing
h	hope, hate	r	run, poor		the sound spelled
i	it, give	s	see, pass		a in above
ī	ice, write	sh	sure, rush		e in sicken
j	joy, ledge	t	talk, sit		i in possible
k	cool, take	th	thin, both		o in melon
l	look, rule	t͟h	this, bathe		u in circus

In the pronunciations an accent mark (′) is used to show which syllable of a word receives the most stress. The word *bandage* (band′ij), for example, is stressed on the first syllable. Sometimes there is also a lighter accent mark (ʹ) that shows where there is a lighter stress, as in the word *combination* (komʹbə·nā′shən).

The abbreviations *n.*, *v.*, *adj.*, *adv.*, and *pl.* stand for *noun*, *verb*, *adjective*, *adverb*, and *plural*.

A

ability (ə·bil′ə·tē). **1.** Talent. **2.** Skill; craft.

aborigine (ab′ə·rij′ə·nē). One of the earliest people known to have lived in a certain area.

absorbed (ab·sôrbd′ *or* ab·zôrbd′). Giving full attention to something.

acceleration (ak·sel′ə·rā′shən). An increase in speed.

accelerator (ak·sel′ə·rā′tər). The pedal that controls the speed of an automobile; the gas pedal.

accelerometer (ak·sel′ə·rom′ə·tər). An instrument that measures and records the increase in speed of an aircraft.

accurate (ak′yər·it). Having no error; exact.

acknowledge (ak·nol′ij). **1.** To show that one is thankful for. **2.** To admit the truth of. **3.** To recognize.

adaptation (ad′əp·tā′shən). A change made to meet new conditions or surroundings.

adventurous (ad·ven′chər·əs). Liking or seeking adventure; fond of taking risks.

agriculture (ag′rə·kul′chər). The raising of crops; farming.

air-speed indicator (âr′spēd′ in′də·kā′tər). An instrument that tells how fast an airplane moves through the air.

almanac (ôl′mə·nak). A yearly calendar giving the days, weeks, and months of the year with facts about the weather, sun, moon, etc.

altimeter (al·tim′ə·tər). An instrument that tells how far above the ground an airplane is flying.

ammunition (am′yə·nish′ən). Bullets, shells, etc., to be shot from a firearm, cannon, or the like.

annual (an′yōō·əl). Happening once each year, usually at the same time.

anthropology (an′thrə·pol′ə·jē). The science that studies the development of man, including his customs and beliefs.

apostrophe (ə·pos′trə·fē). A mark of punctuation looking like this: ’.

apparently (ə·par′ənt·lē). The way it seemed; seemingly.

apply (ə·plī′). To make a formal request. – **applied.**

approximate (ə·prok′sə·mit). Almost exact or correct.

aquanaut (ak′wə·nôt). A person who spends time in the sea in order to study it.

archaeologist (är′kē·ol′ə·jist). An expert in the study of past times and cultures, mainly carried on by digging up and examining remains, as of ancient cities.

artificial (är′tə·fish′əl). Made by man rather than by nature.

assemble (ə·sem′bəl). To gather together.

astronomer (ə·stron′ə·mər). One who is expert in the study of the stars, planets, and other heavenly bodies.

astronomy (ə·stron′ə·mē). The study of the stars, planets, and other heavenly bodies. – **astronomical** (as′trə·nom′i·kəl), *adj.*

atmosphere (at′məs·fir). **1.** The air surrounding the earth. **2.** The air or climate in a place.

attitude (at′ə·t(y)ōōd). A way of feeling, thinking, or regarding.

auburn (ô′bûrn). Reddish-brown.

auction (ôk′shən). A public sale at which each item is sold to the person offering the highest price for it.

auctioneer (ôk′shən·ir′). A person who conducts an auction.

automatically (ô′tə·mat′ik·lē). Done by machines or instruments; without human assistance.

avalanche (av′ə·lanch). The falling of a large mass of snow, ice, or rock down a slope.

aviation (ā′vē·ā′shən). The science of building and flying aircraft.

awe (ô). A feeling of great fear and wonder.

B

bandit (ban′dit). An outlaw, who often wears a mask over the eyes.

bank (bangk). To tilt an airplane so that one wing is higher than the other, as when turning.

baptize (bap′tīz). To make a person a member of some Christian church by performing a rite in which the person is sprinkled with water.

bayonet (bā·ə·net′). A long, knife-like weapon that is attached to the end of a rifle.

A bayonet

belfry (bel′frē). The part of a tower or steeple in which a bell is hung.

bellow (bel′ō). To utter a loud, hollow cry. **–bellowing.**

bid (bid). To offer to pay a price.

billow (bil′ō). To rise or roll in waves; swell; bulge.

bison (bī′sən). A large wild animal related to the ox; a buffalo.

bleak (blēk). Open to the wind and cold; bare.

blockhouse (blok′hous′). A sturdy, heavily protected structure.

board (bôrd). **1.** *v.* To enter (a ship, train, etc.). **2.** *n.* A long, flat piece of wood. **3.** *v.* To cover with boards: to *board* up windows. **4.** *n.* Meals furnished for pay: room and *board.*

boldface (bōld′fās′). A kind of print that looks **like this.**

boom (bōōm). To grow rapidly. **–booming,** *adj.*

bowstring (bō′string′). A strong cord fixed to the ends of a piece of curved wood, used for shooting arrows.

brace (bras). **1.** *n.* Either of two marks { }, used to show that the words, numbers, etc., enclosed between them should be taken together. **2.** *v.* To support firmly in order to absorb a jerk, bump, etc.

breed (brēd). A particular kind, or race, of animals.

brig (brig). A sailing vessel having two masts and square sails.

bruised (brōōzd). Marked by a black-and-blue spot, as from a bump.

burden (bûr′dən). **1.** Something difficult to bear. **2.** An added weight.

burrow (bûr′ō). A hole made in the ground by certain animals.

C

calculate (kal′kyə·lāt). **1.** To figure or measure by using mathematics. **2.** To think out; form an estimate of.

canoe (kə·nōō′). A small, lightweight boat, pointed at both ends and moved by paddles.

canopy (kan′ə·pē). The clear, sliding cover over a cockpit.

capital (kap′ə·təl). Marked by a penalty of death for a crime.

capsize (kap·sīz′). To upset; tip over.

captor (kap′tər). One who takes or holds another by force.

carbon dioxide (kär′bən dī·ok′sīd). An odorless, colorless gas made up of carbon and oxygen. It is breathed out by human beings and animals.

carcass (kär′kəs). The dead body of an animal.

cartilage (kär′tə·lij). A tough elastic tissue that connects some bones and forms part of the skeleton.

cavalry (kav′əl·rē). Soldiers trained to fight on horseback.

cello (chel′ō). A large instrument like a violin, but much bigger and with a deep tone. It is held between the performer's knees.

A cello

century (sen′chə·rē). A period of one hundred years.

ceramics (sə·ram′iks). Objects made from baked clay.

cerebellum (ser′ə·bel′əm). The part of the brain at the back of the head. It causes the muscles to work together properly.

cerebrum (ser′ə·brəm). The largest and most highly developed part of the brain. It controls thought and movement.

ceremony (ser′ə·mō′nē). A formal act or series of actions performed in a set manner: a wedding *ceremony.*

challenging (chal′ənj·ing). Difficult or dangerous.

chamber (chām′bər). A hollow or enclosed space in a piece of machinery or in the body of a plant or animal.

channel (chan′əl). **1.** A body of water connecting two larger bodies of water. **2.** The deep part of a river, harbor, etc.

chemical (kem′i·kəl). Any of a number of substances found on earth which compose in varying amounts the air, water, solids, etc.

chisel (chiz′(ə)l). A cutting tool with a sharp, sloping edge, used to cut or shape wood, metal, or stone.

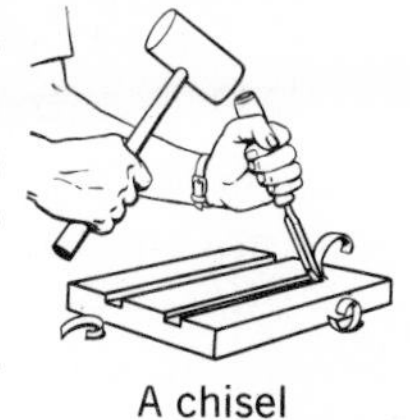
A chisel

cicada (si·kā′də). A large insect with four transparent wings. The male makes a shrill sound by rubbing its legs against its abdomen.

cinema (sin′ə·mə). Motion pictures; movies.

civilization (siv′ə·lə·zā′shən). The kind of living developed by human society.

clamber (klam′bər). To climb using both hands and feet.

clamor (klam′ər). A loud, continuous noise.

classification (klas′ə·fə·kā′shən). Class; group; category.

cleat (klēt). A piece of wood, metal, etc., fastened to a surface to provide strength, support, or sure footing.

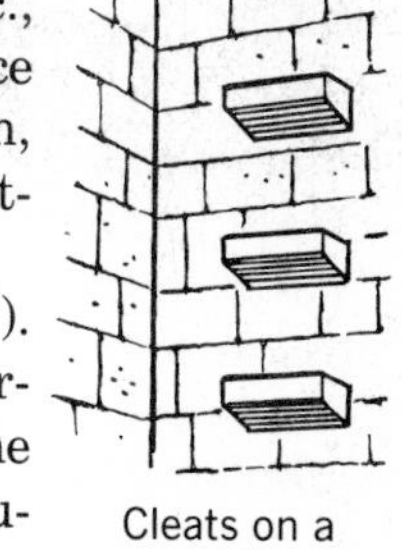
Cleats on a wall

cockpit (kok′pit′). The part of an airplane that holds the pilot and instruments.

cocoon (kə·ko͞on′). The covering spun by the larvae of certain insects while they are growing.

colleague (kol′ēg). A fellow worker in a profession.

colt (kōlt). A young horse or donkey, especially a male.

---

add, **ā**ce, c**â**re, p**ä**lm; **e**nd, **ē**qual; **i**t, **i**ce; **o**dd, **ō**pen, **ô**rder; t**o͝o**k, p**o͞o**l; **u**p, b**û**rn; **ə** = a in *above,* e in *sicken,* i in *possible,* o in *melon,* u in *circus;* **yo͞o** = u in *fuse;* **oi**l; p**ou**t; **ch**eck; ri**ng**; **th**in; **th**is; **zh** in *vision.*

commission (kə·mish′ən). A request for something to be written, composed, painted, etc., along with the necessary funds to do it.

communicate (kə·myōō′nə·kāt). To exchange thoughts.

companion (kəm·pan′yən). One who stays with another person; friend.

company (kum′pə·nē). **1.** A group of people with a common purpose: an insurance *company.* **2.** A guest or guests. **3.** Companionship. **4.** A body of soldiers commanded by a captain.

compensate (kom′pən·sāt). To balance; make up for.

complex (kəm·pleks′ *or* kom′pleks). Made up of many parts; not easy to understand, complicated.

concertina (kon′sər·tē′nə). A small musical instrument like an accordion.

confident (kon′fə·dənt). Having faith; sure; trusting. **—confidently**, *adv.*

consciousness (kon′shəs·nis). A state of awakeness; awareness of one's surroundings.

constant (kon′stənt). Remaining the same; not changing.

construction (kən·struk′shən). The act of building.

consumption (kən·sump′shən). **1.** The act of using up or destroying. **2.** The amount used up.

contemplate (kon′təm·plāt). To look at or consider thoughtfully.

continent (kon′tə·nənt). A large land area of the earth, as North America.

convert (kon′vûrt). A person who has become a new member of a religion.

coordination (kō·ôr′də·nā′shən). A smooth working together, as parts of the body.

corral (kə·ral′). **1.** *n.* A pen for livestock. **2.** *v.* To drive into a pen.

council (koun′səl). A group of people who are called together to make plans or give advice.

counsel (koun′səl). To give advice to. **—counseling.**

cove (kōv). A small, sheltered bay or inlet in a shoreline.

A cove

craftsman (krafts′mən). One skilled in his work, especially hand work.

creed (krēd). A statement of religious beliefs.

critic (krit′ik). A person who judges the quality of books, music, art, dance, etc.

critical (krit′i·kəl). Extremely important; marking a turning point.

crossbreed (krôs′brēd′). A product of mating two different but related animals or plants.

crowbar (krō′bär′). A straight metal bar used as a lever for lifting.

culture (kul′chər). The entire way of life of a certain people, including customs, religion, art, etc.

curious (kyōōr′ē·əs). Eager to know or learn more.

current (kûr′ənt). Water or air that flows in a definite direction.

cycle (sī′kəl). **1.** A series of events that always happen in the same order and return to the beginning position again. **2.** A series of stages in the growth or development of a plant or animal. **3.** A process that takes so long and then begins again.

cylinder (sil′in·dər). A long, narrow circular container or structure.

D

daredevil (dâr′dev′əl). A bold, reckless person.

dead-stick (ded′stik′). Without power; with the engine cut off.

decade (dek′ād). Ten years.

defensive (di·fen′siv). Protecting from attack.

demon (dē′mən). A person having great energy or skill.

deposit (di·poz′it). Material laid down by natural forces, such as a mud or mineral *deposit.*

deprivation (dep′rə·vā′shən). Hardship; suffering.

descend (di·send′). To be born from a certain source: Today's horse *descended* from a much smaller prehistoric animal.

destination (des′tə·nā′shən). The place toward which someone is traveling.

determination (di·tûr′mə·nā′shən). Firmness of purpose; courage.

devise (di·vīz′). To figure out; plan; invent.

diagram (dī′ə·gram). A drawing, chart, etc., that shows how something should look or operate.

dialect (dī′ə·lekt). A form of speech of a certain region that differs in some way from standard speech.

diameter (dī·am′ə·tər). The length or distance across a circular object.

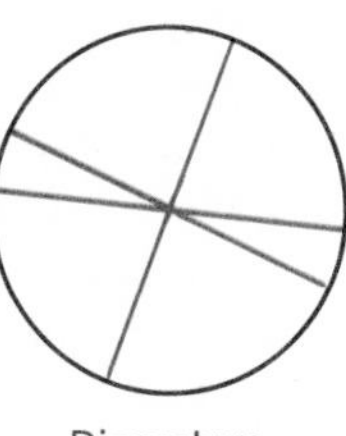

Diameters

discovery (dis·kuv′ər·ē). Something found out or thought out for the first time. —**discoveries,** *pl.*

disdain (dis·dān′). To regard as beneath one; scorn; ignore.

disguise (dis·gīz′). To change the way one looks so as not to be known, or to look like someone else.

dismount (dis·mount′). To get down from.

dispirited (dis·pir′it·id). Unhappy; discouraged.

disprove (dis·prōōv′). To prove to be false or wrong.

distribute (dis·trib′yŏŏt). To spread out.

domestic (də·mes′tik). Tame.

domesticate (də·mes′tə·kāt). To tame for use around the home.

double (dub′əl). **1.** *v.* To take the place of someone whom one closely resembles. —**doubled. 2.** *n.* A person or thing that looks very much like another.

dread (dred). To look forward to with fear. —**dreaded.**

drift (drift). **1.** Slow movement in a given direction. **2.** The course along which something moves.

drifter (drift′ər). A person who moves without purpose from one job or one place to another.

drifting (drift′ing). Moving or being carried along without power.

dropper (drop′ər). A narrow glass tube from which fluid is squeezed out drop by drop.

A dropper

E

electrify (i·lek′trə·fī). To thrill, arouse, startle.

elegance (el′ə·gəns). Gracefulness; beauty; good taste.

---

add, **ā**ce, c**â**re, p**ä**lm; **e**nd, **ē**qual; **i**t, **i**ce; **o**dd, **ō**pen, **ô**rder; t**ŏŏ**k, p**ōō**l; **u**p, b**û**rn; **ə** = a in *above,* e in *sicken,* i in *possible,* o in *melon,* u in *circus;* **yōō** = u in *fuse;* **oi**l; p**ou**t; **ch**eck; ri**ng**; **th**in; **th**is; **zh** in *vision.*

emergency (i·mûr′jən·sē). A sudden event that requires fast action.

enforce (in·fôrs′). To see that rules are obeyed.

engineer (en′jə·nir′). One who is trained in work such as the planning and building of roads, bridges, etc.

enormous (i·nôr′məs). Very large; immense; huge.

enthusiasm (in·thōō′zē·az′əm). Great interest, excitement, or liking.

environment (in·vī′rən·mənt). The conditions and surroundings that have an effect on the development of a person, animal, or plant.

envoy (en′voi). **1.** A messenger on a special mission. **2.** A representative of a government.

equipment (i·kwip′mənt). Things needed for some special purpose.

essential (ə·sen′shəl). Very important; vital.

evaluate (i·val′yōō·āt). To judge or find the worth of. **–evaluating.**

evidence (ev′ə·dəns). Something that supports a belief, conclusion, result, etc. Good grades are usually *evidence* that one has studied.

exact (ig·zakt′). Completely accurate.

exhale (eks·hāl′). To breathe out.

exhaust assembly (ig·zôst′ ə·sem′blē). The system of pipes or other engine parts through which waste gases are released.

exhausted (ig·zôs′tid). Very tired.

exile (eg′zīl). Separation from one's home, usually forced upon someone.

expedition (ek′spə·dish′ən). A journey made for a certain purpose.

F

fanatic (fə·nat′ik). A person who feels so strongly about his beliefs that he will not listen to reason.

fantastic (fan·tas′tik). **1.** Amazing; unbelievable. **2.** Unreal; weird.

fascination (fas′ə·nā′shən). Great interest.

fatal (fāt′(ə)l). Resulting in death.

fearless (fir′lis). Without fear.

fiery (fīr′ē). On fire; burning.

filament (fil′ə·mənt). A very thin thread.

fire extinguisher (fīr ik·sting′gwish·ər). Some kind of device for putting out a fire, often a metal can containing chemical substances.

flabbergasted (flab′ər·gas·tid). Very amazed; astounded.

flint (flint). A hard, dark stone.

flipper (flip′ər). A limb used for swimming by certain animals.

floodlight (flud′līt′). A type of lamp that gives off a very bright and very wide beam of light.

flustered (flus′tərd). Confused; excited; upset.

foal (fōl). A young horse, donkey, etc.

foreigner (fôr′in·ər). A person from a different country.

forerunner (fôr′run′ər). Something that comes before another thing of the same type at an earlier stage of development.

fortnight (fôrt′nīt′). Two weeks.

fortress (fôr′tris). An area enclosed against attack.

fossil (fos′əl). The remains of a plant or animal of an earlier age, hardened and preserved in earth or rock.

A fossil

fragrant (frā′grənt). Sweet in smell.

free-wheeling (frē′(h)wēl′ing). Not bound by any rules or set of manners.

frontier (frun·tir′). **1.** The edge of a settled region that borders on unsettled territory, as in the western *frontier.* **2.** A new or unexplored area, as of knowledge.

fuel (fyo͞o′əl). Something that produces energy in the form of heat when burnt, as wood, coal, oil, etc.

function (fungk′shən). To operate or work properly.

furiously (fyo͝or′ē·əs·lē). At a very fast, energetic pace.

G

gallant (gal′ənt). Bold and courageous.

game (gām). Animals or birds hunted for food or sport.

gantry tower (gan′trē tou′ər). A large framework, which can be moved, used to build and service a rocket on its launching pad.

gauge (gāj). **1.** *n.* An instrument that measures pressure, speed, distance, etc. **2.** *v.* To make an accurate measurement. **3.** *n.* The distance between rails on a railroad.

gear (gir). Equipment for a special purpose, as camping.

generation (jen′ə·rā′shən). A stage in the history of a family of humans or animals, as, parents' *generation.*

geometry (jē·om′ə·trē). The branch of mathematics that studies the relationships between points, lines, surfaces and solids.

goldsmith (gold′smith′). A person who makes articles of gold.

gopher (gō′fər). A squirrel-like animal that burrows holes into the ground.

gossamer (gos′ə·mər). Very fine, filmy, and delicate.

graded (grād′id). **1.** Made to slope slightly, said of a road, in such a way that turning a vehicle is made easier. **2.** Divided into groups by quality or rank. **3.** Given a grade or mark, as in school.

gratitude (grat′ə·t(y)o͞od). Thankfulness.

gravity (grav′ə·tē). The force that pulls objects toward something, usually the earth.

greenhouse (grēn′hous′). A heated building used for growing certain plants, having its roof and sides made partly of glass.

groove (gro͞ov). A long, narrow cut or channel made in a surface; a rut.

grueling (gro͞o′əl·ing). Very tiring.

guardedly (gär′did·lē). Carefully; cautiously.

guitar (gi·tär′). A stringed musical instrument played by plucking the strings with the fingers or a pick.

gully (gul′ē). A channel or ditch, especially one cut in the earth by running water.

H

handicapped (han′dē·kapt). At a disadvantage in doing something because of some physical defect.

hangar (hang′ər). A shelter for storing aircraft.

harmony (här′mə·nē). A pleasant-sounding arrangement of two or more musical sounds played at the same time.

harness (här′nis). An arrangement of straps or bands that holds something, such as a parachute, to the body.

hatch (hach). **1.** An opening in the deck of a ship through which one passes to go inside. **2.** Any similar opening in a sea vessel.

Hatch being opened

hatchway (hach′wā′). Hatch.

hearth (härth). **1.** The floor of a fireplace, furnace, etc. **2.** A small platform for cooking over a fire. **3.** A fireplace.

A hearth

heave (hēv). To throw upward with great effort or force.

helium (hē′lē·əm). A light, colorless, odorless gas that will not burn.

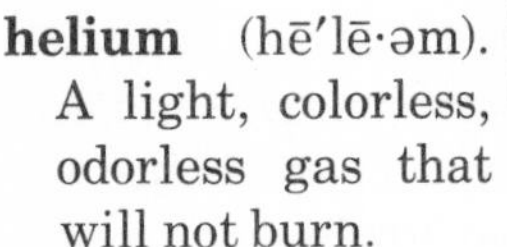

hemp (hemp). **1.** A tall plant with small green flowers. **2.** The fibers of this plant.

herb ((h)ûrb). A plant, often used in seasonings and medicine.

heredity (hə·red′ə·tē). The qualities or characteristics passed on from parents to their young.

heroine (her′ō·in). A woman or girl who has acted bravely.

historian (his·tôr′ē·ən). A person who writes about people and events of the past.

horizon (hə·rī′zən). The line where the earth and the sky seem to meet.

hostile (hos′təl). **1.** Unfriendly. **2.** Not suited to human needs.

hover (huv′ər). To remain in or near one place in the air.

hull (hul). The body or outer frame of a ship or other sea vessel.

humidity ((h)yōō·mid′ə·tē). The amount of moisture in the air.

I

ideograph (id′ē·ə·graf′). A picture symbol that stands for an idea or object.

ignition (ig·nish′ən). Having to do with a system that sets fire to fuel.

impulse (im′puls). A sudden desire to do something.

inadequate (in·ad′ə·kwit). Less than is needed; not enough.

incident (in′sə·dənt). Happening.

inclined (in·klīnd′). Having a preference for; tending toward.

ingenuity (in′jə·n(y)ōō′ə·tē). Skill or cleverness, as shown in inventing or solving things.

initially (in·ish′ə·lē). At first.

inkstand (ingk′stand′). **1.** A rack for holding pens and ink.

inspiring (in·spīr′ing). Causing wonder, awe, or admiration.

instrumental (in′strə·men′təl). Performed on a musical instrument rather than by voice.

intention (in·ten′shən). Purpose.

intercontinental (in′tər·kon′tə·nen′təl). Able to travel between continents.

international (in′tər·nash′ən·əl). Existing between or among nations.

interpretation (in·tûr′prə·tā′shən). A giving of one's own impression or understanding of something.

interpreter (in·tûr′prit·ər). A person who changes one language into another; a translator.

invent (in·vent′). To think out or bring into being for the first time. **—invention,** *n.*

investment (in·vest′mənt). Something for which money is spent in the hope that it will produce a profit in the future.

invisible (in·viz′ə·bəl). Unable to be seen.

irrigate (ir′ə·gāt). To supply water to land through pipes, ditches, etc.

isolate (ī′sə·lāt). To place apart; separate from others. —**isolated,** *adj.*

issue (ish′o͞o). **1.** To send out. **2.** To announce.

J

jackal (jak′əl). An animal similar to a dog, that lives in Asia and Africa.

jitterbug (jit′ər·bug′). Small and fast, as in a lively dance.

journal (jûr′nəl). A written record of daily events.

K

kerosene (ker′ə·sēn). A thin oil made from petroleum, used as fuel.

kimono (kə·mō′nə). A loose robe worn as an outer garment in Japan.

Man in a kimono

L

laboratory (lab′(ə)·rə·tôr′ē). A room equipped for doing scientific work or experiments.

lasso (las′ō). To catch and hold something by throwing a long rope with a loop at one end around it. —**lassoed.**

launch (lônch). To move a boat into water for the first time.

lavatory (lav′ə·tôr′ē). A sink.

legend (lej′ənd). A famous person about whom many stories are known.

litter (lit′ər). The newborn animals born at one time of the same parent.

livelihood (līv′lē·ho͝od). The means of making one's living.

livestock (līv′stok′). Farm animals such as horses, cattle, sheep, etc.

lock (lok). A section of a canal, irrigating ditch, etc., in which the water flow can be controlled. It has a gate at either end.

locomotive (lō′kə·mō′tiv). An engine that moves by its own power, used to pull trains on a railroad.

loyalty (loi′əl·tē). Faithfulness.

lunge (lunj). To make a quick movement toward something; to spring.

luxury (luk′shər·ē). Something that is costly and gives comfort, but is not necessary. —**luxuries,** *pl.*

M

machete (mə·shet′ē). A heavy knife used as a tool or weapon.

management (man′ij·mənt). The way something is run or directed.

Manchuria (man·cho͝or′ē·ə). A region in northeast China.

mare (mâr). A female horse or donkey.

marine (mə·rēn′). Having to do with, or found, in the sea.

marrow (mar′ō). The soft material found in the inner, hollow part of a bone.

Marrow of a bone

meager (mē′gər). Lacking in comfort; poor.

measurement (mezh′ər·mənt). A recording of size or amount.

---

add, **ā**ce, **câ**re, p**ä**lm; **e**nd, **ē**qual; **i**t, **i**ce; **o**dd, **ō**pen, **ô**rder; t**o͝o**k, p**o͞o**l; **u**p, b**û**rn; **ə** = a in *above,* e in *sicken,* i in *possible,* o in *melon,* u in *circus;* **yo͞o** = u in *fuse;* **oi**l; p**ou**t; **ch**eck; ri**ng**; **th**in; **th**is; **zh** in *vision.*

medulla (mə·dul′ə). The lowest part of the brain, near the spinal cord. It controls breathing, circulation, etc.
melody (mel′ə·dē). A series of musical tones arranged in a pleasing way; a tune.
menace (men′is). To threaten with harm.
merchant (mûr′chənt). A trader or storekeeper.
messenger (mes′ən·jər). A person who carries news, instructions, announcements, etc., from one place to another.
metallic (mə·tal′ik). Shiny, as some metals.
microbus (mī′krō·bus′). Looking like a very small bus.
migrate (mī′grāt). To move from one region or climate to another at the change of season. –**migration,** *n.* –**migrating,** *adj.*
military (mil′ə·ter′ē). Having to do with the armed forces.
miller (mil′ər). A person who operates or works in a flour mill.
mineral (min′ər·əl). A natural substance found on earth that is not plant or animal, such as coal or salt.
mingle (ming′gəl). To mix or join.
mischief (mis′chif). One who teases or plays pranks.
mission (mish′ən). The task, business, or duty that a person or group is sent forth to do.
missionary (mish′ən·er′ē). A person doing medical, religious, or educational work in a foreign country.
moccasin (mok′ə·sin). A shoe or slipper with soft soles and no heels, formerly worn by North American Indians.

A moccasin

module (mod′yo͞ol). A unit used as a basis for standardizing the design and construction of parts.
mother country (muth′ər kun′trē). **1.** The country of one's birth. **2.** A country which has set up colonies and has control over them.
mule skinner (myo͞ol skin′ər). A person who drives mules.

N

naturalist (nach′ər·əl·ist). A person who is trained in the study of the earth and living things.
navigate (nav′ə·gāt). To chart or control the course of a ship, aircraft, spaceship, etc. –**navigation, navigator,** *n.*
nesting (nest′ing). Building a nest.
nightfall (nīt′fôl′). The coming of night; close of day.
nitrogen (nī′trə·jən). An odorless, colorless gas that makes up four-fifths of the earth's air.
nominate (nom′ə·nāt). To appoint to some honor, office, or position.

O

obedience (ō·bē′dē·əns). The act or habit of doing as one is told.
obsession (əb·sesh′ən). A thought, feeling, or idea that fills the mind and cannot be driven out.
odds (odz). Chance for success or failure.
offensive (ə·fen′siv). Having to do with attack.
official (ə·fish′əl). Having support from the government.
offspring (ôf′spring′). Something descended from a person, animal, or plant; the young of a parent.
ordeal (ôr·dēl′). A very difficult or frightening experience.

originate (ə·rij′ə·nāt). To bring or come into existence.

outskirts (out′skûrts′). The areas far from the center of a city.

overhaul (ō′vər·hôl′). Complete inspection and repairs.

P

packet (pak′it). A small package.

pampas (pam′pəz). The treeless plains south of the Amazon River.

pamphlet (pam′flit). A booklet on a topic of present interest.

panic (pan′ik). To frighten terribly. **–panicked.**

parachute (par′ə·shōōt). A large, umbrella-shaped device, usually made of cloth, that slows the speed of a falling object. It is usually used for descent from an airplane.

paradise (par′ə·dīs). Any place of great beauty or delight.

partner (pärt′nər). One who shares with another, as work or play.

partnership (pärt′nər·ship). Condition of being and acting together; sharing.

patrol (pə·trōl′). Ships or soldiers that scout and guard an area.

peat (pēt). A substance, used for fuel, made up of dried moss and plants.

penguin (pen(g)′gwin). A black and white swimming bird of Antarctica with flippers, webbed feet, and very short legs on which it stands upright.

permanent (pûr′mən·ənt). Meant to remain without change; lasting.

persist (pər·sist′). To keep on with something, despite difficulty.

persuade (pər·swād′). To coax; urge.

philanthropist (fi·lan′thrə·pist). A person who devotes time and money to helping others.

philanthropy (fi·lan′thrə·pē). A charitable gift or act.

physical (fiz′i·kəl). Having to do with the body; bodily.

pillar (pil′ər). An upright hollow post in the front of a harp frame.

Pillar of a harp

pilot (pī′lət). A person who operates an aircraft during flight. **–test pilot** A person who tries out new aircraft.

pirates (pī′rits). Bands of sailors who rob other ships at sea.

pitch (pich). The level of a sound's highness or lowness.

pivot (piv′ət). **1.** *n.* Something, as a pin or short shaft, on which a part turns. **2.** *v.* To turn as on a pivot. **–pivoted.**

plumb bob (plum bob). The weight at the end of a cord which, when hanging straight, shows whether or not a wall or column is straight up and down.

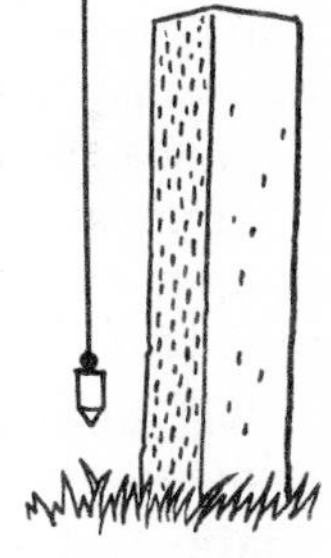
A plumb bob

plummet (plum′it). To fall straight down; plunge.

porpoise (pôr′pəs). **1.** A sea animal like a small whale. **2.** A dolphin.

porthole (pôrt′hōl′). A small window-like opening in the side of a ship to admit light and air.

possession (pə·zesh′ən). Having for one's own; ownership.

add, **ā**ce, c**â**re, p**ä**lm; **e**nd, **ē**qual; **i**t, **ī**ce; **o**dd, **ō**pen, **ô**rder; t**ŏŏ**k, p**ōō**l; **u**p, b**û**rn;
ə = a in *above*, e in *sicken*, i in *possible*, o in *melon*, u in *circus*; **yōō** = u in *fuse*; **oi**l; p**ou**t;
check; ri**ng**; **th**in; **th**is; **zh** in *vision*.

precision (pri·sizh′ən). Having great accuracy; exactly correct.

prehistoric (prē′his·tôr′ik). Belonging to the time before the start of written history.

pressure (presh′ər). The force pushing against a surface over a certain area.

priceless (prīs′lis). Worth more than any price; unable to be replaced by money.

primitive (prim′ə·tiv). Without any comforts; simple; crude.

principle (prin′sə·pəl). **1.** A general rule or truth on which other truths are based. **2.** A law or way of action by which something works in nature.

produce (pro′·d(y)o͞os *or* prō′d(y)oos). Farm products, as vegetables, fruit, etc., grown for market.

professional (prə·fesh′ən·əl). Done for the purpose of earning a living.

prolonged (prə·lôngd′). Made longer; drawn out; lengthened.

prophesy (prof′ə·sī). To state what will happen in the future; foretell.

prosperous (pros′pər·əs). Wealthy.

protection (prə·tek′shən). A shield or defense against harm or attack.

protein (prō′te·in *or* prō′tēn). Any of a group of substances found in food that are necessary for human growth.

Psalms (sämz). A book of the Bible, containing 150 hymns or Psalms.

puncture (pungk′chər). To pierce with a sharp or fast moving object, so as to make a small opening.

Q

quarry (kwôr′ē). A large hole, made by digging, from which stone is taken for use in building.

quavering (kwā′vər·ing). Trembling in an uncertain way, as a voice.

quiver (kwiv′ər). To make a slight trembling motion.

R

raccoon (ra·co͞on′). A small animal with grayish brown fur and a bushy, striped tail. It lives chiefly in trees and is active at night.

radiator (rā′dē·ā′tər). A system of pipes through which steam or hot water passes to provide heat, as for a room.

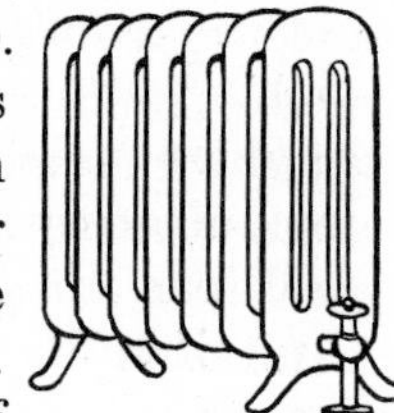

A radiator

rail (rāl). Either of the two parallel steel bars that form a track, as for a train.

raw material (rô mə·tir′ē·əl). Material in its natural condition, from which it is later made into another product. Iron ore is a *raw material* used in making steel.

reassuring (rē′ə·sho͝or′ing). Free from doubt or fear.

recital (ri·sīt′(ə)l). A public performance in which musical works or dances are performed.

reckless (rek′lis). Taking foolish risks; careless.

recur (ri·kûr′). To happen over and over again at regular times. Leap year *recurs* every fourth year.

redcoat (red′kōt′). A British soldier in the Revolutionary War.

refinery (ri·fī′nər·ē). A place where raw material, such as oil, is purified.

reflect (ri·flekt′). **1.** To show or express. **2.** To cause as a result of one's actions.

regalia (ri·gā′lē·ə *or* ri·gāl′yə). **1.** Fancy dress. **2.** The symbols and emblems of a tribe or society.

regiment (rej′ə·mənt). A unit of an army larger than a battalion and smaller than a division, usually commanded by a colonel.

reluctantly (ri·luk′tənt·lē). Unwillingly; not eagerly.

rely (ri·lī′). To place trust or confidence. —**relying.**

remarkably (ri·mär′kəb·lē). In a way that is surprising or amazing.

remote (ri·mōt′). Distant; far off.

repeal (ri·pēl′). The act of doing away with something.

representative (rep′ri·zen′tə·tiv). A person who speaks for a country, organization, etc.

research (ri·sûrch′ *or* rē·surch). Careful, patient study and experiment.

resentful (ri·zent′fəl). Feeling anger or ill will because of a real or imagined wrong or injury.

reservoir (rez′ər·vwär). A place for collecting and storing large amounts of water.

resign (ri·zīn′). To give up an office, position, etc.

respectful (ri·spekt′fəl). Polite; courteous; showing respect.

responsibility (ri·spon′sə·bil′ə·tē). Care; charge; management.

restore (ri·stôr′). To bring back something that has been lost or damaged.

retreat (ri·trēt′). To move back; withdraw.

revere (ri·vir′). To honor.

reverently (rev′ər·ənt·lē). In a manner which shows respect and wonder.

rhythmic (rith′mik). Marked by the repetition of a sound, beat, or accent, as in music. —**rhythmically,** *adv.*

ripcord (rip′kôrd′). The cord that one pulls to make a parachute open.

rivalry (rī′vəl·rē). **1.** A contest. **2.** The condition of wanting the same thing as another.

roadbed (rōd′bed′). The foundation on which railroad tracks are laid.

roundup (round′up′). A bringing together of horses or cattle scattered over an area for the purpose of inspecting, branding, selling, etc.

row[1] (rou). A noisy quarrel.

row[2] (rō). To make a boat move by using oars.

row[3] (rō). An arrangement of things in a line.

rowdy (rou′dē). Rough; loud; disorderly.

rugged (rug′id). Not easy; harsh; difficult.

S

sacrifice (sak′rə·fīs). A giving up of something highly valued.

sacrilegious (sak′rə·lij′əs). Showing lack of respect toward something sacred.

salvage (sal′vij). To save a ship or its cargo from loss or destruction. —**salvaging.**

satisfaction (sat′is·fak′shən). The condition of having what is wanted, needed, or expected.

saturate (sach′ə·rāt). To soak or fill completely.

savage (sav′ij). Wild, untamed, and often fierce.

schedule (skej′o͞ol). **1.** A plan, as of things to be done. **2.** The time agreed upon in a plan.

---

add, **ā**ce, c**â**re, p**ä**lm; **e**nd, **ē**qual; **i**t, **ī**ce; **o**dd, **ō**pen, **ô**rder; t**o͝o**k, p**o͞o**l; **u**p, b**û**rn; **ə** = a in *above*, e in *sicken*, i in *possible*, o in *melon*, u in *circus*; **yo͞o** = u in *fuse*; **oi**l; p**ou**t; **ch**eck; ri**ng**; **th**in; **th**is; **zh** in *vision.*

scholarship (skol′ər·ship). A grant of money awarded to a student to help pay for his education.
schooner (sko͞o′nər). A sailing ship having two or more masts.
scrutiny (skro͞o′tə·nē). Close, careful examination.
scuba (sko͞o′bə). A kind of diving equipment that uses air tanks attached to the diver, so that there is no connection with the surface.
seafarer (sē′fâr′ər). A seaman.
sea lion (sē lī′ən). A very large seal of the Pacific coast of North America.
seize (sēz). To take hold of suddenly and with force.
self-discipline (self′dis′ə·plin). Self-control.
sensitive (sen′sə·tiv). Able to feel quickly and easily.
sentry (sen′trē). A soldier who guards an area.
sequence (sē′kwəns). **1.** The following of one thing after another. **2.** The order of arrangement in which one thing comes after another.
sewage (so͞o′ij). The waste matter which is carried off in sewers.
shaft (shaft). Narrow passageway.
shallows (shal′ōz). A shallow place in a body of water.
shrewd (shro͞od). Sly; wise; cunning; having sharp judgment.
silhouette (sil′o͞o·et′). **1.** The outline of a person or object seen against a light background. **2.** A portrait in outline, cut out of black paper.

Silhouette of Lincoln

simultaneous (sī′məl·tā′nē·əs). Happening at the same time.
singe (sinj). **1.** To burn slightly; scorch. **2.** To burn the ends of, as hair or fur.
singular (sing′gyə·lər). Rare; uncommon.
site (sīt). A place or location.
skydiving (skī′dīv′ing). The sport of jumping from an airplane and falling freely for some distance before opening the parachute.
slither (sli*th*′ər). To slide with an unsteady motion along a surface.
sloth (slōth). A slow-moving mammal of South America that hangs upside down from tree branches by its claws and sleeps most of the day.
specimen (spes′ə·mən). A small amount of something taken as a sample of a whole.
spectacle (spek′tə·kəl). **1.** An unusual sight. **—spectacular** (spek·tak′yə·lər), *adj.* **2.** (*pl.*) A pair of eyeglasses.
spellbound (spel′bound′). Held in one place, as if by a spell; fascinated.
spike (spīk). A very large nail.
spread-eagled (spred′ē′gəld). Positioned with the arms and legs extended; resembling an eagle with its wings spread.
spurt (spûrt). To gush forth in a sudden stream. **—spurted.**
squall (skwôl). A sudden violent outburst of wind and rain.
squawking (skwôk′ing). Giving a shrill, harsh cry.
stake out (stāk′out′). To mark the boundaries of something with wooden posts, or stakes.
stallion (stal′yən). A male horse that can be used for breeding.
stampede (stam·pēd′). A sudden running movement, often due to panic, by a herd of cattle, horses, etc.
steam (stēm). The gas or vapor into which water is changed by boiling. It is used for heating and, under pressure, as a source of energy.

Stone Age (stōn āj). The earliest time known when man existed.

strain (strān). A breed.

subarctic (sub′är(k)′tik). Of the region that surrounds the North Pole.

Subarctic region

subsequent (sub′sə·kwənt). Following after; later.

summon (sum′ən). To make someone or something appear.

supersonic (sōō′pər·son′ik). Traveling faster than the speed of sound.

survey **1.** *v.* (sər·vā′). To measure the size, shape, etc., of an area of land. **2.** *n.* (sûr′vā). The results of such a measurement. –**surveying,** *adj.*

surveyor (sər·vā′ər). One who makes a survey.

survive (sər·vīv′). **1.** To remain alive **2.** To live through something: to *survive* a flood. –**survival,** *n.*

suspension lines (sə·spen′shən līnz). The ropes or cords that extend from the harness of a parachute up to the main part.

T

target (tär′git). The area or object that one aims to hit, land on, etc.

taut (tôt). Stretched tight; not loose or slack.

taxes (taks′·əz). Charges paid on certain goods to a government.

technical (tek′ni·kəl). Having to do with the special skills of a particular art or science.

technician (tek·nish′ən). A person who is skilled in working with machines or scientific instruments.

technique (tek·nēk′). **1.** A skill in handling tools, instruments, materials, etc. **2.** A special way of doing something.

temper (tem′pər). To make less harsh; to moderate.

temperamental (tem′p(ə)rə·men′təl). Easily excited, angered, or upset.

temperate (tem′pər·it). Mild in temperature or climate.

terrace (ter′is). A flat, raised area on the sides of a hill. –**terraced,** *adj.*

Terraces

theory (thē′ə·rē). **1.** An idea or belief that has not been proved. **2.** An idea which suggests an explanation for something.

threaten (thret′(ə)n). To put in danger.

thrive (thrīv). To grow and prosper; be successful.

tie (tī). A wooden board that holds two rails in place.

tilted (tilt′əd). Tipped forward, backward, or to one side.

tone (tōn). A sound having a definite pitch.

tortoise (tôr′təs). A turtle, especially one of the kind that lives entirely on land.

A tortoise

---

add, **ā**ce, c**â**re, p**ä**lm; **e**nd, **ē**qual; **i**t, **i**ce; **o**dd, **ō**pen, **ô**rder; t**ŏŏ**k, p**ōō**l; **u**p, b**û**rn;
ə = a in *above,* e in *sicken,* i in *possible,* o in *melon,* u in *circus;* **yōō** = u in *fuse;* **oi**l; p**ou**t;
check; ri**ng**; **th**in; **th**is; **zh** in *vision.*

tradition (trə·dish′ən). A set of practices, customs, or beliefs passed down from one generation to the next.

traditional (trə·dish′ən·əl). Handed down by custom; following tradition.

transcontinental (trans′kon′tə·nen′təl). Going from one side of the continent to the other.

translate (trans·lāt′). To change words from one language into another.

transplant (trans·plant′). To dig up a plant from where it is growing and plant it again in another place.

tremendous (tri·men′dəs). Unusually large; enormous.

triangular (trī·ang′gyə·lər). Having three sides; shaped like a triangle.

tributary (trib′yə·ter′ē). A stream flowing into a larger stream of water. —**tributaries,** *pl.*

trill (tril). A sound made by changing rapidly between two different tones. Birds often make a trill.

tropical (trop′i·kəl). Of a kind located in the tropics, or very warm lands near the Equator.

troupe (tro͞op). A company of actors, dancers, or other performers.

turret (tûr′it). A tower on an old building or castle. —**turreted,** *adj.*

tussle (tus′əl). A rough struggle.

U

ultimately (ul′tə·mit·lē). In the end; at last; finally.

uncanny (un·kan′ē). So good as to seem beyond human powers.

undaunted (un·dôn′tid). Not fearful; not giving up hope.

unity (yo͞o′nə·tē). The quality of being or acting as a single thing; oneness.

universal (yo͞o′nə·vûr′səl). Happening to everyone; involving everyone.

uranium (yo͝o·rā′nē·əm). A heavy, white, metallic element used to produce atomic energy.

urgency (ûr′jən·sē). Need or demand for prompt action.

V

valve (valv). Any device that controls the flow of a fluid, as through a pipe.

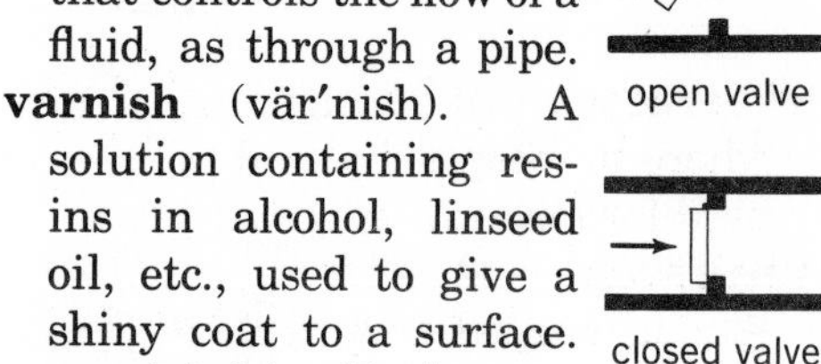

varnish (vär′nish). A solution containing resins in alcohol, linseed oil, etc., used to give a shiny coat to a surface.

vary (vâr′ē). To be unlike; differ.

varying (vâr′ē·ing). Differing; not all the same.

vibrate (vī′brāt). To move back and forth rapidly; quiver. A drum *vibrates* when it is struck.

village green (vil′ij grēn). An open, grassy area in the center of a village or town where people can gather.

vineyard (vin′yərd). An area where grapevines are planted.

vintage (vin′tij). **1.** A season's crop of grapes in a certain district. **2.** The harvesting of a vineyard.

viol (vī′əl). Any of a group of old musical instruments, usually having six strings and played with a bow.

viola (vē·ō′lə). An instrument similar to the violin, but larger and lower in pitch.

visibility (viz′ə·bil′ə·tē). The degree to which things can be seen.

vision (vizh′ən). A dream; a look into the future.

W

warrior (wôr′ē·ər). A man who takes part in fighting; a soldier.

weapon (wep′ən). A tool, part of the body, etc., used for fighting or killing.

Ships at a wharf

weird (wird). Strange; eerie.

wharf ((h)wôrf). A platform built along a shore, where ships may dock to load or unload.

wilderness (wil′dər·nis). A region where no people live and that is not used for farming or industry.

wind sock (wind sok). A flag shaped like an open sleeve that indicates the direction of the wind.

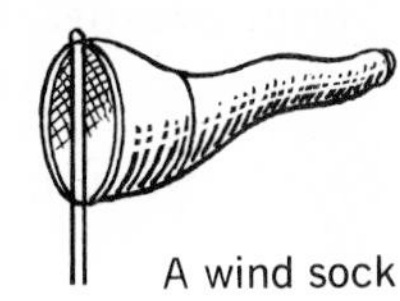
A wind sock

winegrower (wīn′grō′ər). A person who grows grapes that are made into wine.

winepress (wīn′pres). A machine that squeezes juice from grapes for wine.

workmanship (wûrk′mən·ship). **1.** The art or skill of a craftsman. **2.** The quality of work done.

wretched (rech′id). Very unhappy; miserable.

Y

yarn (yärn). A long story of adventure, not always true.